# THE
# HAUNTED SCREEN
## LOTTE H EISNER

# The Haunted Screen

Lotte H. Eisner

*The Cabinet of Dr Caligari*

# THE
# HAUNTED SCREEN

Expressionism in the German Cinema
and the Influence of Max Reinhardt

by Lotte H. Eisner

*'German man is the supreme example of demoniac man.*
*Demoniac indeed seems the abyss which cannot be filled,*
*the yearning which cannot be assuaged,*
*the thirst which cannot be slaked. . .'*
Leopold Ziegler: *Das Heilige Reich der Deutschen*, 1925

University of California Press
Berkeley and Los Angeles

L'Ecran Démoniaque
*first published in France 1952; revised and reissued 1965
by Le Terrain Vague, 14 rue de Verneuil, Paris VII^e*
© *Le Terrain Vague 1965*

*Translated from the French by Roger Greaves
Published in the United States and Canada by
University of California Press
Berkeley and Los Angeles
Translation and new material* © *Thames & Hudson 1969
First California Paperback Edition, 1973*

*ISBN 0 520 02479 6
Library of Congress Catalog Card Number: 68-8719*

*Printed in Great Britain*

# Contents

## Foreword to the English language edition

The German film got off to a comparatively late start. Any judgment on the period up to 1913–14 can only be negative: the dull little moving snapshots turned out by the pioneer Max Skladanowsky have nothing in common with the lively topicalities being produced by Louis Lumière at the same time; in the work of Oskar Messter there is nothing which even remotely recalls the gaiety of the comic films of Pathé or Gaumont, the stylistic perfection of the French *films d'art*, or the poetic fantasies of Georges Méliès. The kinds of patriotic panorama made by Franz Porten – *Königin Luise* and *Deutschlands Ruhmestage 1870–71* (1911–12) – were still mere gropings in the dark; so also were the films of Kurt Stark, whose *Liebesglück der Blinden* (1911) was naturalism of the most naïve and sentimental kind. The screens of the German cinema were swamped by the melodramas of Max Mack, Joe May, and Rudolf Meinert, and by simplistic comedies such as those of Bolten-Beckers. Joe May and Rudolf Meinert were later to direct adventure films, but for anything to approach the charm of the films of Louis Feuillade one has to wait until Fritz Lang's *Die Spinnen* (1919).

But on the eve of the First World War, with a few prophetic works, the German cinema finally got off the mark, though it only really began to move once the war was over; then followed the great period. This great period was shortlived, and did not last much beyond 1925–27. Despite a few later successes, the German cinema was never to know another flowering like this one, stimulated, as it was, on the one hand, by the theatre of Max

Reinhardt and, on the other, by Expressionist art (it is essential not to confuse these opposing styles). It is to this brief period that this book is devoted. I have not set out to write a history of the German cinema. Rather, I have attempted to throw light on some of the intellectual, artistic, and technical developments which the German cinema underwent during these momentous years, the last decade of the silent period. The German sound film is only briefly discussed.

Some questions of terminology need to be mentioned at the outset. The word *demoniac* (German *dämonisch*) is used in its Greek sense – as it was understood by Goethe (and by Leopold Ziegler in the epigraph on the title page of this book) – 'pertaining to the nature of supernatural power'; it is not used in its usual English sense of 'diabolical'. Familiar German expressions such as *Weltanschauung* are used without apology. Key expressions such as *Kammerspielfilm* (page 177), *Stimmung* (page 199), and *Umwelt* (page 186) are discussed when they are first introduced. The anglicized Italian word *chiaroscuro*, which is central to the book and figures throughout, stands, like the also inadequate *clair-obscur*, for German *Helldunkel*, and represents a sort of twilight of the German soul, expressing itself in shadowy, enigmatic interiors, or in misty, insubstantial landscapes. It is a concept dear to Romantic authors and artists, and may be seen for example in the sketches of Robert Herlth, Walter Röhrig, or Walter Reimann.

As an historian of art I have also allowed myself the licence of a few technical terms, such as *grisaille*, a painting in grey monotone to represent objects in relief, and *sfumato*, a softness of shading or outline more delicate than the thinnest smoke. Throughout the book the expression 'titles' is used to describe the explanatory or dialogue captions of the silent film; the term 'sub-titles', now normally used for the translation at the bottom of the screen of a foreign sound film, has been avoided.

For this first English language edition the text has been revised and a number of new illustrations added.

L. H. E.

*'The Germans are odd people, all the same! What with their profound thoughts and the ideas they are forever pursuing and introducing all over the place, they really do make life too hard for themselves. Oh, have the courage to yield to your impressions . . . and do not always think that everything that is not some idea or abstract thought must be vain.'*
Goethe: Eckermann's *Conversations*, 1827.

The years immediately following the First World War were strange ones in Germany. The German mind had difficulty in adjusting itself to the collapse of the imperial dream; and in the early years of its short life the Weimar Republic had the troublesome task of meeting outside demands (the onerous terms imposed on Germany at Versailles) while at the same time maintaining equilibrium internally (the Spartacist revolt of 1919, the unsuccessful Kapp Putsch of 1920). In 1923, after Germany had failed to pay the war reparations laid down at Versailles, French and Belgian troops occupied the Ruhr, and inflation, which had always been a serious danger, could not be stopped. The material conditions which resulted led to a general decline of values, and the inner disquiet of the nation took on truly gigantic proportions.

Mysticism and magic, the dark forces to which Germans have always been more than willing to commit themselves, had flourished in the face of death on the battlefields. The hecatombs of young men fallen in the flower of their youth seemed to nourish the grim nostalgia of the survivors. And the ghosts which had haunted the German Romantics revived, like the shades of Hades after draughts of blood. A new stimulus was thus given to the eternal attraction towards all that is obscure and undetermined, towards the kind of brooding speculative reflection called *Grübelei* which culminated in the apocalyptic doctrine of Expressionism. Poverty and constant insecurity help to explain the enthusiasm with which German artists embraced this movement

9

which, as early as 1910, had tended to sweep aside all the principles which had formed the basis of art until then.

Rather than give an account of Expressionism in terms of sculpture or painting, we need, in order to analyse the phenomenon in all its complexity and ambiguity, to follow its track through the literature of the period. This may appear paradoxical; the reason is that, for the Germans, that 'race of thinkers and poets', every manifestation in art is immediately transformed into dogma: the systematic ideology of their *Weltanschauung* is wedded to a didactic interpretation of art.

But finding one's way through the tangled phraseology of the German Expressionists is not an easy task. At first sight, their telegraphic style, exploding in short phrases and exclamations, seems to have simplified the labyrinthine syntax of classical German; but this apparent clarity is misleading. Expressionist phraseology is ruled by a desire to amplify the 'metaphysical' meaning of words. Its exponents juggle with vague expressions, strings of words which have little orthodox relationship to each other, and invent mystical allegories which amount to little once we attempt to translate them. This language of symbols and metaphors is intentionally obscure, designed to be intelligible only to the initiated.

As an example let us listen to the dithyramb intoned in 1919 by a fervent theorist of this style, Kasimir Edschmid, in his *Über den Expressionismus in der Literatur*. Here we may detect, more clearly than anywhere else, the keystone of the Expressionist conception.

Expressionism, Edschmid declared, is a reaction against the atom-splitting of Impressionism, which reflects the iridescent ambiguities, disquieting diversity, and ephemeral hues of nature. At the same time Expressionism sets itself against Naturalism with its mania for recording mere facts, and its paltry aim of photographing nature or daily life. The world is there for all to see; it would be absurd to reproduce it purely and simply as it is. The Expressionists also oppose the effeminacy of neo-Romanticism.

The Expressionist does not see, he has 'visions'. According to Edschmid, 'the chain of facts: factories, houses, illness, prostitutes, screams, hunger' does not exist; only the interior vision they provoke exists. Facts and objects are nothing in themselves: we need to study their essence rather than their momentary and accidental forms. It is the hand of the artist which 'through them grasps what is behind them' and allows us to know their real form, freed from the stifling constraint of a 'false reality'. The Expressionist artist, not merely receptive but a true creator, seeks, instead of a momentary, accidental, form, the *eternal, permanent meaning* of facts and objects.

We must detach ourselves from nature, say the Expressionists, and strive to isolate an object's 'most expressive expression'. These rather confused stipulations were explained by Béla Balázs in his book *Der Sichtbare Mensch* (1923); an object can be stylized by the accentuation of (in Balázs's words) its 'latent physiognomy'. This will permit the penetration of its visible aura.

Edschmid proclaimed that human life, transcending the individual, participates in the life of the universe; our hearts beat with the rhythm of the world itself and are linked with everything that happens: the cosmos is our lung. Man has ceased to be an individual tied to concepts of duty, morality, family and society; the Expressionist's life breaks the bounds of petty logic and causality. Free from all bourgeois remorse, admitting nothing but the prodigious barometer of his sensibility, he commits himself to his impulses. The 'world-image' is reflected in him in its primitive purity; reality is created by him and the 'world-image' exists solely in him. This intense longing to lose all individuality in a total extravasation of self, to feel pervaded by the destiny of the universe, is a characteristic common to many German intellectuals towards the end of the First World War. Most were beginning to cry out against the absurd slaughter taking place; soon German poets, wishing like Schiller before them to embrace the whole of humanity, were to write, as Werfel had already written in 1910: 'My only happiness, O Man, is to feel myself your brother.'

The contrasts and contradictions in all this will be readily apparent. On the one hand Expressionism represents an extreme form of subjectivism; on the other hand this assertion of an absolute totalitarian self creating the universe is linked with a dogma entailing the complete abstraction of the individual.

The Germans, themselves steeped in contradictions, felt the need for a compromise. Thus the art critic Paul Fechter, in a work called *Der Expressionismus* (1919), distinguished between: (i) an 'intensive Expressionism' characterized by extreme individualism, such as that of the painter Kandinsky who, at the apogee of feeling, deliberately ignores the exterior world and, remote from logic and causality, strives for transcendentality and the chaos of form and colour; and (ii) the 'extensive Expressionism' of a Pechstein, whose creative impulse flows from a cosmic feeling which his will fashions and transforms. On the other hand the Expressionists distinguished between two opposing tendencies. As early as 1910 one of the two groups which had gathered around two literary reviews had taken the name *Aktion*. This group, led by Franz Pfemfert in opposition to the purist ecstatic Expressionists, pursued anti-bourgeois social and political aims while claiming absolute intellectualism with the catchword *Gehirnlichkeit* (cerebrality). The other group had taken the name *Sturm* (storm). Its programme was more artistically inclined than that of *Aktion*, and promulgated the Expressionist doctrine of ecstatic creation based on visions. The leader of *Sturm*, Herwart Walden, wrote in a pamphlet *Die neue Malerei* (1919): 'Expressionism is neither a fad nor a movement; it is a *Weltanschauung*.'

Nature is not alone in being proscribed. Psychology, the handmaiden of Naturalism, is also condemned, along with the laws and concepts of conformist society and the tragedies provoked by petty social ambitions. Edschmid proclaimed the *dictatorship of Mind*. Mind has the mission of giving form to matter. He also exalted the *attitude of constructive Will*, and called for a total revision of the whole of human behaviour. The same sterotyped vocabulary crops up time and again in German Expressionist literature: words and phrases such as 'interior tension', 'force of expansion', 'immense accumulation of creative concentration' or 'metaphysical interplay of intensities and energies'; much is also made of expressions such as 'dynamism', 'density' and above all of the word *Ballung*, a well-nigh untranslatable concept which might be rendered as 'intensive crystallization of form'.

A few words are needed here about the 'abstraction' so frequently referred to by the theorists of Expressionism. In his doctorate thesis *Abstraktion und Einfühlung*, published in 1921, Wilhelm Worringer anticipated many of the Expressionists' precepts, proving how close to the German *Weltanschauung* these aesthetic axioms were.

Abstraction, Worringer declared, stems from the great anxiety which man experiences when terrorized by the phenomena he perceives around him, the relationships and mysterious polarities of which he is unable to decipher. This primordial anguish which man feels when confronted with unlimited space makes him want to detach the objects of the exterior world from their natural context, or better still, to free the individual object from its ties with other objects, to make it 'absolute'.

Nordic man, Worringer continued, is constantly aware of the presence of a 'veil between himself and nature'; this is why he aspires after abstraction in art. Inwardly discordant, always striving for the unattainable, he needs that spiritual unrest which is an incentive to the 'animation of the inorganic'. Mediterranean man, so perfectly harmonious, can never know this ecstasy of 'expressive abstraction'. Such was the paradoxical formula which the troubled mysticism of Expressionism preached.

According to Worringer, Nordic man's desire for abstraction reaches its climax in the living abstraction of Gothic art, in the 'extensive dynamism of energies', and in that intensity of expression which leads him, 'beatified and quivering with spasmodic ecstasy, enthralled by a vertiginious intoxication, towards the heavens opened up for him by a thundering orchestration of mechanical forces'.

To come back to Edschmid, we find him stipulating that everything must remain 'sketchy' and quiver with immanent tension; a perpetual effervescence and excitation must be carefully maintained.

From the *élan* of Gothic art to the Expressionist ecstasy is not such a far cry as might be thought. According to Wolfhart Gotthold Klee (in *Die charakteristischen*

Reinhard Sorge's *Der Bettler*: lithograph by Ernst Stern

*Motive der expressionistischen Erzählungslitteratur*, 1934), Gothic, Baroque, *Sturm und Drang*,★ Romanticism and Expressionism are interrelated: they are periods of the *Werden* (becoming) and not, like the Renaissance for example, periods of the *Sein* (being). Nietzsche maintained that the German *is* not, he *becomes*, he is forever in the process of evolving.

The Expressionists, who liked to call themselves 'apocalyptic adolescents', display an almost childlike love of youth; they abhor old people, those representatives of a chilly conformism which reproves their unbounded high spirits. Two generations separated by an unbridgable gulf bear a mortal hatred for each other: poignant examples are Werfel's poem *Vater und Sohn*, Kafka's novellas *Metamorphosis* and *The Judgment*, and the plays *Der Sohn* by Hasenclever and *Vatermord* by Bronnen.

The paroxysm that the Germans take for dynamism is found in all the drama of this period, which has since been called† the *O Mensch Periode* (the 'O Man period'). Of *Der Bettler* by Reinhard Sorge, a play written in 1912 and a prototype of the genre, it has been said – and the remark holds good for all the artistic activity of this period – that the world has become so 'permeable' that, at any one moment, Mind, Spirit, Vision and Ghosts seem to gush forth, exterior facts are continually being transformed into interior elements and psychic events are exteriorized. Is this not precisely the atmosphere we find in the classic films of the German cinema?

★ It was surely not a coincidence when the group of Expressionist artists pledged to 'ecstasy' and 'vision' took the name *Sturm*. At times they do indeed recall the period of the *Sturm und Drang* of the young Goethe and his companions Klinger and Lenz, in their short, chopped phrases, exclamations, associations of ideas, and violent imagery.

† After Werfel, quoted on page 11.

*The Cabinet of Dr Caligari*

*'Let's talk about* Caligari. *What makes the film compelling is its rhythm. At first slow, deliberately laborious, it attempts to irritate. Then when the zigzag motifs of the fairground start turning, the pace leaps forward,* agitato, accelerando, *and only leaves off at the word "End", as abruptly as a slap in the face.'*
Louis Delluc: *Cinéa*, 1922.

The leaning towards violent contrast – which in Expressionist literature can be seen in the use of staccato sentences – and the inborn German liking for chiaroscuro and shadow, obviously found an ideal artistic outlet in the cinema. Visions nourished by moods of vague and troubled yearning could have found no more apt mode of expression, at once concrete and unreal.

This explains why the first films of second-rate directors such as Robert Wiene or Richard Oswald misled people into thinking them remarkably gifted. These works blithely married a morbid Freudianism and an Expressionistic exaltation to the romantic fantasies of Hoffmann and Eichendorff, and to the tortured soul of contemporary Germany seemed, with their overtones of death, horror and nightmare, the reflection of its own grimacing image, offering a kind of release.

In 1817, in a letter to the archetypal Romantic Rahel Varnhagen, Astolphe de Coustine wrote: 'Behind the lives and writings of the Germans there is always a mysterious world whose light alone seems to pierce the veil of our atmosphere; and the minds disposed to ascend towards that world – which ends with the beginning of this one – will always be alien to France.'

It was in this mysterious world, attractive and repugnant at the same time, that the German cinema found its true nature.

### Das Kabinett des Dr Caligari
### (The Cabinet of Dr Caligari, 1919)

The making of *Caligari* was strewn with incidents, which

17

have been variously reported by the different people responsible for it.

We know from the comments of one of the authors of the scenario – quoted by Kracauer in *From Caligari to Hitler* (1947) – that the prologue and epilogue were added as an afterthought in the face of objections from both authors. The result of these modifications was to falsify the action and ultimately to reduce it to the ravings of a madman. The film's authors, Carl Mayer and Hans Janowitz, had had the very different intention of unmasking the absurdity of asocial authority, represented by Dr Caligari, the superintendent of a lunatic asylum and proprietor of a fairground side-show.

Erich Pommer, who used to claim to have 'supervised' *Caligari*, alleges that the authors submitted the scenario to him and informed him of their intention of commissioning the sets from Alfred Kubin, a visionary designer and engraver whose obsessed works seem to arise from a chaos of light and shadow. Kubin's *Caligari* would certainly have been full of Goyaesque visions, and the German silent film would have had the gloomy hallucinatory atmosphere which is unmistakably its own without being sidetracked into the snares of abstraction. For Kubin, like Janowitz, came from Prague, a mysterious town whose ghetto, with its tortuous back-alleys, was a survival from the Middle Ages. Like Janowitz, Kubin knew all the horrors of an in-between world. In a half-autobiographical, half-fantastic tale, *Die Andere Seite*, published in 1922, he describes his wanderings through the dark streets, possessed by an obscure force which led him to imagine weird houses and landscapes, terrifying or grotesque situations. When he entered a little tea-shop, everything seemed bizarre. The waitresses were like wax dolls moved by some strange mechanism. He had the feeling that his intrusion had disturbed the few customers sitting at the tables; they were completely unreal, like phantoms hatching satanic plots. The far end of the shop, with its barrel-organ, seemed suspicious, a trap. Behind that barrel-organ there was surely a bloody lair wreathed in gloom . . . It is a pity that so vivid a painter of nightmares was never commissioned for *Caligari*.

The practical Pommer relates that while Mayer and Janowitz were 'talking art' at him, he for his part was considering the scenario from a very different point of view. 'They wanted to experiment,' he wrote in 1947, 'and I wanted to keep the costs down.' Making the sets in painted canvas was a saving from every point of view, and largely facilitated production in days when money and raw materials were scarce. On the other hand, at a time when Germany was still going through the indirect consequences of an abortive revolution and the national economy was as unstable as the national frame of mind, the atmosphere was ripe for experiment. The director of *Caligari*, Robert Wiene, subsequently claimed in London to be responsible for the film's Expressionist conception.

Yet it is difficult to be sure of the true details of these remote events.

Here is Hermann Warm's version of the facts about Caligari.★ The producer was not Erich Pommer but Rudolf Meinert, the director of such unknown quantities as *Der Hund von Baskerville*, *Nachtasyl*, *Rosenmontag* and *Marie-Antoinette*. So it was Meinert, not Pommer, who, following the practice current in those days – when the sets were given more importance than everything else – gave the script of *Caligari* to the designer Warm. The latter studied it with two friends employed at the studios as painters, Walter Röhrig and Walter Reimann.†

'We spent a whole day and part of the night reading through this very curious script,' writes Warm. 'We realized that a subject like this needed something out of the ordinary in the way of sets. Reimann, whose painting in those days had Expressionist tendencies, suggested doing the sets Expressionistically. We immediately set to work roughing up designs in that style.'

Next day Wiene gave his agreement. Rudolf Meinert was more cautious and asked for a day to think about it. Then he told them, 'Do these sets as eccentrically as you can!'

This story illustrates one of the basic principles of the German cinema; the essential role played by the author, the designer, and the technical staff. It also helps to explain why, apart from the abstract film, the German silent cinema never had a proper avant-garde such as that found in France. German industry immediately latched on to anything of an artistic kind in the belief that it was bound to bring in money in the long run.

★ In a manuscript sent to the editor of *Der Neue Film* following an article by Ernst Jaeger.

†Lang assures me that Pommer *did* supervise the film, and not Meinert. See, for Pommer and *Caligari*, his comments in 'Carl Mayer's début', *A Tribute to Carl Mayer*, London, 1947.

One of Hermann Warm's sketches for *Caligari*

Today we know that Fritz Lang, who was chosen as the director of *Caligari* before Robert Wiene (he refused because he was still engaged in the filming of *Die Spinnen*), suggested to the production company that a good way of not scaring off the public would be to bring in a kind of *Rahmenhandlung* (framing-treatment), a prologue and epilogue in conventional settings supposed to take place in a lunatic asylum. Thus the main action, related in a conversation between two lunatics sitting in the asylum garden, became the elaborate invention of a fantastic world seen through the eyes of a madman.

When Abel Gance, that eternal pioneer, had made his own attempt at filming a world seen through the eyes of a madman he had gone about it in a quite different way. In *La Folie du Dr Tube*, knowing nothing of anamorphic lenses, he borrowed several concave and convex mirrors from a Hall of Mirrors in a nearby amusement-park and filmed the reflections of people and objects, occasionally obtaining, in addition to 'stretching' effects, mere blobs and wavy lines. This was a fundamentally Impressionistic use of the camera; the distortions of *Dr Caligari* lie in the basic graphic idea, and can therefore be termed *Expressionistic*.

The sets of *Caligari*, which have often been criticized for being too flat, do have some depth nonetheless. As Rudolph Messell says in *This Film Business* (1928), 'the background comes to the fore'. The depth comes from deliberately distorted perspectives and from narrow, slanting streets which cut across each other at unexpected angles. Sometimes also it is enhanced by a back-cloth which extends the streets into sinuous lines. The three-dimensional effect is reinforced by the inclined cubes of dilapidated houses. Oblique, curving, or rectilinear lines converge across an undefined expanse towards the background: a wall skirted by the silhouette of Cesare the somnambulist, the slim ridge of the roof he darts along bearing his prey, and the steep paths he scales in his flight.

In *Expressionismus und Film*, Rudolf Kurtz points out that these curves and slanting lines have a meaning which is decidedly metaphysical. For the psychic reaction caused in the spectator by oblique lines is entirely different from that caused in him by straight lines. Similarly, unexpected curves and sudden ups and downs provoke emotions quite different from those induced by harmonious and gentle gradients.

But what matters is to create states of anxiety and terror. The diversity of planes has only secondary importance.

In *Caligari** the Expressionist treatment was unusually successful in evoking the 'latent physiognomy' of a small medieval town, with its dark twisting back-alleys boxed in by crumbling houses whose inclined façades keep out all daylight. Wedge-shaped doors with heavy shadows and oblique windows with distorted frames seem to gnaw into the walls. The bizarre exaltation brooding over the synthetic sets of *Caligari* brings to mind Edschmid's statement that 'Expressionism evolves in a perpetual excitation'. These houses and the well, crudely sketched at an alley-corner, do indeed seem to vibrate with an extraordinary spirituality. 'The antediluvian character of utensils awakens,' says Kurtz.

* Modern prints of this film (originally tinted in green, steely-blue and brown) give no idea of the unity of composition afforded in the original by the images and their titles, the latter in strangely distorted 'Expressionistic' lettering. A few traces of this are left today in the hallucination scene, when the doctor, swept along by his obsession, perceives the written phrase 'You must become Caligari' flashing and undulating across the narrow entrance to a garden of flat spiny trees.

21

*Caligari*: two of Walter Reimann's sketches

This is Worringer's 'spiritual unrest' creating the 'animation of the inorganic'.

The Germans, used as they are to savage legends, have an eerie gift for animating objects. In the normal syntax of the German language objects have a complete active life: they are spoken of with the same adjectives and verbs used to speak of human beings, they are endowed with the same qualities as people, they act and react in the same way. Long before Expressionism this anthropomorphism had already been pushed to the extreme. In 1884 Friedrich Vischer, in his novel *Auch Einer*, talks about 'the perfidy of the object' which gloats upon★ our vain efforts to dominate it. The bewitched objects in Hoffmann's obsessed universe appear in the same light.

Animate objects always seem to haunt German narcissism. When couched in Expressionist phraseology the personification is amplified; the metaphor expands and embraces people and objects in similar terms.†

So we frequently find German-speaking authors attributing diabolical overtones to, for example, the street: in Gustav Meyrink's *Golem*, the houses in the Prague ghetto, which have sprouted like weeds, seem to have an insidious life of their own 'when the autumn evening mists stagnate in the streets and veil their imperceptible grimace'. In some mysterious way these streets contrive to abjure their life and feelings during the daytime, and lend them instead to their inhabitants, those enigmatic creatures who wander aimlessly around, feebly animated by an invisible magnetic current. But at night the houses reclaim their life with interest from these unreal inhabitants; they stiffen, and their sly faces fill with malevolence. The doors become gaping maws and shrieking gullets.

'The dynamic force of objects howls their desire to be created,' Kurtz declared, and this is the explanation of the overpowering obsessiveness of the *Caligari* sets.

But light, atmosphere, and distance are not the only determinants of the object-distortion which we find in Expressionist art. There is also the power of Abstractionism. Georg Marzynski informs us in his book *Methode des Expressionismus* (1920) that a selective and creative distortion gives the artist a means of representing the complexity of the psyche; by linking this psychical

★ Vischer's term is *Schadenfreude*, hard to translate with its typically German overtones of diabolical persistence and enjoyment of others' misfortunes.

† On the one hand the poet becomes 'a field fissured with thirst'; on the other hand, the 'voracious' mouths of windows or the 'avid' darts of shadow pierce 'shivering' walls, while the 'cruel' leaves of 'implacable' doors slash the 'moaning' flanks of 'despairing' houses.

23

complexity to an optical complexity he can release an object's internal life, the expression of its 'soul'. The Expressionists are concerned solely with images in the mind. Hence oblique walls which have no reality. For, as Marzynski says, it is one of the characteristics of 'imagined images' to represent objects on the slant, seen from above at an acute angle; this viewpoint makes it easier to grasp the whole structure of the image.

The Germans love watching the reflections of distorting mirrors. The Romantics had already observed certain formal distortions. One of Ludwig Tieck's heroes, William Lovell, describes the impression of an unstable, ill-defined universe: 'at such times the streets appear to me to be *rows of counterfeit houses* inhabited by madmen . . .' The streets described by Kubin or Meyrink and those of the *Caligari* sets find their perfect echo in this phrase.

The abstraction and the total distortion of the *Caligari* sets are seen at their most extreme in the vision of the

*Caligari:* Expressionist architecture

prison-cell, with its verticals narrowing as they rise like arrow-heads.\* The oppressive effect is heightened by these verticals being extended along the floor and directed at the spot where the chain-laden prisoner squats. In this hell the distorted, rhomboid window is a mockery. The designers succeed in rendering the idea of a gaol-in-the-absolute, in its 'most expressive expression'.

Hermann Warm stated that 'the cinema image must become an engraving'. But the German cinema's use of light and shade did not issue from this affirmation alone. The serial film *Homunculus*, made three years earlier, clearly demonstrates the effect that can be obtained from contrasts between black and white.

A lack of continuity is apparent between the Expressionistic sets and the utterly bourgeois furniture – the chintzy armchairs in Lil Dagover's sitting-room or the leather armchair in the madhouse yard. The break in style is fatal. Similarly, the façade of the asylum is not distorted, yet the end of the film is seen in the same weird décor. It is hard to say which is the more responsible for this: the Expressionist tendencies of the designers, or the parsimony of the producer.

The stylization of the acting is dictated by the sets. Yet Werner Krauss in the part of the satanic Dr Caligari and Conrad Veidt in that of the sinister somnambulist are the only actors who really adapt themselves to it, and – in Kurtz's words – achieve a 'dynamic synthesis of their being', by concentrating their movements and facial expressions. Through a reduction of gesture they attain movements which are almost linear and which – despite a few curves that slip in – remain brusque, like the broken angles of the sets; and their movements from point to point never go beyond the limits of a given geometrical plane. The other actors, on the other hand, remain locked in a naturalistic style, though, owing to the old-fashioned way in which they are dressed (cloaks, top hats, morning-coats), their outlines do achieve an element of the fantastic.

The characters of Caligari and Cesare conform to Expressionist conception; the somnambulist, detached from his everyday ambience, deprived of all individuality, an abstract creature, kills without motive or logic. And his master, the mysterious Dr Caligari, who lacks

the merest shadow of human scruple, acts with the criminal insensibility and defiance of conventional morality which the Expressionists exalted.

## Genuine (1920)

Though *Caligari* did not establish a genre\* in the strict sense of the word, German film-makers did come under its influence. The very next year Wiene tried to establish 'Caligarism' in his film *Genuine*.

As his scenarist he chose Carl Mayer, who had revealed his great talent and his understanding of the cinema with his first scenario, *Caligari*. Mayer, who did not leave a single novel or short story at his death, whose entire output as a writer went into the cinema, had an extraordinary visual gift: he immediately conceived action in terms of images. But this – and despite the rhythm he conferred on each of his works – did not prevent *Genuine* from being a failure. The set painted by the otherwise interesting artist Cesar Klein was muddled and overloaded; and the naturalistic actors just vanished into it.

The body-wriggling of Fern Andra – a pretty woman but a mediocre actress – would be more appropriate on the stage of a music-hall. Apart from the bald little man with his pale black-ribbed gloves like Caligari's and his old-fashioned clothes emphasizing his satanic aspect, the actors have nothing of the almost Hoffmannesque stylization which Werner Krauss had been able to achieve in *Caligari*.

## Von Morgens bis Mitternachts (1920), Torgus (1920), Raskolnikow (1923)

However, Wiene had realized what was missing from *Genuine* – the third dimension; for his *Raskolnikow* he engaged a talented architect by the name of Andrei Andreiev. Thanks to Andreiev, this film contains certain shots in which sets and characters really seem to stem from Dostoievsky's universe and act upon each other through a sort of reciprocal hallucination. The staircase, with its jagged laths and battens and steps peopled with ghosts, prefigures the serrated shadows on the staircase climbed by Louise Brooks, in Pabst's film *Die Büchse der*

\* *Caligari* had a certain influence abroad. However, *Le Brasier ardent* by Mosjoukine and Baroncelli contains only a few Expressionist elements, and the occasional Expressionism in *Don Juan et Faust* (1922) by Marcel L'Herbier is merely decorative. *La Chute de la Maison Usher* (1928) by Jean Epstein is closer to Surrealism than to Expressionism. On the other hand, a certain measure of influence in the USSR is undeniable: e.g. *Aelita* (1924) by Protazanov and *The Cloak* (1926) by Kozintzev and Trauberg (though the latter is also tinged with elements of the Russian ballet).

27

A poster for *Caligari*

*Genuine:* Expressionist surfaces

*Pandora* (*Pandora's Box*), as she drags Jack the Ripper along with her towards their destiny.

Another film betrays a more artificial conception: *Von Morgens bis Mitternachts* (*From Morn to Midnight*), directed by Karl Heinz Martin, the stage-producer. Here the sets and even the faces and costumes of the actors were striped or spotted in white and dark tones. But instead of emphasizing the third dimension of the forms this artifice merely blurred the outlines.

In *Torgus*, a rather poor film by Hans Kobe, Expressionism is limited to the decorative elements, and all the basic outlines are respected. However, as in *Von Morgens bis Mitternachts*, the furniture is striped. This solitary attempt at destroying the normal relationships obtaining between objects is a clear example of the dissonance which stamps many Expressionist films (*Caligari*, more unified than the others, excepted). This dissonance is unavoidable when the aim is to create an enhancing atmosphere for elements which are almost impressionistic, and when the attempt at abstraction stops short at a stylization of the setting. Thus in *Torgus* the Expressionistic ornamentation on the walls of an inn seems to blur into the smoky glow of a hanging lamp.★

In *Caligari* the distortion was justified, since the images represented the vision of a madman; in *Von Morgens bis Mitternachts* the viewpoint is different. We see objects and people as they are conceived by the cashier whom chance has torn from his honest humdrum world and who is led astray by vague, ambitious yearnings. The forms which take on importance for him become gigantic and, in accordance with the precepts of Expressionism, lack proportion or any logical connection with the context. Other objects, those which have no meaning for him, become blurred or shrink almost to nothing.

We can already observe signs of this Expressionist narcissism in the Romantics. In *Titan*, Jean-Paul Richter says of his hero, dreaming under a tree, that in his imagination the tree was becoming enormous, unique in the universe.

Here we are close to the secret of the fantastic effects in many German films; we come across it again in the swirling images of Murnau's film *Phantom* and in the visions of the crowd seen through the eyes of an acrobat

★ See p. 187.

*Raskolnikow:* Expressionist depth

in Dupont's film *Varieté* (*Variety*). It is also the main-spring of a film such as *Narkose* (1929) by Alfred Abel, in which we see the images emerging in the unconscious of a young woman on an operating-table.* And in certain respects it was to be the technique used by Ernö Metzner in 1928 for his short film *Überfall*, in which the dreams of a wounded man knocked unconscious by a thug are reflected in concave or convex mirrors.

But there is one film in particular in which the director, while taking advantage of all the previous Expressionist experiments, transposes the traditional technique: *Geheimnisse einer Seele* (*Secrets of a Soul*, 1926) by Pabst. Certain shots representing the dreams of a repressive could never have been filmed had it not been for Expressionism. In this style Pabst discovered a means of giving a luminous and unreal relief to objects or people, of deforming architectural perspective, and of distorting the relative proportions of objects.

The conception of *Von Morgens bis Mitternachts* is not so much structural as ornamental. There are hardly any true perspectives, and on the rare occasions when we come across a real landscape, there is an embarrassing break in tone. In all the other shots the background remains black, and a few details of the set – a piece of furniture, a strong-box, a door – appear like paper cut-outs, without depth, in a crude attempt at abstraction.

Sometimes this concern for abstraction takes more sophisticated forms. A set suddenly emerges from the darkness in an effect recalling Max Reinhardt's productions at the Grosses Schauspielhaus in Berlin. Perhaps this is why the film appears so close to Georg Kaiser's play.

Only Ernst Deutsch, with his contorted miming and behaviour, acts in a truly Expressionistic manner; the acting of the other players is, if anything, naturalistic. Inevitably this stylized realism clashes grotesquely with the abstract tendencies of the Expressionist set. And owing to this unintentional naturalism certain scenes with scant detail lose all relief.

There remains an effect which is remarkable for the period: the six-day cycle race, filmed as the avant-garde was to film later. Anamorphosed into shimmering facets by the magic of lighting-effects and the deforming lens, astounding in those days, the cyclists bound forward

* The trick photography was by Eugen Schüfftan and included an entire flash-back sequence contained in a drop of water.

Architecture and furniture: *Torgus*

Architecture and furniture: *Von Morgens bis Mitternachts*

and are distorted into a mere symbol of speed, in the almost abstract rush of the race. Yet this 'pre-avant-garde' sequence was less revolutionary than one might think. As early as 1916 that great pioneer actor and director Paul Wegener had defined in his lecture 'The artistic possibilities of the cinema'★ what he called a *kinetische Lyrik* or 'cinematic lyricism' inspired by photographic technique. 'You have all seen films', he said, 'in which a line appears, then curves and changes. This line gives birth to faces, then disappears. Nobody has ever thought of attempting an experiment of this order in a full-length film. I can imagine a kind of cinema which would use nothing but moving surfaces, against which there would impinge events that would still participate in the natural world but transcend the lines and volumes of the natural'.

Wegener considered it would be possible to use 'marionettes or small three-dimensional models which could be animated image by image, in slow or rapid

★ Given on 24 April 1916, at an Easter Monday conference, and printed in Kai Möller: *Paul Wegener*, Rowohlt Verlag, Hamburg, 1954.

33

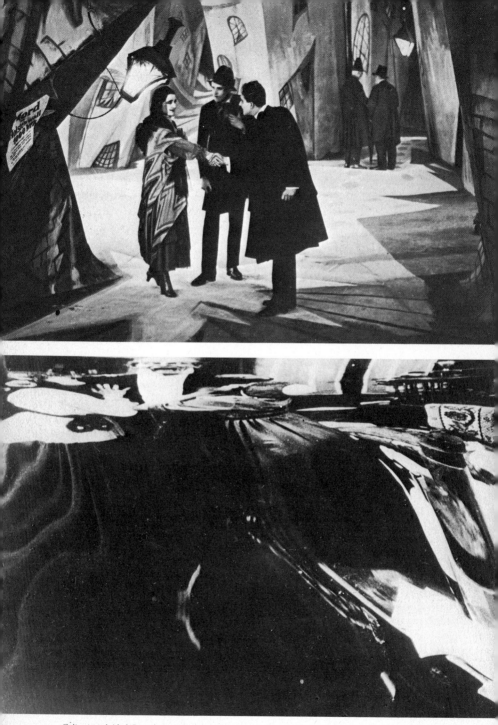

*Caligari*, and Abel Gance's *La Folie du Dr Tube* (1916): forms of distortion

*Secrets of a Soul:* the dreams of a repressive

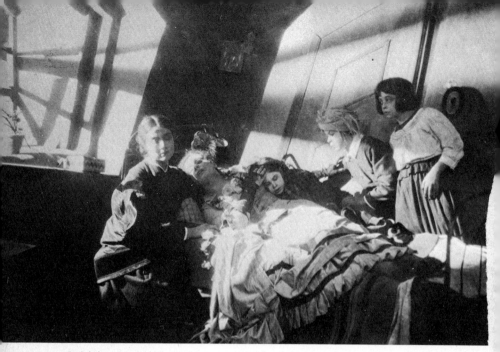

*Raskolnikow:* 'sets and characters act upon each other through a sort of reciprocal hallucination'

motion depending on the speed of the montage. This would give rise to fantastic images which would provoke absolutely novel associations of ideas in the spectator.

'Microscopic particles of fermenting chemical substances could be filmed together with small plants of various sizes. It would be impossible to distinguish the natural elements from the artificial ones. In this way we could enter a new fantastic domain of *pure kinetics*, the universe of optical lyricism.'

Wegener also imagined an empty surface on which phantom-like forms would come into being, and on which, in continual evolution, cells would burst open disclosing other cells which would revolve faster and faster until they looked like a firework display.

This is the formulation of the 'absolute film' which Hans Richter and Ruttmann were later to imagine and which is anticipated in the trick sequence of the six-day relay in *Von Morgens bis Mitternachts*.

One of the secrets of the success of the classical German

film was the perfect technical harmony achieved by long *Regiesitzungen*, discussions on the *mise-en-scène* of the film to be made which sometimes lasted for two months or more before the actual filming began, and to which the director invited everybody due to work on the film, from the chief designer and chief cameraman to the workmen in charge of the lighting.

A British designer expressed his astonishment when the German cameraman Günther Krampf, before starting filming in a studio near London, asked to see his sketches ('an unusual way of going about things in our country') in order to study them carefully to gauge the shooting angles and to be able to supervise the lighting. This 'way of going about things', of appreciating and familiarizing oneself with the designer's intentions, does not effectively detract from the value of the work of the great cameramen such as Guido Seeber, Karl Freund, Carl Hoffmann, Fritz Arno Wagner, Curt Courant, Günther Rittau, Franz Planer, Reimar Kuntze, and Eugen Schüfftan, to mention only the most important. For at these *Regiensitzungen* everyone was heard; like everybody else, the cameraman could ask for changes in the sets if he thought he saw a way of achieving a better result.

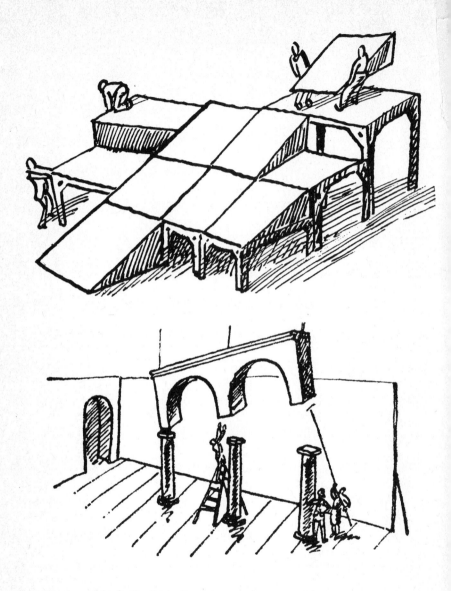

Ernst Stern: two sketches for Max Reinhardt

# 3  The Spell of Light: the Influence of Max Reinhardt

The word 'Expressionist' is commonly applied to every German film of the so-called 'classical' period. But it is surely not necessary to insist yet again that certain chiaroscuro effects, so often thought Expressionist, existed long before *Caligari*; and that this film, contrary to what many people seem to think, was hardly the first film of value to be made in Germany. As early as 1913, some writers started campaigning for the *Autorenfilm*, that is, the idea of a film being judged as the work of an author. This is not surprising in a country with so marked a literary bias as Germany.

These writers' origins and talents were very diverse: among them was Gerhart Hauptmann's brother, Carl Hauptmann, likewise a playwright, misunderstood and stunted by the greater fame of his brother; there was also Hanns Heinz Ewers, author of strange tales of blood and lust. (Nobody was surprised when this then over-rated individual turned his hand to the *Blut und Boden* – blood and soil – conception of the Nazis.)

The future German cinema was to owe to this concept of the *Autorenfilm* one of its main strongpoints: the 'literary scenario'.

## Der Student von Prag (The Student of Prague, 1913)

Ewers wrote the script of *The Student of Prague*, a much more restrained piece of work than his novel *Alraune*, filmed by Henrik Galeen in 1928. Ewers was evidently inspired by *Peter Schlemihl*, a story by Chamisso in which a young man sells his shadow, and by *Das Abenteuer*

39

*der Sylvester-Nacht* in which E. T. A. Hoffmann sends Chamisso's hero on a journey with his own Erasmus Spikher, 'the man who lost his reflection'. (The name Scapinelli, which Ewers gives to the diabolical and mysterious character who buys the reflection, is surely a harking back to the bewitched world of Hoffmann.)

When *The Student of Prague* came out, it was immediately realized that the cinema could become the perfect medium for Romantic anguish, dream-states, and those hazy imaginings which shade so easily into the infinite depths of that fragment of space-outside-time, the screen.

Paul Wegener, who was for some years an actor with Max Reinhardt, had been the first to grasp this. In his public lecture in April 1916 on the artistic possibilities of the cinema, already quoted, Wegener told the following anecdote. In 1913 a series of comic photographs of a man fencing and playing cards with himself had made him realize that the cinema was better equipped than any other art-form to capture the fantastic world of E. T. A. Hoffmann – above all, the famous theme of the *Doppelgänger*,* the shadow or reflection which takes on an independent existence and turns against its model

'*The Student of Prague*,' Wegener said, 'with its strange mixture of the natural and the artificial, in theme as in setting, interested me enormously.'

He went on to say that the cinema had to free itself from the theatre and novel and create in its own medium, with the image alone. 'The real creator of the film must be the camera. Getting the spectator to change his point of view, using special effects to double the actor on the divided screen, superimposing other images – all this, technique, form, gives the content its real meaning.'

He continued: 'I got the idea for my *Golem* from the mysterious clay figure brought to life by the Rabbi Loew, according to a legend of the Prague ghetto, and with this film I went further into the domain of pure cinema. Everything depends on the image, on a certain vagueness of outline where the fantastic world of the past meets the world of today. I realized that photographic technique was going to determine the destiny of the cinema. Light and darkness in the cinema play the same role as rhythm and cadence in music.'

* In a book published in 1927, *Das Problem der Magie und der Psychoanalyse*, Leon Kaplan remarks that the adult members of primitive races are like children distressed by the exterior world, which to them seems mysterious and hostile. They take refuge in a reassuring narcissism. And narcissistic man, prey to his dreams and predisposed to magic, is always prone to create a double of himself.

40

This first *Golem* of 1914, which mixed contemporary events (the Golem being discovered in Prague) with the legend of the Rabbi Loew, in the year 1580, creating the giant, is unfortunately lost. The *Golem* we know is that of 1920, which limits itself to the legend.

But the first (1913) version of *The Student of Prague* has survived, and this film, coming six years before *Caligari*, already exhibits many of the properties which one finds in the so-called 'classical' films of the twenties. In the early days nothing prevented German film-makers from working on location. The Expressionist style which had been the ruling taste in all the other arts since 1910 had not as yet got through to the cinema, which was still regarded with scorn. The director, with no reason to distort the natural appearance of objects, had no use for studio towns and landscapes.

Yet the Romanticism to which *The Student of Prague* so faithfully subscribes – fascinated as Paul Wegener was by the limitless expressive powers of this new

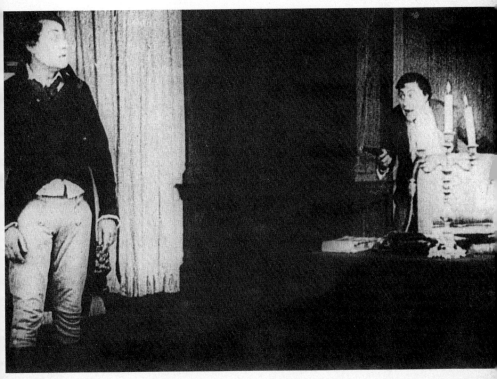

*The Student of Prague* (1913): the *Doppelgänger*

*The Student of Prague* (1913): the forest cemetery

art-form – already strives for the unusual. Stellan Rye, the
Danish director, who was called upon by Union Film★ for
the *mise-en-scène* (Wegener was to work in close collaboration with him) shot his film in the old town in Prague,
where dark, mysterious relics of the Middle Ages can
still be seen. He filmed in the narrow back-alleys and
on the old bridge in front of the bristling silhouette of
the cathedral. Wegener was to remember this when
making his second *Golem*, this time in the studio.

However, for religious reasons, the Jewish com-
munity refused to allow filming in the old cemetery. It
could have been reconstituted in the studio, as was done
for the later *Student of Prague*; but significantly it was
decided to erect the enormous medieval tombstones
(facsimiles, of course) in a real forest.

Nowadays the photography of what is probably the
only copy to have survived seems rather grey. One has to
remember that the contemporary prints, toned in brown,
green or (for night scenes) dark blue, were more subtle.

★ Under Paul Davidsohn
Union Film produced some
remarkable films; the Asta
Nielsen films were made
here. The company was
later bought up by Decla
Bioskop.

Of course the images – by Guido Seeber, the best cameraman of his day – lack the quality and depth of focus to which the German cinema of the twenties has accustomed us: the real interiors filmed in the Lobkowitz palace seem rather flat. There are a few shots, however, which anticipate the great films to come, notably the 'lovers' secret meeting on a castle terrace among the heavy shadows of columns, while, on the wall below, the ominous shadow of Scapinelli appears, spying on them from the darkness. Also worth noticing are a few interiors with an impressive measure of atmosphere. They were created in the studio from *maquettes* by Kurt Richter: the stark bedroom of the poor student into which Scapinelli comes skipping, then his study, heavy with anguish and nostalgia, when he has become rich, are bathed in mysterious shadows, and the candle-light flickers in the gloom. The lighting is already provided for in the sketches.★ Thus *The Student of Prague* already exhibits that preoccupation with setting and atmosphere which was to be characteristic of the entire German cinema.

In his lecture in 1916 Wegener insisted that the only effective acting was discreet acting: restrained movements, calm and expressive faces, eloquent eyes, and a dignified naturalness of bearing. Anything in the nature of affectation or gratuitousness would be exposed at once on the vast surface of the screen, where 'the actor is seen as if under a microscope'.

His own acting as the Student of Prague, three years before this lecture, shows that he still had everything to learn about the cinema. Judging from the few rare stills that have come down to us, he must have corrected his style for the inscrutable, enigmatic, claylike being he played in the first *Golem*. That he did so is also borne out by his acting in the same part in the 1920 version.

In the first *Student of Prague* there was already one actor – the obscure and Hoffmannesque John Gottowt – who seemed admirably suited to the cinema. In some respects he foreshadowed the extraordinary character of Dr Caligari played six years later by Werner Krauss.

It is worth mentioning a film made in 1921 by Rochus Gliese (who was later to design *Sunrise*): *Der Verlorene Schatten*; it recalled the story of Peter Schlemihl, and

★ See the sketch published by Edward Carrick in *Designing for Films*, Studio Publications, London and New York, 1949.

43

Wegener played the main part. Stylistically, it is an archaic film, and the acting is curiously stiff and clumsy. This may have been, as Lyda Salmonova told me in Prague, because Wegener quarrelled with the director, who promptly lost interest in the film. It certainly seems to belong to a period earlier than that of *The Student of Prague*.

Our knowledge of the period between *The Student of Prague* and *Caligari* is very limited. All we can do is mention the titles of some artistic films made by Stellan Rye or Wegener and leave the question of their value open: *Das Haus ohne Tür* (1914), *Evinrude – Geschichte eines Abenteuers* (1914), *Der Yogi* (1916), *Der Golem und die Tänzerin* (1917), *Der Fremde Fürst* (1918), *Der Galeeren-sträfling* (1919), and a few years later *Herzog Ferrantes Ende* (1923) and *Lebende Buddha* (1924).

Only a few fragments remain of the *Märchenfilme* (films on legendary or magical subjects) which Wegener made during the war, such as *Rübezahls Hochzeit* (1916) and *Rattenfänger von Hameln* (1918). *Hans Trutz im Schlaraffenland* (1917) has also disappeared. Wegener made them, again on location, among the rocks of the Silesian Riesengebirge, on the sunny slopes and in those small medieval towns along the banks of the Rhine.

Among the surviving images from these lost films there is one of a girl dancing in the silvery sunlight on a grassy flower-spangled hill. Her dress, patterned in different shades of the same tone, harmonizes with the tints in the meadow, as she dances to the magic pipe of Hamelin. The young Lyda Salmonova under the spell of the music bears a resemblance in this costume to the Ophelias and Juliets of the Deutsches Theater. The lines of this slim 'Gothic' figure recall the bearing of those frail maidens in German Primitives as evoked by Max Reinhardt's actresses.

## Max Reinhardt

The links between Max Reinhardt's theatre and the German cinema were obvious as early as 1913, when all the main film actors – Wegener, Bassermann, Moissi, Theodor Loos, Winterstein, Veidt, Krauss, Jannings, to mention but a few – came from Reinhardt's troupe.

*Das Haus ohne Tür (The House
without a Door,* 1914), a
forerunner of *Dr Mabuse.*
Realistic in style, these stills
nevertheless show tendencies
towards decorative composition,
studied grouping and a sharp
contrast between black and white

*Der Ratten fänger von Hameln* (Paul Wegener, 1918): Lyda Salmonova dancing to the magic pipe

We should remember that Max Reinhardt, from 1907 to 1919 (when the revolution brought Piscator and his Constructivist theatre to the fore),★ was a sort of 'Kaiser' of the Berlin theatre. He had become so important that in solid middle-class families everybody skipped the newspaper headlines to read Alfred Kerr's article on the previous night's performance. Berliners often went to the Reinhardt theatre several times a week, for the programme changed daily.

When the cinema became an art-form, it quite naturally took advantage of Reinhardt's discoveries, using the chiaroscuro, the pools of light falling from a high window into a dark interior, which people were used to seeing every evening at the Deutsches Theater.

But Max Reinhardt was far from being the sole source of the German cinema's celebrated treatment of light and shade. There was also the contribution of the Nordic film-makers (the Danes in particular) who invaded the German studios: Stellan Rye, Holger Madsen, Dinesen, for example. They brought with them, at a time when Expressionism had still not crystallized into a recognizable style, their love for nature and their feeling for chiaroscuro.

Since the appearance of Kracauer's book *From Caligari to Hitler*, many cinema enthusiasts have imagined that this much-discussed chiaroscuro was an essential attribute of Expressionism, and that it originated in an Expressionist drama, *Der Bettler* (1912) by Reinhard Sorge, directed for the stage in 1917 by – if I remember correctly – one of Max Reinhardt's collaborators.

This play did in fact have everything: the contrast – or, more precisely, the collision – between light and shadow; the sudden spotlighting of a character or object to concentrate the spectator's attention; and the tendency simultaneously to leave all the other characters and objects in vague darkness. This was the visual translation of the Expressionist axiom stipulating that a sole object chosen from the chaos of the universe must be singled out and plucked from its links with other objects. And everything, even the phosphorescent halo following the outline of a head and shading out towards the regions of darkness, even the slash of piercing light screaming at the blur of a white face, was anticipated in this play.

★ Besides Piscator there were of course three other great stage-directors: Karl Heinz Martin and Jürgen Fehling, both tending towards Expressionism, and Leopold Jessner, who often used Expressionism when it suited him but who, with his famous onstage staircases, was mainly a Constructivist.

47

Yet it is incorrect to claim Reinhardt himself as an Expressionist. Benno Fleischmann writes in his *Max Reinhardt*:* 'Reinhardt was always chary of the young Expressionist poets. They were far different from him as regards both temperament and style. Yet he let them into his theatre for Sunday matinée performances called *Das Junge Deutschland* in Berlin and *Das Theater des Neuen* in Vienna. He himself had little to do with these productions. The great, the indefatigable experimenter stood aloof from these experiments.'

Max Reinhardt, that profound 'Impressionist', could legitimately ignore the experiments of the Expressionists. He had already mastered all the secrets of lighting. He had always been fond of clothing shapes in warm light spilling from innumerable invisible sources, of rounding, melting and hollowing his surfaces with velvety shadows. Here his sole aim was to do away with the Verism and meticulous Naturalism of the previous generation. Before 1914 Reinhardt used innumerable kaleidoscopic effects to appeal to his audience's imagination. The stage would become a vast expanse bustling with life. Bare wings and curtains would frame the gentle curve of a *Rund-horizont*, a horizon whose concave surface was flooded, first with moonlight, then with brilliant sunlight, then immediately plunged into darkness; stars flickered while a kind of magic lantern covered the sky with moving clouds.

During the later years of the First World War, Max Reinhardt, who had frequently been criticized for giving too much importance to his sets, was obliged by shortage of raw materials and lack of money to discontinue the grandeur of his productions. Plays supposed to take place in several different spots were placed in a fixed setting, preferably between two immense columns. Light and darkness then took on a new meaning, by replacing structural variety and by animating and transforming a single set; shifting lighting-effects, crossing and clashing with one another, were the only means of disguising the mediocrity of the ersatz materials used for the sets and of varying the intensity of the atmosphere to suit the action. Darkness was also used to divide one stretch of action from another: a short scene would flash on and then off, and immediately

* Paul Neff Verlag, Vienna, 1948.

Max Reinhardt's stage production of *Hamlet* (1909)

*Homunculus* (1916) and *Metropolis* (1926): the superman

be followed by another. Rapid changes were possible owing to the revolving stage at the Deutsches Theater and the vast arena at the Grosses Schauspielhaus. From the incidental circumstance of war shortages Reinhardt evolved a new manner of grouping characters and giving them depth by means of light. Moreover, crowds could be made to appear denser in the secrecy of shadows. (Lubitsch learned this lesson from Reinhardt, and put it effectively into practice when filming *Das Weib des Pharao*.) Lighting of this kind heightens atmospheric tension, increases the pathos of tragedy, and even enhances the spicy burlesque of a *commedia dell'arte*.

So German film-directors had no need to recall the production of *Der Bettler* in order to use in their turn chiaroscuro effects which had been familiar to them for years.

Proof can be found in the serial film *Homunculus* which, made as it was long before *Caligari*, has not had the attention it deserves. In this pioneer work the contrasts between black and white, the collisions between light and shade – all the classical elements of the German film, from *Der Müde Tod* (*Destiny*) to *Metropolis* – are already present.

The German soul instinctively prefers twilight to daylight. In *The Decline of the West* Oswald Spengler exalts the mist, the enigmatic chiaroscuro, the '*Kolossal*', and infinite solitude. The unlimited spaces cherished by the 'Faustian soul' of northern man are never clear and limpid but swathed in gloom; the Germanic Valhalla, symbol of a frightful solitude, is a grisaille* ruled by unsociable heroes and hostile gods.

Spengler asserts that solitaries are the only men to know the 'cosmic experience'; they alone are capable of experiencing the inexpressible isolation and nostalgia of the forest. Jean Cassou said of Lang's *Nibelungen*, shortly after it came out in France, that it was 'a new and poignant testimony of man's solitude'.

Spengler's 'Faustian soul', enamoured of this gloom, has a predilection for the colour brown – 'Rembrandt's atelier brown'. This brown, a 'protestant colour' missing from the rainbow, is consequently the 'most unreal of all colours'; it is the colour of the soul, it becomes the symbol of the transcendental, the infinite and the

* Grisaille: decorative painting in grey monotone to represent objects in relief.

The influence of Max Reinhardt: Eichberg's *Monna Vanna*, Oswald's *Lukrezia Borgia*

The influence of Max Reinhardt: Oswald's *Carlos und Elisabeth* and *Lukrezia Borgia*

The influence of Max Reinhardt: *Lukrezia Borgia* and Buchowetzki's *Danton*

'spatial'. The adoration of brown and its tints and, inevitably, of shadow, goes back to the famous book by Julius Langbehn *Rembrandt als Erzieher*, published in 1890, which argues that Rembrandt represents the authentic Aryan with the instinct for chiaroscuro characteristic of the Low German. Consequently, like the Germans, Rembrandt, the master of melancholy and the 'bilious black', is, according to Langbehn, always in quest of 'the dark side of existence, the twilight hour when the dark seems darker and the light lighter'. And he goes on to allege that chiaroscuro is the perfect Low German colour, the German being 'simultaneously both harsh and tender'!

Reading certain passages in Jean-Paul Richter (that Romantic all too often neglected by those who are forever quoting Hoffmann), particularly in *Titan*, written in 1802, one has the distinct feeling that one is watching a German film. For instance, he talks about a shadowy bedroom in which his soul starts shivering on account of a sunbeam falling through the high-set window, and a swirl of dust continually shifting like a live thing about to take on concrete form.

Landscape obviously participates in this obsession with chiaroscuro. 'Often', says Hölderlin in his *Hyperion*, 'my heart feels at ease in this twilight. Contemplating unfathomable Nature I know not why this *veiled idol* draws sacred, blessed tears from my eyes.' And he asks, 'Could this twilight be our element?' Or again, 'Is shadow our soul's Fatherland?'

To the glory of this eternal love for the uncertain, hence for the night, Novalis composed langorous hymns, finding in it a refuge far from the 'poor and puerile' light, far from the attacks of hostile life. Attracted by the dark maternal bosom of this dream- and death-dispensing night, all that Novalis ultimately sought there was the echo of his own disquiet. 'I am light. Ah, if only I were night! Why am I not shadows and darkness! How I would quench my thirst at the breast of light.'

Spengler, the theorist of mysticism, tried to see clearly what was what in the motives for these preferences. Daylight imposed limits on the eye and created corporeal objects. Night dissolved bodies, daylight dissolved souls. In this sense darkness has an appeal for the German mind. The Scandinavian *Edda* already bore 'the trace of those midnights when Faust ponders in his study'.

Nordic man's Faustian soul is committed to gloom, whereas Reinhardt – we should remember that he was Jewish – created his magical world with light, darkness serving only as a foil to the light.

This was the twofold heritage of the German film.

## Der Golem (The Golem, 1920)

Paul Wegener had too strong a personality to be content with merely imitating Reinhardt's style. His treatment of the magical lighting-effects found at the Deutsches Theater was to adapt them to the needs of the cinema. From his previous work in natural settings he kept a fluidity of atmosphere which he managed to bring to his studio-made *Golem* (1920). An airy lightness hangs about the shots of the flower-garlanded children playing in front of the ghetto gates.

Wegener uses every one of Reinhardt's lighting-effects: the stars glinting against a velvety sky, the fiery glow of an alchemist's furnace, the little oil-lamp lighting a corner of a darkened room when Miriam appears, the servant holding a lantern, the row of blazing torches flickering in the night, and, in the synagogue, the light trembling over the prostrate, indistinct forms wrapped in cloaks, with the sacred, haloed seven-branched candelabra emerging from the darkness.

The spell of these subtle effects is never broken by clashing contrast or exaggerated Expressionist brio. A warm Rembrandt-like light floods the interiors, modelling the old Rabbi's ravaged face and casting the young disciple into gentle relief against the dark background; the shadow of a barred window stands out across a garment. The scene of the appeal to the demon with its circles of flames is even more poignant than the corresponding scene in Murnau's *Faust*: the demon's phosphorescent head, with its sad empty eyes, is suddenly transformed into a huge Chinese mask looming up in profile at the edge of the screen with a kind of prodigious ferocity.

Paul Wegener always denied having had the intention of making an Expressionist film with his *Golem*. But this

56

*The Golem* (1920): the rabbi's furnace

*The Golem* (1920): the flower-garlanded children

has not stopped people from calling it Expressionist, doubtless because of the much-discussed settings by Poelzig, the creator of the Grosses Schauspielhaus in Berlin.★

Kurtz says something to the effect that Poelzig expresses all a building's dynamic, ecstatic, fantastic and pathetic elements in the façade without extending any renewal of forms to the layout itself.

This explains why the sets of *The Golem* are so far removed from those of *Caligari*. The original Gothic forms are still somehow latent in these houses with their steeply-pitched thatched roofs. Their angular, oblique outlines, their teetering bulk, their hollowed steps, seem the none too unreal image of a distressingly insanitary and overpopulated ghetto where people actually live. The success of these sets owes very little to abstraction. The narrow gables are somehow echoed in the pointed hats and wind-blown goatees of the Jews, the excited fluttering of their hands, their raised arms clutching at the empty yet restricted space. This alternately terrified

★ Compared with other modern architects such as Le Corbusier or Mies van der Rohe, Professor Hans Poelzig cuts a rather surprising figure: in his Grosses Schauspielhaus, the reconstruction of a Berlin circus (transformed into a Greek arena for Reinhardt), the interior suggested a kind of mysterious, stalactitic cavern; in the foyer and corridors, the style was Egyptian, with the lotus-flower shining from floodlit capitals; while outside, the narrow arcades vaguely recalled the style of the Colosseum, though with a Gothic element.

58

*The Golem* (1920): in the synagogue

★ Mme Marlene Poelzig, Professor Hans Poelzig's widow (whom I was able to contact through the kindness of Mr Standish D. Lawder, Yale University, Hans Richter's son-in-law), recently sent me the following information.

In 1918 Paul Wegener re-encountered Hans Poelzig, whom he had known before the war. In the aftermath of defeat, the great architect was without work. He gladly accepted Wegener's offer to draw up some sketches for the setting of the second *Golem*. He made a number of sketches, which he had modelled in greater detail

and exultant crowd at times recalls the flamboyant outlines and disjointed movement of a painting by El Greco. The brio of these masses has nothing in common with the mechanical use of extras found in Lubitsch, or the geometric groupings of crowds found in Fritz Lang. The shaping effect is particularly successful when the ornamental derives from the natural, as in the high-angle shot of the thora-tabernacle bordered by the great sacred trumpets.

In the interiors, a tracery of Gothic ribs and ogives transformed into oblique semi-ellipses composes a framework for the characters. This gives stability to the fluctuating intensity of the atmosphere, which is at times curiously 'Impressionistic' for this authentically 'Expressionistic' structure.

We do find from time to time Expressionistic shock lighting effects: for instance the conch of the spiral staircase glaring out abruptly from the darkness of the laboratory; the sudden glow of the seven-branched candelabra; or the livid, anguished faces of the faithful in the synagogue.★

59

The Golem (1920): two sketches by Hans Poelzig, *left*, 'how he came into the world', *right*, the ghetto

### Die Chronik von Grieshuus (1925)

It is a quite remarkable fact that the 'Nordic invasion' – the arrival of so many Danish actors and directors in the Berlin studios – did not leave so deep a mark on the German cinema as it might have done – though it did open the way to chiaroscuro. On the whole, the white magic of the Scandinavians was conquered by the black magic of the Germans.

It was perhaps because he took *Die Chronik von Grieshuus* from a typically Nordic tale by Storm, a writer from Schleswig-Holstein (long a Danish possession), that Arthur von Gerlach succeeded in creating one of the few German films to capture the feeling of fresh air and nostalgic poetry characteristic of the Swedish cinema. Even the rather melodramatic scenario with its clumsy captions (the work of Thea von Harbou) and the battered Expressionistic castle built on the vast location at Neubabelsberg cannot attenuate this melancholy *Ballade-*

by his wife Marlene, who was a sculptress (and who, incidentally, sculpted the columns for Reinhardt's Grosses Schauspielhaus). On large tables in her studio, she constructed clay models which were later taken to the film studios to be made up.

*The Golem* (1920): the crowd

*The Golem* (1920): model for the rabbi's laboratory, made by Marlene Poelzig from her husband's sketches. *Below*, part of an actual set

like lyricism, which is also found in Paul Wegener's fantasy films.

The Lüneberger Heide in northern Germany lends its natural setting of bleak open country to this grim tale of unhappy love, fratricide and expiation. Across the plains dotted with blackish storm-rent shrubs horsemen gallop in vast billowing cloaks, huge equestrian frescoes sculpted against a pale sky. Their mounts rear and stamp the air: the storm of the heart and Nature become one. In the interiors, darkness, light, and superimposed apparitions weave their dense veil of atmosphere. This tonality is the perfect continuation of the rather 'Impressionistic' chiaroscuro already found in *The Golem* which was to be brought to its perfection in Murnau's *Faust*.

## Vanina (1922)

All we know about Arthur von Gerlach is that he produced for the stage, but not in Berlin.★

After the two lost films for Fern Andra, and three years before *Die Chronik von Grieshuus*, he made a sublime film which is astonishingly mature for its day, taken from a scenario by Carl Mayer, *Vanina*. It is a work whose quality of light comes through even in mediocre 16 mm duplicates, and it is characterized by audacity of movement, especially in the scenes between the revolutionaries and the Governor's troops; the screen comes to life in the powder-smoke of the cannon and the darkness slashed by fire. Eloquent, austere use is made of a columned gateway through which the streams of combatants pass. No one gives the impression of wearing fancy dress. And the snatches of exteriors, skilfully edited, give space to this stark drama which makes but little use of Stendhal's *nouvelle*.

These scenes of movement contrast with the dark, multiple, inextricable corridors – created with all the fervour of Expressionism by Walter Reimann – through which the lovers wander in their despair. The main action, set in sumptuous halls, recalls some of Buchovetzki's better costume films.

If this film is more astonishing for us today than many others, the reason is that Nielsen's acting is intensely modern – her eyes, her hands, the sweep of her figure

★ Professor Rolf Badenhausen of the Institut für Theaterwissenschaft at Cologne University, and of the Theatermuseum, has kindly given me the following information on Gerlach: born *c.* 1877, died 1925. Producer and director in Bromberg 1906–11, then in Elberfeld. Produced, among others, Shakespeare and Strindberg, and staged Mozart and Wagner operas for festival weeks in Holland. Made two other films, now lost (both with Fern Andra) before his two masterpieces *Vanina* and *Die Chronik von Grieshuus*.

*Die Chronik von Grieshuus:* fresh air and nostalgic poetry

betraying an immense sorrow, give a violent intensity and resonance to this Kammerspiele of souls, even if at times the great Wegener (and also Paul Hartmann) does not quite succeed in freeing himself from certain theatrical qualities to which Gerlach, as a stage director, may still have been sympathetic.

Gerlach died young, but these films already reveal a master hand: had he lived, he would surely have risen to the heights attained by Lang and Murnau.

## Carl Boese on the special effects for The Golem (1920)

I have often been asked what my part was in the making of Paul Wegener's second version of *The Golem.* Primarily an actor, Wegener had always preferred to have a craftsman at his side, as was the case for *The Student of Prague* in 1913, made by Stellan Rye.

When I filmed *Die Tänzerin Barberina* in 1919, there was, besides a still unknown young actor, Otto Gebühr, a very beautiful novice actress who played the famous dancer – Lyda

Landscape: in the studio (*Siegfried*) and in nature (*Die Chronik von Grieshuus*)

*Die Chronik von Grieshuus:* darkness, light, and superimposed apparitions

*Die Chronik von Grieshuus:* the battered Expressionistic castle

Salmonova, then the wife of Paul Wegener. Thus the latter
often came along to the studios and one day he suggested that
I work with him on a new *Golem* for Union Film. I accepted
with pleasure.

I proposed the extraordinary architect Hans Poelzig for the
sketch-designs; the great designer Kurt Richter had the job of
supervising the actual making of the sets. The whole was freely
built in rough-cast vaults and ogives.

As Guido Seeber was ill we fell back on another very good
cameramen, Karl Freund, who was splendid at composing
images, but unwilling to risk his hand at executing trick shots.
So I had to take care of them myself, while Freund helped me
with the lighting.

The whole was, moreover, filmed with a normal Debrie
(Parvo) camera. We used diaphragms for shutter dissolves, iris
diaphragm dissolves, and superimpositions, which in those days
were prepared and executed in the camera itself during the
actual shooting.

*The sunbeams*
It had always been difficult to film sunbeams falling from a

67

*Vanina*: darkness slashed by fire

high window, a shot often used in films at that time. I had frequently had to explain to cameramen that only in the early morning or late in the evening did sunbeams fall from the window as flat as they were usually shown in films. The sun being higher during the hours of work, another way of showing sunbeams had to be found.

One of Poelzig's sketches in the Rabbi's laboratory showed sunbeams falling almost vertically from the window. These rays of light were quite conspicuous and swirling with dust. To obtain this effect Freund asked for very powerful light sources, for these rays had not merely to illuminate, but to be luminous themselves.

Yet we had to work with a single light source with rays falling on a parallel. Thus we could give the illusion of rays having sharp shadow-outlines. I had the idea of using a natural source of light – the sun itself. For we still worked in glass studios in those days.

So we had to place the laboratory in such a way that the real sunbeams could be captured. Of course, we only had a few hours to take advantage of them.

68

*Vanina*: Asta Nielsen

However, everything was not altogether settled even then. The fine particles of dust in the air did not reflect sufficiently to make the sunbeams luminous on the film-emulsions then used. We thus had to grind down a special dust composed principally of mica. When we scattered this dust in the air it stayed there for quite some time. As this dust was highly reflective, we had to mask the lamps and spots serving for the ensemble lighting, i.e. we had to create a kind of dark zone around the sunbeams.

*The invocation of the demon*
You will remember that the Rabbi Loew had to trace in the laboratory itself a magic circle of three metres diameter, which neither he nor his assistant were to leave. Then the ground split and flames rose up. To attain this effect the whole laboratory had been built on scaffolding. Technicians, installed in a kind of underground passage, sent smoke and blazing matter up through the slits. They wore gas masks and pushed small grates along a track to feed the smoke and flames. At the same time, spotlights were tilted down on to the smoke-flames; in this way we got the impression that they were themselves incandescent.

For the thunderstorm bursting outside the magic circle, we used high-tension flashes. We first filmed the Rabbi and his disciple in the magic circle, then we counted the frames and superimposed the flashes on to the same negative in the camera. When we had to present flashes in the background, we used lens masks. But we had to show at the same time the reflections of the flashes on the two actors' faces. To obtain this effect we printed from the developed negative one positive and three excessively thin double-negatives; then we superimposed one of the negatives and, immediately afterwards, the flashes of the two images of the other negative; in this way we obtained some parts less luminous than the others. In the eyes of the spectators these parts seemed to be produced by the flashes. These two copies only served, moreover, for the trials. Then we superimposed the master negative and, after each flash, two images of the third double negative, which gave us the effect we wanted.

The transparent ghosts were superimposed on the master negative. For them we had created in another corner of the studio a kind of enormous mountain covered with black velvet. Rochus Gliese had invented fantastic shapes and faces, which glided and dived towards the magic circle. We filmed these apparitions at double or even triple speed, which made their movements extremely slow and unreal. What is more, our camera was already mobile [*sic*!],★ we moved forward

★ *Author's Note*: Karl Freund assures me that he had *not* used the mobile camera before using it, for the first time, in *The Last Laugh* (1924).

with it instead of hanging the ghosts on wires and making them swing. Scraps of the magic word that the Rabbi sought had to come out of the mouth of a demoniac mask. This effect was also executed by a mobile camera in front of black velvet, using dissolves and lap dissolves, and the whole was super-imposed on the negative in the camera itself, as we were used to doing, by counting the frames. The letters of the word were cut out in yellowish cardboard, they were harshly lit, and we used the same effects as for the flashes, while using two negative emulsions from time to time in order to light some more than others and to make them dip and sway.

*The burning mantlet*

It had been decided that the Rabbi's assistant would wear a light mantlet which the storm would lift and which ghostly hands would grip when it floated out of the magic circle. Then the mantlet had to burst into flames on the body of the young man in the circle.

What were we to do? How were we to film cloth burning on a person's body?

Nothing but chemical techniques could give us such an effect. I remembered that nitrocellulose burned excessively fast. It was less dangerous than people generally think, in an open space, for thus the danger of a severe explosion is averted.

So I had several mantlets made in cellulose, like paper handkerchiefs. They were dyed dark grey, almost black. (We needed several mantlets because if they had burned too fast, the camera would only have captured the smoke instead of the flame.)

These mantlets were rigged on a copper wire mounting which gave them the necessary support and served as the conductor wire for ignition. This mounting was joined to another invisible conductor wire which was introduced into the interior of the mantlet and led down from the neck to the shoe and to a small copper plate under the sole of Ernst Deutsch's shoe. Under Deutsch we had fixed another copper plate in the magic circle, larger this time, to allow him to move around at will. This second plate was joined by a well-insulated lead to a secondary pole of the high-tension coil of a magneto. The ghost which was to touch the mantlet was fitted with a lead from the other secondary pole of the magneto, running from the trousers to the sleeve of its costume and traversing one of its gloves which ended in a metal claw. When the ghost touched with this claw the copper wire at the edge of the mantlet, heavy sparks burst out, capable of igniting the powder cotton of the mantlet.

Finally the six mantlets were steeped in a specially pro-
portioned mixture of nitric and sulphuric acids. They were
carefully dried and put into little tin boxes; the firemen brought
them to the studio at the last minute.

To reassure Ernst Deutsch, who was uneasy, we asked for a
volunteer to put on one of the mantlets which was slightly
defective and undergo the 'ordeal by fire'. The trial was
successful. And the film proves that this effect of the mantlet
touched by the ghost's claw and bursting into flames is effective.

Afterwards Deutsch had to fall down in the magic circle.
An explosion had to take place, then a dark cloud of smoke
had to rise up gradually. Beneath it the spectator then had to
see the two characters stretched out senseless on the floor where
the magic circle had been shortly before this scene.

This effect was to be resolved by exploiting physical
properties, a light gas necessarily passing through a heavier
one.

All the openings in the laboratory walls were blocked with
tarpaulins from the outside up to a height of two metres;
screens and sheets were set up around the camera. All that
was left open was the window and the spiral staircase in the
background.

Two dummies dressed in the actors' costumes were then
placed on the floor. Next, eight cylinders of carbon dioxide
were installed. This could be led through pipes into the interior
of the laboratory. The carbon dioxide, transparent like air,
but much heavier than air or smoke, filtered from the cylinders,
lifting the smoke, and the camera filmed the forms stretched
out on the ground beneath this cloud of smoke. Then the smoke
slowly cleared through the opening of the window, as day
dawned.

### The Golem comes to life

Our final special effect was the bringing to life of the inert
matter of the Golem. This time the effect was neither technical,
chemical, or physical. I appealed quite simply to the illusion and
imagination of the spectator himself.

Rabbi Loew, having discovered the magic word, has to
write it on a parchment and slip it into a capsule fixed on the
chest of the clay Golem. Then the Golem comes to life and
opens his eyes wide.

We were unwilling to cut this shot, which would have
simplified the replacement of the clay statue by Wegener
himself.

Consequently, we had to proceed as follows: the Rabbi
stares at the statue which, a moment previously, had still been
tottering. Then he removes the capsule from the Golem's

*The Golem* (1920): special effects

chest and goes with it to the table. The camera tracks back in the air and keeps the Golem in the field of vision, even when it tilts to film what the Rabbi is doing.

The Rabbi takes the parchment with the magic word, rolls it up and slips it into the capsule. Then he goes back towards the Golem. The camera follows him, still keeping the Golem in the field of vision, and approaches it until it frames it in life size. At the edge of the image we still partly see the Rabbi and at the bottom his hands which are putting the capsule back in the Golem's chest. At the same moment the Golem opens his eyes and looks around. The inert matter starts breathing.

Nobody seeing the film will believe that at a certain moment, in front of the camera, which continues rolling, the immobile statue of the Golem was removed by four men and swiftly replaced by Wegener.

I had suggested that Steinrück, the Rabbi, should pretend to be clumsy while rolling up the parchment and almost drop it, then finally succeed in lodging it into the capsule. At this critical moment all eyes were intent on this action in the foreground, and I got Wegener to take the place of the statue in the background without the audience noticing.

*'At first sight he may appear a trifle rough, even vulgar. But you have to remember that he spent more than half a century in Berlin, where there lives – as many a detail has made me realize – a species of the human race so bold that little can be gained by treating them with nicety; on the contrary, you have to bare your teeth and resolve to be brutal yourself if you don't want to go under. . . .'*
Goethe, speaking of his friend Zelter, who before turning musician was a stonemason in Berlin: *Eckermann's* Conversations, 1827.

## Madame Dubarry (1919), Sumurun (1920), Anna Boleyn (1920), Danton (1921), Othello (1922)

The flood of historical films that swamped the German cinema from 1919 to 1923–24 – usually designated, rather significantly, by the term *Kostümfilme* – was an expression of the escapism of a poverty-stricken, disappointed nation which, moreover, had always been fond of the glitter of parades. Despite what Paul Rotha says of these films in his book *The Film Till Now* – he calls them 'commercial products of the property-room and Reinhardt' – all that the majority of them retain of the Reinhardtian *mise-en-scène* is a rather superficial treatment of certain purely exterior elements. Many a *Kostümfilm* merely imitates the things easiest to filch: a few nicely symmetrical decorative groupings and a stylization which it promptly debases through an unimaginative lack of variety.

Max Reinhardt's influence did lead to many costume films being set in the Renaissance: *Die Pest in Florenz*, one of the episodes in *Der Müde Tod*, *Lukrezia Borgia*, and *Monna Vanna*, for example. We sometimes find the recollection of a Reinhardt production leading second-rate directors to film a few effectively framed shots: in Richard Oswald's *Lukrezia Borgia*, for example, a row of soldiers forming a thick hedge prickling with lances recalls a scene from Shakespeare's *Henry IV* in Reinhardt's production of 1912. There also soldiers deployed along the stage contrived to give the impression of an entire army. As in Reinhardt, a few tooled sets of armour and a flag drifting in the wind establish points

*Madame Dubarry*

of reference in the design. If these compositions seem to reflect one of Uccello's famous battle-scenes, this is due to Reinhardt.

In the *Monna Vanna* of Richard Eichberg, who was later to content himself with directing insipid comedies, we come across magnificent shots such as that of the semicircle of soldiers levelling their lances at a single character who holds the mob at bay. Leaving an empty space between the main character and the extras and guiding the spectator's eye by means of salient features towards the centre of interest is another of Reinhardt's devices. Everything in this shot betrays his technique; even the palazzi bordering the piazza recall the stage of a theatre. (One can compare, in passing, that famous square market-place, around which Lubitsch was so fond of moving his crowds, in *Madame Dubarry*, *Sumurun* and *Anna Boleyn*. In each of these instances, the imitation of Reinhardt effects is of an almost documentary fidelity.)

76

Oswald had realized long before Lubitsch what the
cinema had to gain from the magical effects of Reinhardt's
lighting. For his film *Carlos und Elisabeth* (1924) he used
as his model the production of *Don Karlos* which was put
on several times at the Deutsches Theater.

As in Reinhardt, the characters suddenly surge out of
the darkness, lit by invisible sources of light; in a room,
a flood of light falls from a high central window, piercing
the darkness without destroying it. The rich costumes
and trimmings glitter and glow – lamés, gilt dentelles,
velvets. The Hamlet-like sadness of the pallid face of
Veidt as the Spanish Infanta leaps from the darkness.
But these extremely evocative images contrast unfavour-
ably with others which lack this magic, and the mediocrity
of the *mise-en-scène* and the indifferent direction of the
actors (though they all belonged to Reinhardt's troupe)
becomes immediately all too apparent.

These films based on more or less forgotten memories
of productions at the Deutsches Theater soon came up

*Anna Boleyn*

*Anna Boleyn*

against their limitations. In *Othello* by Dimitri Buchovetzki, a Russian director working in Germany, nothing remains of the opalescent Venice evoked in *Destiny*. The fluid doom-laden rhythm which Reinhardt was able to achieve is made impossible by the constant intrusion of distractingly naïve titles.

The only thing left is the character of Iago, which Werner Krauss had already played on the stage. Krauss plays Iago as a sort of buffoon, with a close-fitting tunic of gleaming silk setting off his plumpness to odd effect. Part ballet dancer, part Harlequin, part mephistophelian demon, Iago excites the spectator's curiosity with his frantic capers, his *entrechats*, and the evil pleasure he takes in intrigue.

Lubitsch, who was for a long time a member of Max Reinhardt's troupe, was less sensitive to his influence than other German film-makers. A typical Berliner, who began his career in the cinema with rather coarse farces, Lubitsch saw the pseudo-historical tragedies as so many opportunities for pastiche.

Before Hitler came to power Berliners were considered to be realistic and even materialistic people, with a keen sense of the ridiculous and a fondness for back-chat. To their naturally positive and down-to-earth attitudes the arrival of the Huguenots had added a grain of French wit. At the beginning of the nineteenth century, during the period of Rahel Varnhagen's salon, the wealthy Jewish bourgeoisie contributed their intellectual drive and insight. Later, towards the end of the century, the nonchalant, rather cynical humour of the *Konfektion*, the Jewish lower middle-class engaged in the ready-made-clothing trade, came in with that sense of comic fatalism peculiar to people used to enduring pogroms and persecutions.

Such were the ingredients that went to make up the 'Lubitsch touch'. Subsequently, in the United States, Lubitsch was to become more refined and to understand that it was time for him to rid himself of a certain 'Central European' vulgarity. He radically modified the frequently oafish effects in his middle-class comedies, hastily adopting an elegant gracefulness in which there always remained a little of the vainglory of the *nouveau-riche*. But all these factors contributed to the elaboration

*Madame Dubarry*

of very skilful elliptical techniques based on what Lewis
Jacobs calls the 'rapier-like comments of his camera'.
All in all, in order to perfect his famous 'touch', Lubitsch
had merely to develop his Germanness: his Berliner's
presence of mind, his taste for realistic detail, and his
Jewish liking for the suggestive implication leading
quite naturally to images with a double meaning.

Even at the start of his career, when he was still in
Berlin, Lubitsch already knew how to exploit ridicu-
lousness by suggesting a comic trait with an image
which scarcely touched upon the action but which hinted
at the essence of a situation or character. The contrast
between a character's overall importance and the absurdity
of some accessory detail was to be used several times
over in films such as *Madame Dubarry* or *Anna Boleyn*.
Visual double meanings which, when the time came,
he was to enrich with a kaleidoscopic use of sound, were
thrown into relief by skilful editing.

In a way Lubitsch turned into the proverbial valet for

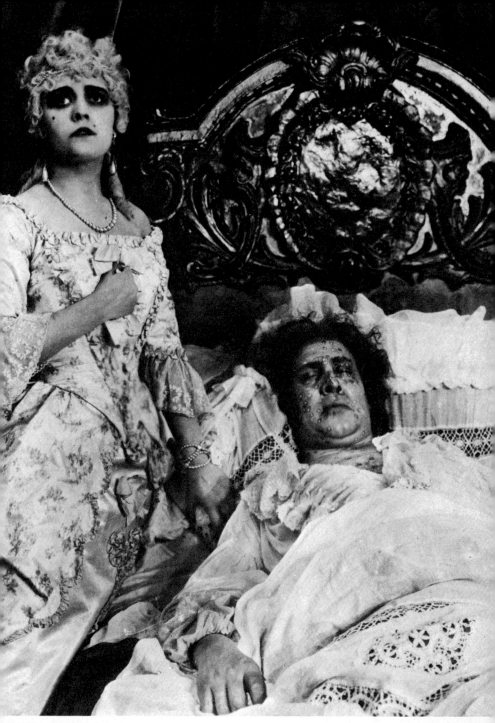

*Madame Dubarry*

whom no man is a hero. Non-Germans can find this a rather disconcerting attitude, but the glance into the wings, however superficial it may be, does give a breath of humanity to his characters. This is why the Americans, who are not given to respecting historical truth (especially other people's), could think that Lubitsch was 'the great humanizer of history', and call him the 'German Griffith' who with 'a realism in no wise fictitious reconstitutes history in all its barbaric grandeur'.★ But a king manicuring his mistress or artlessly pinching a pretty wench is hardly Unadorned Reality, and even less History As It Was Lived.

For Lubitsch, one-time shop assistant, History was never to be more than a pretext for telling love stories in sumptuous period costume: silks, velvets and trimmings delighted his knowing eye.

Preoccupied with incidentals, Lubitsch rarely resorts to the use of contrast between light and shade which his contemporaries pursued. His typically Berliner mentality, never tempted by dreaming or mystery – Heaven and Hell can *both* wait – is at the origin of his sometimes offhand technique up to the day his shrewdness made him realize what there was to be gained from using the famous chiaroscuro. He also learned to value his leading actress, Pola Negri, who played the leading roles in many of his films.

## Pola Negri

*She is the Magnani of the silent era, full of exuberant vitality.*

*She does not act; she is scarcely an actress. Quite simply, she exists. She has that intangible quality called 'presence'; she is her role.*

*At a time when women on the screen often appeared to have botched their make-up, her full clear-featured face is photogenic in itself and brimming with life.*

*For she represents healthy sensuality in all its spontaneity. Instinctive and uncomplicated, Pola Negri is the opposite of the subtle intellectuality of the great Asta Nielsen.*

*Ingenuous, yes, but Polish, and knowing much of love.*

*In the days of the rounded figure she is almost robust, but at the same time supple as a panther.*

★ His aim in *Madame Dubarry* was not, as French histories of the cinema still affirm, to 'ridicule, mock and vilify French monarchs and the great figures of the Revolution'; nor, in *Anna Boleyn*, was it to 'undermine the traditional English respect for royalty and set American puritanism against Merrie Olde England', as Georges Sadoul claims. In 1919–20 Germany was interested above all in foreign currency, and the reactionary forces of heavy industry, which controlled production, considered these pseudo-historical films less as instruments of revenge than as instruments of profit. What is more, certain over-stereotyped French Revolutionary characters – a ruffian with a knife between his teeth, a ragged harridan – are also found in Griffith's *Orphans of the Storm* and Carl Th. Dreyer's *Blade af Satans Bog* (*Leaves from Satan's Book*, 1920).

82

*Nowadays we have to try to understand what she meant for a cinema often still too close to the theatre. For above all she lends her abounding freshness to the rather fusty world of the costume film; next to her, actors coming to films from the stage, and more experienced, sometimes seem mannered. Impulsive, intuitive, she adapts herself better than they to the improvization of the new art-form.*

*Lubitsch and she met in a kind of tacit complicity like that which, some years later, brought together Sternberg and Marlene Dietrich.*

Yet one has to admit that the *mise-en-scène* of *Madame Dubarry* does contain certain nuances. While the great court receptions have a certain dryness despite a wealth of draperies, parquets and stuccoes, the revolutionary passages bear the trace of two productions by Reinhardt, Büchner's and Romain Rolland's plays on Danton. Moreover, in the shots portraying the conspiracy against the Favourite, the grouping of the characters, jutting

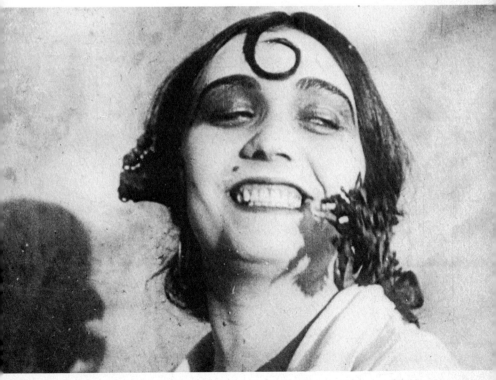

Pola Negri

*Sumurun*

from the shadows, relates them to those in Buchovetzki's *Danton*, though this followed its models more faithfully.

Recollections of Reinhardt's art prevail above all in something for which Lubitsch is famous: his handling of crowd scenes. Yet stills and frame enlargements clearly reveal the arid regularity behind the groupings and the mechanical application of Reinhardt's techniques. From time to time this excessively preconceived orderliness does however come to life when Lubitsch gives it an ebb-and-flow movement – for example, the jostling crowd in front of the cathedral in *Anna Boleyn*.

The town-square architecture in *Anna Boleyn* or *Madame Dubarry* is more realistic than in Reinhardt. Moreover Lubitsch has absolutely no scruples about taking his settings from where he sees fit: in *Sumurun*, for example, we come across an almost exact reproduction, complete with its neighbouring houses,

The costume film: *Die Flamme* (*The Flame*, also known as *Montmartre*, 1923)

of the claylike staircase invented by Poelzig for *The Golem*.

In *Madame Dubarry*, the revolutionary masses clamouring around the guillotine for the death of the former favourite raise their right arms, a formalized movement frequently seen in German films whenever a crowd of extras has to express fury or exultation. Reinhardt gave these gestures to the classical chorus in his production of *Oedipus Rex*, performed in a Berlin circus in 1910. They lose all value in the majority of German films in which inspiration has deteriorated into mere technique.

More than the two *Dantons*, it was *Sumurun*, a favourite pantomime of Max Reinhardt's (he first produced it in 1909, affectionately remodelling it in all its Arabian Nights splendour for each subsequent revival), which left its mark on Lubitsch's style.

In *Sumurun* Lubitsch himself plays the hunchback, a tragic buffoon. When he launches into a bizarre, disjointed, robot-like dance in which his arms and legs seem to have a life of their own, he is inspired by the stage version of the famous pantomime. Wherever this light rhythm comes through, so rare in a German film, it is to Reinhardt that we should render homage.

A few passages in *Sumurun* foreshadow the elegance of the americanized Lubitsch. For example, the clownish assistants in a haberdashery unroll rich materials and spread them out with a 'nothing up my sleeve' look, and the wink at the audience their director is so fond of. The 'Lubitsch touch' is also unmistakable in the high-angle shots of a few cushions laid out on a carpet around which a flock of pretty servant-girls suddenly flutter up and disperse in graceful circles. The American musical was to pattern itself on these delicate arabesques.

Though more superficially than people usually think, the German costume film underwent another influence – that of the Italian historical spectaculars. It can usually be detected in the crowd scenes in the old epics, whether those of Joe May (*Veritas Vincit I/III*, 1918, and *Das Indische Grabmal* I/II, 1921) or a distinctly late film such as *Helena oder der Untergang Trojas*, 1923–24, by the third-rate director Manfred Noa.

We have already noted the Scandinavian contribution, though it should not be overestimated. As for that of the Russian émigré directors working in Germany, one needs only to look at the striking example of Buchovetzki. His *Peter der Grosse*, based on the national history of Russia, is an entirely German film.

'Expressionist man seems to wear his heart painted on his chest' wrote
Kasimir Edschmid. This poster by Hans Werkmeister dates from about 1920

# 5  The Stylized Fantastic

'Young people engaged in the cultural fields, myself among them, made a fetish of tragedy, expressing open rebellion against the old answers and outworn forms, swinging from naïve nineteenth-century sweetness and light to the opposite extreme of pessimism for its own sake.'
Fritz Lang: 'Happily ever after', *Penguin Film Review*, No. 5, 1948.

## Der Müde Tod (Destiny, 1921)

The difference between the Germans and other races, said Clemenceau, is that the Germans have a taste for death, whereas other nations have a taste for life. But the truth of the matter is perhaps – as Hölderlin implies in *Hyperion* – that the German is obsessed by the phantom of destruction and, in his intense fear of death, exhausts himself in seeking means of escaping Destiny.

Lang's silent films and the scenarios which he wrote for Rippert frequently return to the theme of Death, treated in a minor key; it is the leitmotiv of *Der Müde Tod* (*The Weary Death*, usually called *Destiny* in Britain and America). Framed by a main plot (the young woman who tries to wrench her lover from the hands of Death), the three episodes set in different periods and countries are variations on this theme, leading to the same conclusion: all the girl's efforts to save her lover lead him to his destruction.

Death, masculine in German, is not presented in a cruel light. 'The angel of the final hour', says Jean Paul in his *Quintus Fixlein*, 'he whom we call so harshly Death, is the tenderest and best of the angels, chosen to gather up the wilting human heart with delicate gestures. Detaching it from life, extracting it from our frozen bosoms, he bears it off without bruising it, in his gentle hands, to Eden, where it will be warmed again.'

*Destiny:* the Quattrocento through Max Reinhardt

Lang evolved. In 1948, in his Penguin article on the happy ending, he insists several times on his refusal to make any more films in which 'man is trapped by fate'.

Of all the German film-makers it was Fritz Lang who felt Max Reinhardt's influence the most. Nevertheless, like Wegener, he adapted it to his own needs.★

This stylistic origin is especially apparent in one of the episodes in *Destiny*, the one set in Venice during the Renaissance. Rising diagonally, a flight of steps traces its clear outline against a limpid background; down it comes a joyful crowd, moving with the particular rhythm and brio of extras in Reinhardt. Night carnival scenes, in which torches gleam in the trembling darkness, recall the iridescent Impressionism with which that great magician of the theatre treated Shakespeare. Again through Reinhardt we find in Lang traces of the fresh and ardent Quattrocento as it has lived on in the panels of Florentine bridal coffers. The carefree attitudes

★ In his Arabian Nights episode the eclectic Lang uses a detail from *Cabiria*. Douglas Fairbanks, for his part, 'borrowed' the flying-carpet scene in the Chinese episode for his *Thief of Baghdad*. Murnau was later to transpose the same scene masterfully into his *Faust*.

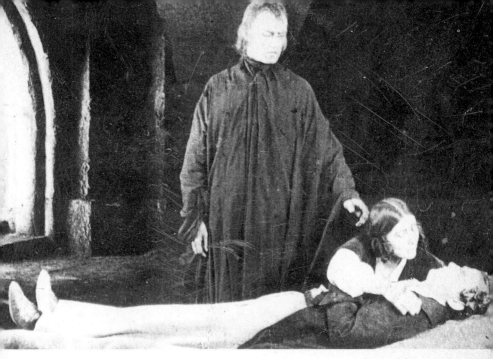

*Destiny:* lighting

of slim young men in short tunics and cloaks leaning against an arcade, skirting a wall, or striding up a staircase after an adversary, betray this source.

Lang is an architect (he was in fact trained as one). He makes the ogival fluting of the Gothic doorway of a crypt stand out in luminous relief contrasting with the dark walls. Compared with such effects the sets of *Caligari* appear reduced to purely linear arabesques, totally lacking the magic of chiaroscuro.

Extraordinary oddness of appearance is found in the laboratory of the little apothecary. A real alchemist's laboratory this, with bottles and innumerable utensils glimmering mysteriously; skeletons and stuffed animals jut out from the darkness like phosphorescent phantoms. In the satanic atmosphere of this place, straight out of Hoffmann, one feels that horrid plots must inevitably be hatched. (Yet the apothecary is a harmless old man who snatches the goblet of poison from the hands of the young inamorata.)

91

*Destiny*: stylization

This technique of emphasizing, often of over-emphasizing, the relief and outline of an object or the details of a set – it was not apparent in *The Golem*, where the atmosphere had more density – was to become one of the most easily recognizable characteristics of the German film. From this time onwards sets were lit from the base, accentuating the relief, deforming and transforming the shapes of things by means of a mass of dazzling and unexpected lines. Another technique was the placing of enormous spotlights to one side, at an angle, so as to flood the architecture with light and use the projecting surfaces to produce strident effects of light and shade. German directors and cameramen were to begin juggling with lighting effects to such an extent that Kurtz could legitimately say that light sometimes created 'abgrundlose Tiefen' – depths without depth. Outlines and surfaces were fragmented irrationally, light and shadow were exaggerated. This interplay of contrasts and counter-contrasts culminated in the half-tangible, half-

*Destiny*: the Chinese magician

unreal 'féerie de laboratoire' mentioned by Jean Cassou. Similar violent oppositions can be found in Romantic authors such as Eichendorff.

Lang soon realized what the judicious handling of light could bring to an atmosphere. He opens up a wall and erects a steep staircase whose steps compose a ladder of light in an arch; a bamboo thicket with its smooth shafts bathed in a swirl of phosphorescent light is a prelude to the crescendo of light in the forest crossed by Siegfried. As Kurtz says, German film-makers fond of the effects of light treat it as a *raumgestaltender Faktor*, a space-forming factor.

These notions no doubt had some influence on Lang, but it would be wrong to consider his first films as essentially Expressionistic. A Chinese landscape in the third episode of *Destiny*, with its twisted trees and curving roofs and bridges, is an obvious target for Expressionistic distortion, but here it is only used to bring out the light–operatic aspect of this episode, which

93

*Destiny:* the Chinese episode

is in the style of *Die Bergkatze*, a film by Lubitsch. Lang's intense feeling for the physical character of objects and his skilful use of lighting effects to bring out architectural line were the only contributions he was to make to the evolution of Expressionism.

# 6    The Symphonies of Horror

'Leave to us Germans the
horrors of delirium, the
dreams of feverishness and the
kingdom of ghosts. Germany
is a country which suits old
witches, dead bears' skins,
golems of each sex and
especially fieldmarshals such
as little Cornelius Nepos who
by birth is a root which the
French call Mandragore.
Such spectres can only
succeed on the other side of
the Rhine; France will never
be a country for them. . . .'
Heine: Die Romantische
Schule, II, 1833.

'We now turn to discuss that
inexhaustible source of
poetical effects in Germany:
terror. Ghosts and wizards
please the people as much as
men of culture.'
Madame de Staël: De
l'Allemagne.

The weird pleasure the Germans take in evoking horror
can perhaps be ascribed to the excessive and very
Germanic desire to submit to discipline, together with a
certain proneness to sadism. In *Dichtung und Wahrheit*
Goethe deplores the 'unfortunate pedagogical principle
which tends to free children early in life from their fear
of mystery and the invisible by accustoming them to
terrifying spectacles'.

In a novel by Karl Philipp Moritz, an eighteenth-
century precursor of the Romantics, a little boy, Anton
Reiser, is kept awake for hours on end by a terrifying
fairy tale about the Man with No Hands who haunts the
chimney on windy nights. Lying in bed, the little boy
imagines with relish the decomposition of his own body
after death.

Most German children delight in tales of horror. As a
child, Tieck's William Lovell dreams of murdering his
little playmates. Nathanael, the tragic hero of Hoffmann's
tale *Der Sandmann*, says that nothing gave him more
pleasure than 'hearing or reading frightening stories of
ghosts, witches and dwarfs. . . .' He could hear again and
again the tale of the Sandman, who tours children's
bedrooms at night and throws sand in their eyes if they
are still not asleep. He then plucks the eyes from their
sockets and bears them off, dripping with blood, to the
moon. There he feeds the eyes to his owl-beaked offspring, who squat in their nest and watch out avidly for
his return.

What are we to make of the child in Eichendorff's
*Ahnung und Gegenwart* who wallows in his nurse's tale

95

ALRAUNE UND DER GOLEM

RIESENBIOSKOPFILM

KÜNSTLERISCHE OBERLEITUNG:

NILS CHRISANDER            GUIDO SEEBER

AUFNAHM

about a poor lad beheaded by his stepmother (she slams the lid of a chest on him), and shudders with pleasure while watching the blood-red evening fall beyond the dark forests? There is a curious ambiguity in the German soul. 'We create fairy tales', says Tieck, 'because we prefer to populate the monstrous emptiness and horrid chaos.'

Quite naturally the Nazis preferred the national poet Schiller to the world-citizen Goethe who, despite *Faust* – turned by Spengler into a symbol of Germanic Man – was considered 'unreliable'. Talking about Faust with Eckermann in 1826, Goethe said that this was the only occasion in his life when he had used 'sorcery and devilry'; afterwards, satisfied with having eaten his Nordic inheritance, he had gone to sit at the table of the Greeks.

Schiller, on the other hand, whose *Geisterseher* (he who sees ghosts) anticipates the Romantics, has a predilection for the imagery of darkness. In fact Goethe criticized Schiller for 'a certain taste for cruelty which revealed itself as early as *Die Räuber*'. He told Eckermann that he had been forced to reject a rather sadistic innovation proposed by Schiller for the production of *Egmont*. Schiller had wanted to have the Duke of Alba appear at the back of the prison, a dark figure masked and draped in a cloak, gloating upon Egmont's reactions to the death-sentence.

What a scene for a film!

## Nosferatu (1922)

The complete title of Murnau's film is *Nosferatu, eine Symphonie des Grauens* (*Nosferatu, a Symphony of Horror*). And in fact, seeing this film again today, one cannot fail to be chilled by what Béla Balázs called 'the glacial draughts of air from the beyond'. The terror emanating from *Caligari* seems somehow almost artificial by comparison.

In Friedrich Wilhelm Murnau, the greatest film-director the Germans have ever known, cinematic composition was never a mere attempt at decorative stylization. He created the most overwhelming and poignant images in the whole German cinema.

97

Alraune (Mandrake) and the Golem were favourite characters during 'the demoniac epoch'

Murnau was trained as an art-historian. Whereas Lang attempts to give a faithful reproduction of the famous paintings he sometimes uses, Murnau elaborates the memory he has kept of them and transforms them into personal visions. The foreshortened view of a prostrate man stricken with plague in *Faust* (the shooting angle makes the soles of his feet become enormous) is the transposed reflection of Mantegna's Christ. And when Gretchen nurses her infant in the snow among the ruins of a cottage, with her head wrapped in her cloak, this image is no more than the vague reminiscence of a Flemish Madonna.

Murnau had homosexual tendencies. In his attempt to escape from himself, he did not express himself with the artistic continuity which makes it so easy to analyse the style of, say, Lang. But all his films bear the impress of his inner complexity, of the struggle he waged within himself against a world in which he remained despairingly alien. Only in his last film, *Tabu*, did he seem to have found peace and a little happiness in surroundings which abolish the guilt-feelings inherent in European morality. Gide, once his *Immoraliste* had delivered him from Protestant austerity and its con-comitant scruples, could then indulge his natural in-clinations. But Murnau, born in 1888, lived under the ominous shadow which the inhuman Paragraph 175 of the pre-1918 German Penal Code, lending itself to all the horrors of blackmail, cast over him and those like him.

Murnau, a conscientious artist, German in the good meaning of the word, never resorted to the little shifts and subterfuges which can facilitate the creator's task. This is why his films seem rather heavy in places – the underlying meaning of their rhythm only becomes apparent little by little. At other times, when the big businessmen of Ufa★ put pressure on him for a happy ending, as in *Der Letzte Mann* (*The Last Laugh*, 1924), he scamps it with disgust, pulling the coarsest threads of comedy, and becomes as crass as the audiences that slapped their sides at Lubitsch's *Kohlhiesels Töchter*, one of his least refined farces.

In any case one is forced to admit that Murnau's genius – I think we can talk about genius in his case –

★ Ufa (Universal Film A.G.), Germany's national film-production enterprise, was founded by merger in 1917.

98

has surprising weaknesses. Normally so sensitive, he sometimes commits extraordinary errors of taste and lapses into mawkishness. In *Faust*, for example, insipid images follow powerful visions bursting with creative vigour. His shy nature, burdened with a weighty heritage of typically German sentimentality and morbid timidity, led him to admire in others the muscular strength and vitality he himself lacked. This is why he allowed Jannings to show off outrageously in the role of Mephisto and failed to moderate the exuberance of Dieterle.

Murnau came from Westphalia, a region of vast pastures where enormous peasants breed heavy-boned plough-horses. The landscape had a great influence on him. Even when he was prevailed upon to film in the studio he kept his nostalgia for the countryside; and this homesickness gives *Der Brennende Acker* (*The Burning Earth*, 1922) a wild flavour which is still perceptible in *Sunrise*, made in the USA.

The landscapes and views of the little town and the castle in *Nosferatu* were filmed on location. This was far from being the usual practice in German films at that time. Directors such as Lang or Lubitsch built vast forests and entire towns so as to be able to film in the studio or, at a pinch, a few yards away on a strip of waste ground; and the reason was not merely that the frontiers were closed to them through a lack of foreign currency and sympathy. They could easily have found Gothic towns on the Baltic coast or Baroque towns in Southern Germany; but Expressionist precepts turned them away from reality.

Murnau, however, making *Nosferatu* with a minimum of resources, saw all that nature had to offer in the way of fine images. He films the fragile form of a white cloud scudding over the dunes, while the wind from the Baltic plays among the scarce blades of grass. His camera lingers over a filigree of branches standing out against a spring sky at twilight. He makes us feel the freshness of a meadow in which horses gallop around with a marvellous lightness.

Nature participates in the action: sensitive editing makes the bounding waves foretell the approach of the vampire, the imminence of the doom about to overtake the town. Over all these landscapes – dark hills, thick

99

forests, skies of jagged storm-clouds – there hovers what Balázs calls the great shadow of the supernatural.

In a film by Murnau every shot has its precise function and is entirely conceived with an eye to its participation in the action. The momentary close-up of a detail of billowing sails is as necessary to the action as the image preceding it – the high-angle shot of the current sweeping away the raft and its sinister cargo.

The grisaille of the arid hills around the vampire's castle recalls, with its extreme and almost documentary restraint, certain passages in the films of Dovzhenko. A few years later, when Ufa obliged him to use pasteboard, Murnau filmed the famous air journey in *Faust* in the studio, with the aid of models. This prodigious chain of artificial mountains is complete with valleys and torrents; the only thing that makes them tolerable – and sometimes even admirable – is the talent of Murnau. He masks his materials with those combinations of mist and light to which the Germans are so sensitive and which they interpret with the same skill they bring to portraying the gentle glow of a hanging lamp in a stuffy room. *Faust* is the large-scale deployment of all the artifice of the cinema by a man who knows every detail of his craft; but how one regrets the greyish expanses of *Nosferatu*.

In the full maturity of his talent Murnau could achieve in the studio such visions as the vast snow-covered plains against which a storm-rent tree stands out; a post in all its sad nudity rises above a demolished fence – a precarious refuge for Gretchen nursing her child. Similarly, in the studios in America, he was to create for *Sunrise* such realistically desolate marshes that it takes the eye a long time to discern their artificiality. Murnau was one of the few German film-directors to have the innate love for landscape more typical of the Swedes (Arthur von Gerlach, the creator of *Die Chronik von Grieshuus*, was another), and he was always reluctant to resort to artifice. When he made *City Girl* (1930), according to Theodore Huff, he was moved to exaltation when he felt his camera running over the wheatfields of Oregon and sliding through the ocean of ripe grain at the height of the harvest. The coming of the sound film and the commercial ruthlessness of Hollywood destroyed this

*Nosferatu*: the grisaille of the arid hills around the vampire's castle

dream. To escape, Murnau fled to the South Seas, and *Tabu*.

The architecture in *Nosferatu*, typically Nordic – brick façades with stubby gables – is perfectly adapted to the film's strange plot. Murnau did not have to distort the little Baltic townscapes with contrasting lighting effects: there was no need for him to increase the mystery of the alleyways and squares with an artificial chiaroscuro. Under Murnau's direction the camera of Fritz Arno Wagner required no extraneous factors to evoke the bizarre. When Nosferatu is preparing a departure in the courtyard, the use of unexpected angles gives the vampire's castle a sinister appearance. What could be more expressive than a long narrow street, hemmed in between monotonous brick façades, seen from a high window, the bar of which crosses the image?

The undertaker's mutes dressed in top hats and skimpy frock-coats move slowly over the crudely hewn cobbles, black and stiff, bearing, two by two, the slim

*Nosferatu:* brick façades and stubby gables

coffin of a victim of the plague. Never again was so perfect an Expressionism to be attained, and its stylization was achieved without the aid of the least artifice. Murnau was to return to this theme in *Faust*, but there the men in cowls have a quality of artificial picturesqueness rather than the starkness of the earlier composition.

But it was in the portrayal of horror that the camera of Murnau and Fritz Arno Wagner excelled. In *Caligari* the forms of the satanic doctor and Cesare often slant up in a shot left deliberately out of focus, which Kurtz defined as 'the ideal and pure shot of the transposed expression of objects'. But Murnau created an atmosphere of horror by a forward movement of the actors towards the camera. The hideous form of the vampire approaches with exasperating slowness, moving from the extreme depth of one shot towards another in which he suddenly becomes enormous. Murnau had a complete grasp of the visual power that can be won from editing, and the

*Nosferatu:* the portrayal of horror

virtuosity with which he directs this succession of shots has real genius. Instead of presenting the whole approach as a gradual process, he cuts for a few seconds to the reactions of the terrified youth, returns to the approach, then cuts it off abruptly by having a door slammed in the face of the terrible apparition; and the sight of this door makes us catch our breath at the peril lurking behind it.

It is true that the opening shots of *Caligari* show the evil doctor walking straight at the camera and drawing up his replete figure in a menacing attitude; for a second his face swells up diabolically. But a diamond-shaped lens mask immediately tones down the effect. The images of Cesare advancing in the booth and crossing Lil Dagover's bedroom, or the robot coming towards us from the back of the screen in *Metropolis*, are less violent than that of the vampire slowly emerging from the darkness. (But Lang was to learn how to use this effect to advantage; in the first *Mabuse* the doctor's head appears, at first small and remote on a black background, only to be suddenly projected forward, as if by some supernatural agency, filling the whole screen.)

Murnau could also enhance the effect of a transversal movement by spreading it over the whole screen: for instance, the dark phantom vessel speeding with all sail set over a surging sea, and ominously entering the harbour; or again, the low-angle shot of the enormous silhouette of the vampire crossing the vessel to reach his prey. Here the camera angle confers on him, in addition to his gigantic proportions, a kind of obliqueness which projects him out of the screen and makes him into a sort of tangible, three-dimensional menace.

People have often wondered why Wiene never used for *Caligari*, in addition to lens masks of various shapes, the trick techniques that Méliès had already developed, which would have increased the impression of mystery and terror. In *Destiny* Lang took full advantage of superimpositions and fade-outs. The superimposed march of the dead towards the great wall, and the various transformations and apparitions, show that he had understood the resources of a technique capable of freeing itself from the limits imposed by this apparently two-dimensional art-form.

*Nosferatu*

In *Nosferatu* the jerky movements of the phantom coach which bears the young traveller off to the land of the undead, or those of the coffins being piled up with an atrocious rapidity, were rendered by the 'one stop one' (stop-motion) technique. The spectres of bare white trees, rearing up against a black background like carcasses of prehistoric beasts, during the rapid journey to the monster's castle, were rendered by an insertion of a few feet of negative.

Murnau used the obsession with inanimate objects much better than many fanatics of Expressionism. In the haunted hold of the sailing vessel in which all the sailors have been struck down by death, the empty hammock of the dead sailor goes on gently swinging. Or again, stripping down the details to the very minimum, Murnau shows nothing but the reflection of the sustained, monotonous swinging of a suspended lamp in the deserted captain's cabin. Murnau was to use the same effect when his rejuvenated Faust takes the proud Duchess of Parma: a chandelier swinging above the sumptuous bed.

## The demoniac bourgeois

The haunted universe of Hoffmann was reborn in a film by Karl Heinz Martin, *Das Haus zum Mond*, in which a waxwork modeller bears a similar resemblance to his creations. In *Narkose*, which employed a contemporary setting, there is a character who resembles Caligari, feature for feature. In *Orlacs Hände* (*The Hands of Orlac*, 1924) Robert Wiene makes use of all those Romantic characteristics which seemed to him Expressionist in kind: shadowy, ambiguous streets, a strange house with a long corridor peopled by weird figures, a devilish magician and his Hoffmannesque servant. He even includes a cavernous inn, dimly lit by the uncertain light of a hanging lamp, where Orlac is helplessly swallowed up.

The taste for lugubrious characters influenced even Lang, in *Destiny*; the apothecary seeking the mandrake by night is set in a framework of macabre elements: trees with bared roots and twisted silhouettes rear up like phantoms. This wretched creature, a shabby individual not admitted to the dinner-tables of the well-to-do bourgeois, tricked out in his heavy cape and elongated top hat (recalling the extravagant headwear in *Caligari* or *Torgus*), has a distinctly strange appearance. Turning essentially rather inoffensive characters into sinister ones was a pleasure no German film-maker was eager to give up. Thus the characterization of the kindly proprietor of a fairground sideshow in Paul Leni's *Das Wachsfigurenkabinett* (*Waxworks*, 1924) is ambiguous. And again, that odd little gentleman in *Genuine*, with his skimpy morning-coat, white spats and light gloves – is he really as candid as we are led to believe when the young man, his nephew, awakens from a nightmare?

In Romantic literature, one frequently does not know whether a character will eventually prove sympathetic or a wicked demon. In Hoffmann's *Der Goldene Topf*, Archivist Lindhorst, prince of the powers of Good, scares the student Anselme with the piercing gaze of his eyes, rolling in their hollow sockets. Heine says that Hoffmann saw a grimacing spectre under every wig in

The demoniac bourgeois:
painting by Caspar David
Friedrich (1774–1840)
with frames from
*The Student of Prague* (1926)
and *Destiny*

The demoniac bourgeois:
two frames from *Caligari*,
one from Abel's *Narkose*

Berlin; he changed men into beasts and beasts into town councillors. German films belong to the same hybrid, half-real world.

The Romantics also have a tendency to place these unreal creatures of their imagination in hierarchies, related to ordinary middle-class hierarchies. Among those gentlemen practising well-defined professions and flaunting pompous official titles, can one ever be sure that there is not one who leads the double life which fanciful minds find so agreeable? All those town-clerks, municipal archivists, qualified librarians and magistrates must surely hide beneath their municipal exteriors some vestige of sorcery liable to come to the surface at any moment.

In this context one can more easily understand certain German film characters whose vulgarity recalls the buffoonery in those little humorous magazines of which Germany was once so prodigal. In *Destiny* and *The Last Laugh*, Lang and Murnau delighted in portraying the coarseness of the lower middle-classes, besotted with eating and drinking and reeling under the effects of the fresh outdoor air. (The same middle-class drunkards were to appear again in *Hintertreppe* (*Backstairs*) by Jessner, and in Lupu Pick's *Sylvester*.)★

Is this another instance of the Faustian tragedy of the dual soul? And is a whole nation split by this duality?

## The sway of the Doppelgänger

The traces of the 'Doppelgänger, du finst'rer Gesell' (Heine) are numerous. In *Titan*, Librarian Schoppe, a neurotic character, avoids glancing at his hands and feet for fear of perceiving that they belong to 'the other'! In another novel by Jean Paul, *Hesperus*, the hero, Victor, shudders at the waxwork figures, 'those flesh-coloured shadows of the Self'; as a child, when he had been put to bed, he had the gift of leaving his body, conscious of the distance separating him from his 'outer bark of alien flesh'. And in the days of Expressionism the hero of *Der Spiegelmensch* (*The Mirror-Man*), a play by Werfel, was also subject to the perpetual anguish of the *Doppelgänger*. In *Elixire des Teufels*, Hoffmann, terrified by his own ego, exclaims: 'My whole being, turned into

★ Stroheim worked in the same vein in *Greed*, when he satirized the ignoble voracity of Germanic philistines incapable of adjusting to the United States.

the capricious toy of a cruel fate, surrounded by strange phantoms, floated without rest upon a sea of events whose enormous waves broke over me, roaring. I can no longer find myself . . . I am what I seem, yet I seem not to be what I am. I cannot solve the problem myself: my "self" is split in two.'

This dualism appears in many German films: Caligari is both the eminent doctor and the fairground huckster. Nosferatu the vampire, also the master of a feudal castle, wishes to buy a house from an estate agent who is himself imbued with diabolism. And the character Death in *Destiny* is also an ordinary traveller in search of land for sale. It would seem from this that for the Germans the demoniac side to an individual always has a middle-class counterpart. In the ambiguous world of the German cinema people are unsure of their identity and can easily lose it by the way.★ Thus Homunculus, a kind of Führer, can even split his personality at will; disguised as a worker, he incites the poor to rebel against his own dictatorship. The same morbid taste for split personality is also found in Fritz Lang's two *Mabuse* films and *M*.

The hairless face and almost indecently bald head of Nosferatu haunted the German film-makers for a long time. In the more middle-class ambience of *Tagebuch einer Verlorenen* (*Diary of a Lost Girl*, 1929), a film made by Pabst although he was the champion of a certain 'social realism', the director of the house of correction looks like Nosferatu's brother. This vigilant and obsequious supervisor is everywhere at once, popping up like a jack-in-the-box, tall and stiff and proper in his dark frock-coat, recalling the enigmatic manservant embodied by Fritz Rasp in *Metropolis*.

Nosferatu's baldness, which we encounter again in the little man in *Genuine*, seems to come straight out of *Titan*, the novel by Jean Paul in which we are shown, suddenly appearing among the drinkers in a beer-cellar (an altogether propitious spot ever since Faust's 'Auerbachs Keller' with its diabolical apparitions), 'a stranger as bald as a skull, without eyebrows, and with pink but flabby cheeks'. This character folds his repugnant skin into convulsive grimaces in such a way that at every instant a different personality seems to take shape beneath this changing mask.

★ Hoffman says that the devil bestrews walls, cradles and rose-hedges with thorns and hooks so that 'we always leave a few shreds of our precious person behind when passing'.

The sway of the *Doppelgänger*: *The Student of Prague* was made three times. This is the second (1926) version, directed by Henrik Galeen

The bald man predicts to Librarian Schoppe, one of the drinkers fuddled by a glass of punch, that in fifteen months and a day he will go mad. Similarly, Cesare in *Caligari* was to predict to a happy man that he would die before dawn.

*Titan* contains all the elements of the sinister fantastic vein which the cinema was to seize on a century later: the bald man opens a waxworks cabinet in Madrid and, being a skilful ventriloquist, hides among his dolls swathed in a black cloak; or again, when the young Count follows the bald man down the corridor, he perceives his own head surrounded by flames in a mirror.

It is worth noticing the singular costume, at once old-fashioned and rather unreal, of the middle-class characters in *Caligari* or *Destiny*. The demoniac gentleman in Chamisso who buys Peter Schlemihl's shadow wears the grey, very old-fashioned frock-coat: similarly old-fashioned is the ash-grey morning-coat of another lugubrious character, Lawyer Coppelius in *Der Sand-mann*, whose physical appearance seems to prefigure that of Dr Caligari. In many German films we encounter characters dressed in Biedermeier costume dating from the conformist period, which in Germany began after the fall of Napoleon and continued until 1848. It is this Hoffmannesque period which films such as *The Student of Prague* or *Nosferatu* – the latter specifically set in 1838 – try to bring to life, whereas the middle-class characters in *Caligari* and *Destiny* merely show a vaguely adapted recollection of it.

Costume was always to be a dramatic factor for the German cinema. Homunculus, that artificial creature born in a laboratory, seems to owe all his being to the contrast between the black of his cape and top hat and the white of his mask-like face and clenched fists. The costume of Dr Caligari, with its billowing cape, gives him the appearance of a bat. In *The Student of Prague* the Devil – played by Werner Krauss – looks like a cross between a demon and a scarecrow when he appears at the height of the storm, which buffets the skirts of his frock-coat, near one of the artificially twisted trees similar to those in *Destiny*. The honourable citizen he has hitherto appeared to be is suddenly changed, and he brandishes his umbrella like a weapon.

We also need to remember the student Anselme, hero of *Der Goldene Topf*. Watching the worthy Archivist Lindhorst go off into the twilight he sees him glide, rather than walk, over the valley, then suddenly notices a grey-white vulture rising into the air in his place, and wonders whether he is not the victim of a hallucination. Surely we have here the forerunner of Scapinelli's change in appearance, when he becomes somebody else simply in the way his morning-coat swells, wrinkles, and stretches as if in a deforming mirror.

Such transformations carry the phenomenon of split personality to its extreme. Wrapped in a cloak 'of a very particular shade of brown' (!) which flaps around him forming innumerable folds and re-folds, the odd little man in *Die Abenteuer der Sylvester-Nacht*, deprived of his reflection as the result of diabolical machinations, skips around the tavern; the image seems to multiply itself. 'In the lamplight those present had the impression

112

of seeing several superimposed figures cavorting like those in the phantasmagorical scenes of Ensler.'

Romantic authors such as Novalis or Jean Paul, while anticipating the Expressionist notions of visual delirium and of a continual state of effervescence, also seem almost to have foreseen the cinema's consecutive sequences of images. In the eyes of Schlegel in *Lucinde*, the loved one's features become indistinct: 'very rapidly the outlines changed, returned to their original form, then metamorphosed anew until they disappeared entirely from my exalted eyes.' And the Jean Paul of the *Flegeljahre* says: 'The invisible world wished, like chaos, to give birth to all things together; the flowers became trees, then changed into columns of cloud; and at the tops of the columns flowers and faces grew.' In Novalis's novel *Heinrich von Ofterdingen* there are even super-impositions.

It is reasonable to argue that the German cinema is a development of German Romanticism, and that modern technique merely lends visible form to Romantic fancies.

FILM
„WAXWORKS"

JVAN
THE
TERRIB.

# 7 'Decorative' Expressionism

'*Expressionistic stylizations
have no decorative aims; if
they had, they would be
nothing but an abuse of art
and the world.*'
Paul Fechter: *Der
Expressionismus*, 1914.

## Das Wachsfigurenkabinett (Waxworks, 1924)

If Paul Leni, the Expressionist painter and film-maker,
patterned the essence of his *Waxworks* on the title of
*Das Kabinett des Dr Caligari*, he did so deliberately, for
he was to amplify, in his own playful manner and using
a more skilful technique, the fairground ambience which
had already proved so conducive to mystery. Leni was a
designer, and he knew what could be done for a film by
variations in costume and setting. He was thus to adopt
the formula Lang had chosen for *Destiny*: three episodes
set in different periods and countries.★

In *Waxworks*, Leni's style, which was to develop
once he reached the United States, had still not crystallized. He went further than Lang had done in varying
the elements to suit the ambience of each episode. The
main action is set at night in a fairground booth. Tents
with mysterious shadows, innumerable electric signs,
the merry-go-round and a gigantic wheel turning in a
welter of lights, the whole multiplied by the superimpositions which thread across the screen like spiders'
webs, show how far the German cinema had come since
the rather arid abstraction of the *Caligari* fairground.
The third episode – in contrast to the two others which
are simply interpolated into the narrative – continues
the main action, the nightmare of the young poet who
falls asleep instead of writing the story of the three wax
figures.

## The concept of space

The puffy dough-like settings in the episode of the
baker's wife are full of rotundities and cockled walls and
seem to have no interior framing: the corridors, stair-

★ Leni, who had worked
with Reinhardt as a
set-designer and as poster-
designer for the cinema and
had already directed films
such as *Dornröschen*, *Prinz
Kuckuck*, *Die Verschwörung
von Genua*, and *Backstairs*
(with Jessner), had
originally planned a fourth
episode for *Waxworks*:
*Rinaldo Rinaldini*, whose
wax effigy can, in the film,
still be seen in the booth.

*Waxworks*: sketch by Ernst Stern for Ivan the Terrible

*Waxworks:* The four characters: Haroun Al-Raschid, Ivan the Terrible, Rinaldo Rinaldini, Jack the Ripper. The Rinaldini episode was not in fact made.

cases (vaguely patterned on *The Golem*) and the soft, yielding arches seem to anticipate the creations of Antonio Gaudí. These sets are skilfully matched to the bloated physique of Jannings, whose face is depersonalized by a coarse make-up. Tricked out in an immense turban, his clothes padded and looking like some huge spinning-top, his Haroun Al-Raschid trundles his belly around a studio Orient. Kurtz very pertinently calls attention to a divergence in style: at times Jannings is the perfect Expressionist actor, but these times are in contradiction with others in which his 'psychological drollery' is not far from Naturalism.

The Ivan the Terrible episode is set entirely in a misty chiaroscuro: specks of dust float in pools of light and there is a new Impressionism, softening the harshness of Expressionist contrast. Out of the half-light emerges an ornamental beam, a door, an ikon, and suddenly there looms up the glinting shell of a ceremonial bed.

*Waxworks:* the Haroun Al-Raschid episode, with Emil Jannings

*Waxworks:* lighting in the Ivan the Terrible episode

Architectural details in the first two episodes reveal Leni's skill as a designer. The roundness of the oriental cupolas has a lively counterpart in the heavy turbans worn by the caliph's courtiers. When the town of Baghdad appears, all light transparent curves, it is flat like the little diagrammatic town in *Caligari*, which has often been compared to the architecture in the paintings of Lyonel Feininger. Similarly the Russian cupolas, corms with no apparent structure, are purely and exclusively decorative elements; they appear everywhere, flanking the palace entrance, concealing a secret door in one of the rooms.

At the same time, Leni embraces the traditional idea of the heavy-beamed, low-ceilinged Russian cottage. Even in the imperial palace it is necessary to stoop on account of the squat archways everywhere: the wedding guests in the Voivode's hall seem overwhelmed and stifled by its massive proportions.

One needs to grasp the full implications of this style.

The low ceilings and vaults oblige the characters to stoop, and force them into those jerky movements and broken gestures which produce the extravagant curves and diagonals required by Expressionist precept. If the Expressionism in the caliph episode is confined to the settings, in the Russian episode it completely withdraws into the attitudes of the characters, as when the blood-thirsty Tsar and his counsellor move in front of a wall in carefully stylized parallel attitudes, with their trunks jack-knifed forward.

A few years later Leni was to use the same attitude in *The Man Who Laughs*, made in America, when his King of England creeps down a corridor accompanied by his sadistic jester.

Throughout the Russian episode Leni strives after this movement-restricting architecture. There are vaults and low doorways; there is also a narrow, plunging stairwell, whose ominous walls make the lack of space even more stifling than before. Even the torture-chamber in the vast palace is nothing but a steep staircase which gives the Tsar a clear view of his victims' reactions.

Eisenstein's *Ivan The Terrible* shows the influence of the decorative stylization in Leni's film. Eisenstein used *Waxworks* as a model, particularly in the disposition of the figures on the screen, and the way in which they are reduced to ornaments, their gestures frozen to the point of a carefully elaborated abstraction.

## The obsession with corridors and staircases

One could say a lot about this taste the Germans have for staircases. The attraction exerted on them by the mysteriousness of long, dark, deserted corridors – von Gerlach's film *Vanina* positively swarms with them, as does Paul Leni's *Cat and the Canary*, made in America – is easier to account for. In any case corridors are ideal opportunities for chiaroscuro: in his tale *Das Majorat*, Hoffmann says: 'We crossed long, high-vaulted corridors; the wavering light borne by Franz threw a strange brilliance in the thickness of the gloom. The vague forms of the coloured capitals, pillars and arches seemed suspended here and there in the air. Our shadows moved

The obsession with staircases: *Raskolnikow*

forward at our side like grim giants and on the walls the fantastic images over which they slipped trembled and flickered. . . .'

I prefer to leave it to the psychoanalysts★ to discover what repressions they please in this fondness for stairs and corridors. But, remembering the German fascination with *Werden* (becoming) rather than *Sein* (being), it could perhaps be granted nevertheless that their stair-cases represent an upward movement, the degrees of which are represented by the stairs themselves. And we can perhaps infer from the striking German respect for symmetry that the symmetry of a staircase embodies ideas of balance and harmony.

On the other hand, it is possible that these images, which recur so frequently, have no implications and are purely decorative. In *Genuine* Wiene again exploited the hallucinatory power of the staircase he had originally used in *Caligari*, the steps of which seem to climb to infinity. It is true today that in certain German films the staircase has as much importance as the steps the Cossacks march down in *Potemkin*.

But was it really necessary for Lang to set the chases in the oriental episode of *Destiny* up and down in-numerable staircases, or to show the last survivors of Kriemhild's revenge, Hagen and Gunther, walking down a staircase littered with bodies? (Leni repeats the *Destiny* chases in his Haroun Al-Raschid episode.) When Murnau set the plague victims scene in *Faust* on the steps of an interminable flight of stairs, was it merely in order to accentuate the picturesqueness of his medieval town?

In a book called *Aktuelle Dramaturgie*, published in 1922, Herbert Ihering, the theatre critic, attempted to analyse the meaning of the famous *Jessnertreppen*, the stylized staircases which Leopold Jessner, the stage-director, used for his productions, particularly that of *Faust*. Ihering said that the people who object that stair-cases, terraces or arcades are not 'action-places' had not understood that these elements need to be interpreted, the 'division of space' being a 'dramaturgical function', and that there is no question here merely of obtaining a pictorial effect. We know very well, he added, that the famous lane in *Wilhelm Tell* is not a staircase, and that

★ Otto Rank has claimed that staircases are 'representations of the sexual act', while cellars and corridors stand for the female sexual organ.

121

the action of *Richard III* does not take place on a flight of steps. Jessner brings them in because they give him fresh possibilities – for the attitudes of his characters; for the structure, division and co-ordination of the scenes and groupings – and because he knows that word and gesture need to be *raumbildend*: they need to build, or create, space.

In his excellent analysis of German Expressionism, *Le Théâtre Allemand d'Aujourd'hui* (1933), René Lauret interpreted the *Jessnertreppen* in a quite different way. He said that Jessner used his staircases, not only to vary the disposition of the groups of characters, but also to symbolize their moods, to express their exaltation or depression in visual terms. He also used them during the dialogues to emphasize psychological or social inferiority or superiority. So, for Lauret, the *Jessnertreppen* are a symbol rather like that which Paul Rotha and Kracauer see in the image of the unapproachable secretary perched on a tall stool in *Caligari*.

Moreover, what the Germans call *Raum* is a conception which is half metaphysical, half real: the *Bühnenraum* which the critics were often to discuss can just as easily mean the limited space perceived by the eye of the spectator as the notion of an unlimited space created on the stage by the poet and the extensions of the imagination. In both cases the actor's body 'builds space'; flights of steps allow his dynamism to assert itself.

Setting aside all the psychological implications, this is the real reason for the importance of staircases in German films.

The most Expressionistic episode in *Waxworks* is incontestably that of Jack the Ripper, with its sliding corners, its continually shifting surfaces, its walls yielding without revealing what they conceal. It is a chaos of forms: triangles and rhomboids pierce space, sudden cascades of light collide against an infernal darkness. The sequence of all these unconnected objects is completely incoherent, their form offering no point of support. Through the turmoil of this setting glides the phantom of Jack the Ripper (Werner Krauss), elusive, insubstantial. Like the surrounding space the ground is without limits, it dissolves underfoot, cracks, congeals, becomes unreal. The Big Wheel and the merry-go-round

The obsession with staircases: *The Golem* (1920), *Von Morgens bis Mitternachts*

The obsession with staircases: *Dr Mabuse der Speiler, Die Weber*

The obsession with staircases: *Asphalt*

become decorative forms for a few moments, casting shadows which resemble birds of prey.

Yet despite its manifest virtuosity this film marks a regression, as this last episode clearly shows. Although Jack the Ripper moves forward threateningly and the sets open up like sliding doors, the depth-effect is botched; there is no more depth here than in *Caligari*. In addition, a sort of resolute perfection, an over-refined composition, an excessive mannerism, can make the spectator feel uncomfortable. Purely 'decorative' Expressionism here ends in the same impasse as *Genuine* had done.

In the United States Paul Leni was to realize the necessity of intensifying the 'mood' and of going beyond mere enjoyment in the Baroque and in the use of a super-abundance of forms. The set stops being a game or a subterfuge and becomes part of the action. In *The Cat and the Canary* a long dark corridor, light-coloured richly-draped curtains falling over the numerous windows, the enigmatic housekeeper holding an oil-lamp in

The obsession with staircases: *Die Strasse, Hintertreppe (Backstairs), Pandora's Box*

the foreground while her black form throws a heavy shadow – all these details provoke an inexpressible feeling of horror. Having learnt how to master his settings, Leni made films which have close links with the universe of Hoffmann. He no longer needed facile accessories.

## Paul Leni on set designing

If the designer merely imitated photography to construct his sets, the film would remain faceless and impersonal. There has to be the possibility of bringing out an object's essential attributes so as to give the image style and colour . . .

This is particularly necessary for films set wholly in a world of unreality. For my film *Waxworks* I have tried to create sets so stylized that they evince no idea of reality. My fairground is sketched in with an utter renunciation of detail. All it seeks to engender is an indescribable fluidity of light, moving shapes, shadows, lines, and curves. It is not extreme reality that the camera perceives, but the reality of the inner event, which is more profound, effective and moving than what we see through everyday eyes, and I equally believe that the cinema can reproduce this truth, heightened effectively.

I may perhaps cite the example of *Caligari* and *The Golem*, in which Hans Poelzig created a town's image. I cannot stress too strongly how important it is for a designer to shun the world seen every day and to attain its true sinews . . .

It will be seen that a designer must not construct 'fine' sets. He must penetrate the surface of things and reach their heart. He must create mood (*Stimmung*) even though he has to safeguard his independence with regard to the object seen merely through everyday eyes. It is this which makes him an artist. Otherwise I can see no reason why he should not be replaced by an adroit apprentice carpenter.

(From *Kinematograph*, No. 911, 1924)

Shadows: *The Student of Prague* (1926)

# 8 The World of Shadows and Mirrors

'What do I care about my shadow! Let it chase after me! I run away and I escape from it . . .
   But when I looked in a mirror I gave a cry and my heart shook; for it was not myself I saw but the grimacing face of a demon. . . .'
Nietzsche: *Also Sprach Zarathustra*.

'Nothing can scare us more than chancing to see our face in a glass by moonlight.'
Heine: *Harzreise*.

For the Romantics, portraits, mirror-images and shadows merge into one vision. Hoffmann sends Erasmus Spikher, the man with no reflection, on a journey with Peter Schlemihl, the man with no shadow: Schlemihl hugs the torch-lit walls so that nobody will notice that he has lost his shadow, and Spikher has all the mirrors veiled with crêpe.

This eternal obsession with mirrors is linked to a fascination with lights. The man who detaches the crêpe from the looking-glass veiled by Spikher is at first unable to recognize himself, he is so pale and disfigured; then he makes out a floating figure, 'gleaming with some magical light', heading towards him from the depths of the mirror. The same effect is to be found in *Undine*, the tale by de La Motte Fouqué, when the Chevalier sees, in a looking-glass next to the wavering flame of a candle, the doors slowly opening and a white figure entering the room.

Mirrors which face each other across a room are a good opportunity for evoking the famous double: Jean Paul's Librarian Schoppe is scared out of his wits by the four-fold reproduction of himself he sees mirrored in a deserted room, and tries to smash the illusive surfaces.

But is a mirror always a mirror? We never quite know whether the magical mirror which Dr Prosper Alpanus, another of Hoffmann's characters, uses to produce apparitions is really a mirror or just the crystal knob of his walking-stick. In *Der Goldene Topf* the 'mirror' formed of sparkling rays of light turns back into Archivist Lindhorst's emerald ring.

In German films windows, glazed doors and puddles can also act as mirrors. Paul Leni juggled with the numerous facets of the stone in a magic ring, reflecting the face of the baker Assad in *Waxworks* in a dozen or so simultaneous images. In *Variety* the lenses of several pairs of binoculars were to reflect the image of a group of acrobats. Similarly Pabst, in *The Love of Jeanne Ney*, multiplies the lover's image in the facets of a diamond.

In their trips through the looking-glass the meta-physically-inclined Germans go much deeper than Alice (that essentially very materialistic little girl), and of course much further than Cocteau. The rhyme of *Schein* (seeming) with *Sein* (being), leads them, like Tieck, to 'juggle with reality and dreams until the forms born of the darkness seem the only genuine ones'. Life is merely a kind of concave mirror projecting inconsistent figures which vacillate like the images of a magic lantern, sharp-focused when they are small and blurring as they grow. 'Somewhere, in a brighter world, there must exist that magic lantern whose slides are painted with landscapes, springtimes and human groups', says Jean Paul. Could what we call a novel, a life, be nothing but shadows cast by these jerky sequences of fuzzy slides?

In Franz Werfel's Expressionist drama *Der Spiegel-mensch*, the 'mirror-man' struggles desperately to escape from the 'mirror-world' which reflects nothing but frightening malformations.

'Finally he saw a shadow moving along the wall. This shadow grew in the moonlight, with every step growing higher, broader, until, gigantic, it disappeared into the forest.' When Eichendorff writes this it is difficult to decide whether his taste is more for ornament or for mystery.

Max Reinhardt had realized what power there was behind that kind of shadow which fuses decoration and enigma into symbol. In his first production at the Kammerspiele in 1906 – Ibsen's *Ghosts* – in the scene in which the panic-stricken mother runs after her delirious son, Reinhardt got them to pass in front of a light-source, and immense shadows shot around the walls of the stage like a pack of demons.

In German films shadow becomes an image of Destiny: the sleepwalking Cesare, stretching out his murderous

hands, casts his gigantic shadow on to the wall in the same way as Nosferatu, leaning over the traveller's bed or going up a staircase.

At the entrance to the chamber where Siegfried's body lies Hagen is preceded by his shadow, which betrays him as the killer. While the lovers exchange a kiss in *The Student of Prague* the huge shadow of Scapinelli is cast on to the high wall of the terrace. In *M* we see the elusive murderer's shadow outlined on a reward notice, hovering above the little girl who knows nothing of the sinister warning over her head.★

Occasionally shadow is replaced by silhouette, as in *Pandora's Box*, where the dark back-lit outline of Jack the Ripper is seen in front of a notice listing his crimes. Or again, in *Metropolis*, the gigantic figures of the stretcher-bearers removing the accident victims form a ghostly frame around the rich young man dressed in white. And the young woman in *Sylvester* keeps glancing apprehensively at the frosted-glass window against the

★ Pabst's use of shadow in *Die Freudlose Gasse* (*The Joyless Street*), where the police inspector's shadow appears on the bawdy-house wall before he goes inside, is more decorative. But the shadow he uses in *Dreigroschenoper*, when Peachum harangues the mob, is meant to indicate that Peachum still has the upper hand.

Shadows and silhouettes: *M, Pandora's Box, Nibelungen*

appearance of the ominous silhouette of her mother-in-law. In *Tabu* Murnau was to use shadow as an element of foreboding: the spear-like shadow of the priest who will destroy the lovers' happiness slips across the sands and falls on the bamboo hut where they are sleeping. Murnau has a marked liking for shadows: in *The Four Devils* all we see of the clown and the circus-manager wrestling are immense shadows flickering above the heads of the terrified children. In *Tabu* the garland that Matahi manages to throw over his loved one's head is immediately torn away from her. Murnau shows this white crown lying on the deck of the boat – a shadow hovers over it for a second. Then we just see a hand which has picked it up again, the only indication that Matahi has understood. This passage is more expressive than any image of a suffering face; it was used by Maya Deren in one of her 'psychoanalytic' films.

Most film-makers of Germanic origin share this taste for shadows. It was surely no accident when Stroheim brought into *Greed* the surface of a glazed door which profiles a man's head just as he is about to enter the room to commit his crime.

## Schatten (Warning Shadows, 1923)

A complex use of shadows is met with also in *Schatten* (*Warning Shadows*, 1923) by Arthur Robison, an American brought up in Germany, who handles phantoms with the same mastery as his strange illusionist, the central character of the film. In addition to the evocative ornamental shadows cast by the little illusionist's lighted candles and skilful hands, we have shadows passing behind the lighted window which German film-makers are so fond of (and which even Murnau was to bring into *The Last Laugh*), and that shadow of doom proclaiming the imminence of a menacing but still unseen character, a shadow which slips across the floor and reaches the person threatened before the real contact occurs.

Robison has a very personal treatment of misunderstandings caused by the interplay of shadows. Behind the curtains of a glass door the jealous husband spies upon shadowy hands approaching, then touching, the shadow of his wife. Another shot shows us the reverse of the

Shadows and silhouettes: *Warning Shadows, Metropolis*

*Warning Shadows:* illusion and reality

*Warning Shadows:* momentous phantasmagoria

situation: the vain young woman primping and preening herself at her looking-glass and, behind her, several feet away, her admirers sketching the curves of her figure in the air with their hands. Later, the husband bursts in upon what he believes to be two hands joining, when in fact they only touch as a result of the prolongation of their shadows.

The ambiguity of the shadows in this film has a Freudian inspiration. The little illusionist steals shadows and opens the flood-gates of the repressed unconscious desires of the other characters in the film, who suddenly start acting out their secret fantasies. In a momentous phantasmagoria shadows temporarily replace living beings, who become for a time passive spectators. The pace of the film increases, and the slow rhythm of the opening is left far behind.

'Often', says Tieck in *William Lovell*, 'the world, its people, and its contingencies flicker before my eyes like flimsy shadows; often I appear to myself to be a shadow playing a part, coming and going and doing without knowing the motives for its acts.'

The mirror-illusions represent mirages of thought. In *Warning Shadows* Robison makes masterful use of the reflections of mirrors set at the corners of a dark corridor. Fritz Arno Wagner's skilful camera catches in their clear bright surfaces the undulating form of the young woman as she goes towards her bedroom, and one of them shows the opening and shutting of the door by which her lover comes and goes. In this same mirror the deceived husband perceives the adulterous embrace which – significantly – he first sees merely as a shadow cast on the curtain of the glazed door. And then the lover in his turn discovers in the mirror the presence of the spying husband.

After the murder, the husband comes back to the mirror, whose impassive surface has kept no trace of the image of the crime. By the flickering light of a chandelier which he carries in his trembling hand he perceives the reflection of his chaotic soul. Bewitched, turning round and round, on all sides he sees his disfigured face reflected in other mirrors. Where can he hide? Where can he hide from himself? There is no way out. To destroy himself he does what Librarian Schoppe tried to do, he breaks the mocking polished surface. But the half-broken mirror still reflects the other mirror, which has remained intact.

*Warning Shadows* is full of eroticism, yet there is no vulgarity in Robison's style, even when he exploits the transparent effect of a flimsy Directoire gown with the halo of a chandelier unwittingly wielded by the jealous husband.

Thanks to an exceptional vigour of inspiration the characters in this film free themselves from the abstract uniformity imposed by Expressionism. They act with an almost animal intensity: the young woman, for example, in every movement of her hips, in every curve of her arm, is the embodiment of temptation and promise – an eternal Eve.

## The Expressionist actor

However, the acting, perhaps because the actors apply

137

*Warning Shadows*

The Expressionist actor: Werner Krauss in *Caligari*, Fritz Kortner in *Warning Shadows*

themselves to bringing out the notion of the wholeness of the personality, calls for some explanations.

The brusque, exaggerated gestures of actors in an Expressionist film frequently make modern audiences laugh. This is not merely due to its being shown at the speed of sound projection (24 frames per second); at the original speed (often 16 frames per second) the effect can be just as astonishing. And even in films of this period which are not in the least Expressionistic, Delluc's *La Femme de Nulle Part*, for example, or the Italian film *La Donna Nuda*, the actors' effusions seem over-emphatic. The theatrical ecstasy and entirely exterior emotionalism, the solemn, flowery titles remain alien to us; they belong to an outworn period when all opposition to middle-class conformism paraded as *noblesse*, not to say heroism. To this facile exteriorization there was added a nation's innate exaltation carried to its paroxysm by the fever of Expressionism.

One can picture those excited minds. It was a period of inflation when everybody wanted to live at any cost, to drink the cup of pleasure to the dregs, to keep his balance somehow and anyhow on the debris of normal life. But no one could free himself from the anguish of the morrow. The cost of pleasure went up from minute to minute, billions of marks becoming mere scraps of paper.

For the fancy-dress balls held in many of the fashionable Berlin houses, dimly-lighted cubby-holes were provided for the convenience of lovers, whose affairs were to have no morrow. The bawdy-houses in *The Joyless Street* and *Diary of a Lost Girl* dispense the implacable images of a society on the wane.

German films were long to wear the trace of this period. In *Pandora's Box* the lesbian, in order to save her girl-friend, is forced to seduce the fat acrobat; she does so with the jerky movements of a robot, with her head and trunk thrown back at a sharp angle to the rest of her body. In Joe May's *Heimkehr* Dita Parlo stiffens beneath the embrace of Lars Hanson in a paroxysm which can only be described as totally Expressionistic. And in Murnau's *Sunrise*, during the great love scene in the swamps, the vamp twists and turns like a will-o'-the-wisp, with the exaggerated movements characteristic of Expressionism.

According to Edschmid, Expressionist Man is to such an extent the Absolute Being, the Original Being, and capable of so many direct feelings, that he seems to 'wear his heart painted on his chest'. This remark can be applied to a whole generation of actors who exteriorized emotions and psychic reactions in the most extreme manner.

The views of an Expressionist dramatic author, Paul Kornfeld, were exactly opposite to those of Hamlet. The actor should not attempt to give the impression that word and idea are born simultaneously at the moment he expresses himself; he should dare to stretch out his arms in a grandiose manner and give the phrase its full declamatory vigour, as he would certainly never do in daily life; he should in no wise be an imitator, and there is no need for him to go and take notes at the hospital or tavern in order to play a dying man or a drunkard. The rhythm of a large gesture has a power which is much more charged with meaning and emotion, according to Kornfeld, than most impeccable natural behaviour.

Leontine Sagan, the director of *Mädchen in Uniform* and a former Expressionist actress, writing retrospectively in *Cinema Quarterly* (Summer 1933), said that she and the other actors of her day concentrated a whole complex of thought and emotion into a single word which they catapulted at their audience. She described how actors, tied to their own bodily naturalism, started behaving Expressionistically, reducing their gestures to a minimum of active movement; and she showed how their ambition to become abstract led them to go too far and become 'stiff and academic'.

Some Expressionists recommended a slight hesitation between cues to avoid naturalistic dialogue. Others put the accent on 'the music of the word', on its direct effect stripped of all logical or grammatical values.

If we replace stage direction by the mime of the screen-actor, we get the expressions and gestures with no transitions or intermediary nuances, the abrupt incisive movements, brusquely galvanized and broken half-way, which composed the usual repertoire of the Expressionist actor. The Germans, who have so pronounced a taste for exclamation marks, cannot help

The Expressionist actor: *Secrets of a Soul, Metropolis, Die Frau im Mond*

The Expressionist extra: *Madame Dubarry, Metropolis*

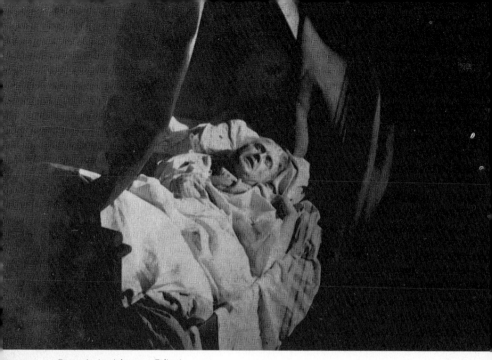

Expressionist nightmare: *Caligari*

liking unfinished gestures. The Expressionist film goes even further in this direction than the 'ecstatic theatre'. Once etched with the emulsion, gestures take on a definitive shape, stereotypes for the future.

This is why, even in 1926, when Expressionism already seemed outmoded, in a film like *Metropolis* Klein-Rogge, playing the magician-inventor, was still to display those jerky movements and puppet-like gesticulations. The aim was not to reveal the madness of an exalted character, as has been supposed, for Brigitte Helm expresses the sorrow or fright of the real Maria with such brusque body-movements and changes of expression that she resembles the bogus Maria, the robot. Similarly, the rioting workers show faces deformed by savage grimaces, gaping, crevice-like, unnatural. Homunculus, in 1916, had worn the same features of savage despair and shaken the same clenched fists. Similarly, in Wiene's *Hands of Orlac* Conrad Veidt, like Homunculus in feature and similarly dressed in black,

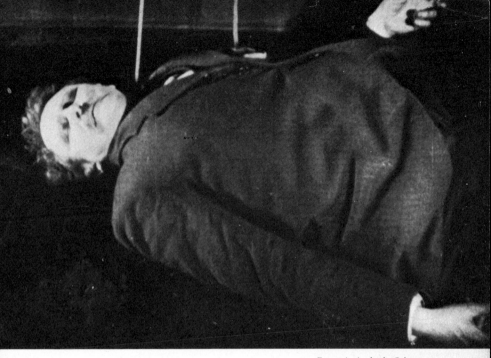

dances a kind of Expressionist ballet, bending and twisting
extravagantly, simultaneously drawn and repelled by
the murderous dagger held by hands which do not seem
to belong to him.

Still further back, Romantic authors had presented
character animated by the same perpetual agitation:
Jean Paul's Bald Man, or Erasmus Spikher, the man with
no reflection, who seems to work on elastic springs, are
forever on the move. And in Leni's *The Last Warning*,
made in the United States in 1928, Erasmus Spikher
seems to have gained a brother, a frightened little man
who hops around like an automaton.

Kurtz stressed that the rules established by the
Expressionist artist for the formation of space must be
equally valid for the use of the human body: the
passion in a situation must be expressed by an intense
mobility, and abnormal and excessive movements must
be invented. For the inner rhythm of a character's life
is transposed into his gestures. The Expressionist actor,

145

Expressionist gesture: *Metropolis, Backstairs*

Expressionist gesture: *The Hands of Orlac*

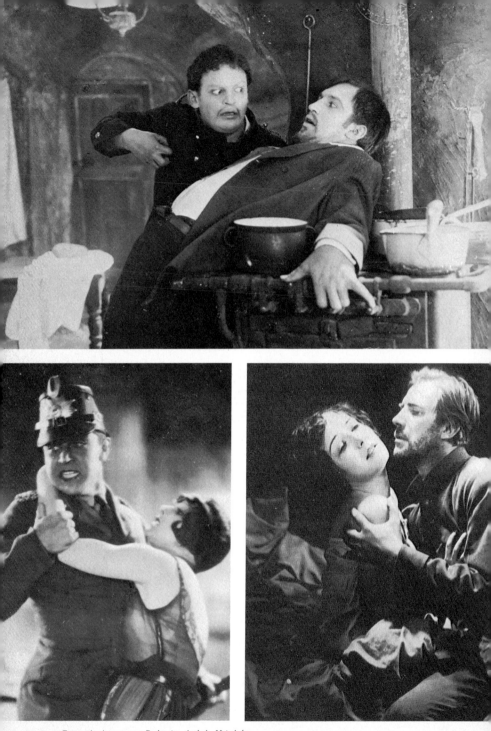

Expressionist gesture: *Backstairs*, *Asphalt*, *Heimkehr*

said the critic Herbert Ihering, had the aim of 'intensively compressing his role and not of interpreting it with intermediary nuances; it is in this sense that he synthesizes his role'.

These commentaries help to explain Kortner's acting in *Hintertreppe* (*Backstairs*) and even better his interpretation of the jealous husband in *Warning Shadows*: the close-up of his enormous face twisted into a frightful sneer makes it resemble some African demon-mask; the crazed spinning of his body in front of the mirrors, and his habit of projecting his arms or trunk as if to rid himself of them, take on a partly abstract quality.

The Expressionistic distortion of gestures is the counterpart to the distortion of objects.

Arnold Böcklin's painting *The Isle of the Dead; Siegfried*

## 9 Studio Architecture and Landscape

### Die Nibelungen

Writers such as Kurtz or Kalbus frequently referred to
the films made by their compatriots in terms of *beseelte
Landschaft* or *Landschaft mit Seele*, which means 'landscape
imbued with soul'. For non-Germans, this landscape
is a mere thing of the studio, smacking of plaster, pasteboard and insufficient oxygen, though they will often
admit that a judicious use of lighting can sometimes
lend these artificial constructions a semblance of life and
atmosphere.

The declared aim of the Expressionists was to eliminate
nature and attain absolute abstraction. But this was not
the only issue at stake during this period. Béla Balázs
held that the soul of a landscape or milieu did not
always present itself in the same way. It was up to the
director to seek 'the eyes of the landscape': thus the
black silhouette of a bridge above a swaying gondola,
and a flight of steps plunging into the dark lantern-
reflecting water could convey the atmosphere of Venice
far better, even if built in the studio, than a scene filmed
live in the Piazza S. Marco.

Fritz Lang submitted to the ruling of Ufa which,
at that time, absolutely refused to use exteriors. Yet the
borders were open again, and currency could be
exchanged once more. The weather factor was less
important than people thought since the monumental
constructions too big for the studio were always erected
on waste ground (the *Gelände*) around the studios at
Tempelhof, Staaken or Neubabelsberg; shooting necessitated suitable weather in any case, despite the huge

151

*Siegfried:* approaching Brunhild's castle

scaffoldings for lights. But of course many landscapes
were built inside the studio, with the shooting stage
covered with earth, rocks, trees, moss, or artificial
snow.

Kurtz, for his part, declared that for a film to become
a work of art nature had to be stylized. In a film, human
destiny did not always lend itself to a natural framework,
the neutral reality of which was only suited to the
documentary film. In order to make man's destiny
understood, *Stimmungsbilder* – 'mood pictures' – should
be used. (The word *Stimmung* is complex and cannot
readily be translated: English 'mood' and French
'atmosphere' do not quite convey the meaning. It stands
for an atmosphere permeated in some sort by the
emanations of the German *Gemüt* – a highly particular
mixture of sensibility and sentimentality.) According to
Kurtz, only when a director builds his own landscape
can he give it a soul and make it play an active role in
the plot.

152

*The Vengeance of Kriemhild*: Attila, the black knight

On a par with lighting, which gives depth to people and objects, landscape becomes a 'dramatic' or 'dramaturgic' factor in German film-making. Kurtz maintained that there are close links between landscapes and human beings. The appearance of the set should emphasize and accentuate the tension of the *scene*. Expressionism constructs its own universe, it does not adapt itself to a world already in existence. ('Every landscape', Novalis said, 'is the idealized Body of some form of Mind.') The veil separating Nordic man from Nature cannot be torn down; so the Germans, narcissistic in the extreme, construct an artificial Nature, the only one to which they have access.

Seen in this light, the most successful of *Die Nibelungen's* landscapes★ (designed by Otto Hunte and Erich Kettelhut, and built by Karl Vollbrecht) are, not surprisingly, those which approximate to the atmosphere of a barbaric Valhalla. The arid and desolate décor of desert-like rocks through which the heroes make their

★ *Die Nibelungen* was made in two parts: *Siegfried* and *Kriemhilds Rache* (*The Vengeance of Kriemhild*). The two parts were released together early in 1924, being shown on consecutive evenings.

Part of Arnold Böcklin's painting *The Silence of the Forest*; *Siegfried*

way towards Brunhild's castle, looming before them like a flame-shrouded rock, and the horizon of cold sky behind the sombre stones where the struggle with the untamed virago is taking place, are visions stemming straight from the Germanic conception of Darkness. The landscape of gnarled branches in which the underworld creature Alberich, flexing his spidery fingers, lies in wait to strangle the Bright Hero, is vibrant with mystery.

For his studio landscapes, the artist in Lang attempted to bring to life certain famous paintings. When Siegfried crosses the forest on his white charger the model is Arnold Böcklin's nymph on a unicorn: light spills against the tree-trunks, between which mists rise, shadowy and indistinct beneath a trellis-work of subdued light filtering from above.

In the same way, the flower-flecked meadow lined with young birches, whose slim white trunks stand out against the rocks, is a synthesis of two other pictures by Böcklin. And the shot of the knight, Attila, clad in his black armour, rising up against a spring sky near a band of naked, garlanded children, is a faithful replica, as far as I can recall, of an engraving by Max Klinger. Lang places his actors in these landscapes with a precise feeling for space, transforming them into points of reference in the design. In *The Revenge of Kriemhild* he was to remember the decorative value of these trees: in a winter landscape Siegfried's widow kneels at the sacred spot where her hero died, framed by two birches above the snow.

The décor of the flowery meadow in which Hagen kills Siegfried has the same mellowness as that in which the love-scenes between Siegfried and Kriemhild take place, beneath a tree in full blossom. This liking for cloth, paper or wax flowers (an artifice which Stroheim with a kind of Germanic nostalgia and not a little irony brought into his films) sometimes results, in the hands of German film-makers, in an extreme mawkishness. Even Murnau is not free from it, as shown by the burgesses' Easter stroll through a picture-postcard village, or the flower-crowned children dancing round Gretchen and Faust in a studio-springtime meadow.

The more restrained Wegener never succumbs to the

Paul Richter as Siegfried

temptation of the *Edelkitsch* of Böcklin and of so many
German film-makers. He does not sugar the *Stimmung*
bathing the marvellous dance in the *Rattenfänger von
Hameln* (*The Pied Piper of Hamelin*), nor the image of
flower-crowned children in a studio-shot sequence in
*The Golem*. But other German film-makers were deeply
affected by this false naïvety, this *Butzenscheiben-
romantik,* a *fin-de-siècle* Gothic. The influence of Moritz
von Schwind, the nineteenth-century painter, and the
engraver Ludwig Richter, whose compositions abound in
blonde-tressed, opulent-bosomed and curving-waisted
châtelaines leaning over the battlements to wave a
tender farewell to some beplumed troubadour – what
the Germans call *sinnig, innig, minnig* – was disastrous.
How far all this is from the flower-garden and ideal
nature of the setting which in *Gösta Berlings Saga* harmonizes so well with the fragility of Greta Garbo!

Expressionist landscapes are much harder to do well
than purely architectural abstractions. Never again was

156

Kriemhild and Siegfried

Studio Nature: Siegfried in the forest, and the cement trees under construction

a film able to attain the plainness of *Caligari*, so simply won by the use of flat trees and of paths whose subtle variations in texture even achieve an impression of colour.

Lang's masterly chiaroscuro has produced some poignant images: on the drawbridge, where we have already seen the glorious hero at the head of his vassals, a group of warriors bears Siegfried's body home on a stretcher. The procession is distorted by the flickering lights of the torches, shrieking across the dusk like cries of grief; Siegfried's charger is ghostly-white, and the wind plays in the luminous locks of hair framing the shining face of the dead hero.

The same wind of ill omen, which had swirled among the dust on the drawbridge before the appearance of the procession, buffets the curtains in Kriemhild's bedroom. The menace of destruction is always lurking in the inorganic world: it is the wind that shakes the bedroom curtains at the approach of Nosferatu, the wind one notices when Gretchen is on the point of yielding to

158

*Siegfried*

Faust's embraces. Even Pabst, the so-called realist, cannot forbear to use its psychological effect in *The Love of Jeanne Ney*: the curtains quiver in the room where old Ney lies murdered. Paul Leni was also to use this device: in *The Cat and the Canary*, a ghostly wind billows through a row of heavy curtains lining a narrow corridor. The wind again plays a dramatic role in *Destiny*: it swirls among the dusty grass on a barren slope before the appearance of 'weary Death'. It is a device which has gone into the language of the cinema.

### Geometric grouping

The counter-balanced architecture in *Die Nibelungen* is not in the least Expressionist, although Expressionist principles govern the stylization of the vast surfaces found in this film. Lang's theme necessitated the use of massive frescoes, for the composition of which he resorted to the monumental proportions seen as befitting the Germanic mind.★ Langbehn, the author of *Rembrandt als Erzieher*, had already held that German *Kultur* was wrought in granite, from which material it was impossible to carve anything but massive shapes, which was why the Germans' ultimate aim was to 'monumentalize' (*monumentalisieren*).

The massive architecture in *Die Nibelungen* constitutes an ideal setting for the stature of its epic heroes. Aiming for spectacular effects, Lang brought life to the grandiose rigidity of the architecture with a skilful use of lighting.

He has a marked preference for symmetrical and contrapuntal arrangements: the heavy gateway leading to the Nibelungen's treasure-vault is flanked by two tall characters (Kriemhild and Hagen); on another occasion, a single figure stands carefully framed in a doorway under an arch. He arranges the actors in his landscapes according to an ornamental design of which they become the points of reference: Siegfried leaning towards the spring is placed in such a way that his head comes just in front of the birch in the centre of the screen; when he is wounded he rises up for a moment in line with the same tree.

In *Die Nibelungen* nothing is left to chance: Hagen, on

★ In *The Film Till Now* Paul Rotha writes pertinently that the architecture of German films, which is above all an architecture of façades, resembles a 'tapestry' of hieroglyphics expressing the structure of the soul in terms of space.

Geometric grouping: *Siegfried*

the look-out for the arrival of Kriemhild, sits as still as a statue, with his sword resting across his lap. Brunhild, standing among the rocks on the look-out for the heroes and their escort, is no more than an oblique silhouette against the grey sky, with the aurora borealis glimmering in the background. If some scenes in the film were inspired by paintings, others, if the film were stopped at the right moment, might well be paintings in their own right.

The grouping falls under the heading of pure ornamentation, as in many German films. Two identical wings are often placed about a more imposing centre: Caligari seated at his desk is like an enormous spider, with his arms resting on two piles of books of equal height; in *Destiny*, in front of an impassable wall, the burgesses walk backwards and forwards together on either side of 'weary Death'. The effect is achieved by rapid cutting.

A strictly 'heraldic' composition of symmetrical, juxtaposed masses shows itself to be even more expressive – that in which Siegfried and Günther perform the age-old rites of blood-brotherhood, flanked along parallel lines by the king's two brothers and Siegfried's two brothers-at-arms; the tall stature of Hagen behind them gives a final emphasis to this methodical arrangement in three dimensions.

Although Lang takes decorative stylization a step further than Reinhardt, the latter's influence remains apparent. Traces of the way in which groups were treated at the Grosses Schauspielhaus are to be found in the scene in which the two queens clash on the cathedral steps: the separate ranks of Brunhild's and Kriemhild's followers, dressed respectively in uniform dark and light tones, come violently together in the form of an inverted V. But the rectangles or squares of the groups of warriors – sometimes filmed in bird's-eye view, when they form gigantic mosaic designs similar to those which Leni Riefenstahl was to film in her *Triumph des Willens* (*Triumph of the Will*, 1935) are not entirely drawn from Reinhardt, but may well be a reminiscence of the tight groupings of the *Sprechchöre*, the Expressionist rhythmical choruses.

In *Die Nibelungen* also, the isolated human body is

163

*Siegfried:* the aurora borealis

*Siegfried:* Brunhild walks across a pontoon composed of shields

treated as a decorative element, absolutely static, deprived of individual life and frozen in its symmetry. The horn-blowers, for example, stand out against the limpid sky as architecturally as the gleaming drawbridge jutting into space. The numerous extras are also dehumanized: for instance the row of warriors, spaced at regular intervals, draw themselves up into strictly identical postures following a very precise rhythm, and flanked by their swords and shields; a rising zigzag pattern turns their chain-mail coats into plane surfaces barely seeming to cover human figures at all, and seen from behind their helmets give them the appearance of indestructible pillars. They take up position in front of the kings and heroes like a palisade, giving these shots a certain depth while seeming to mask the background altogether.

A similar depersonalization is to be found in a sequence from *The Vengeance of Kriemhild*: in the chapel where Siegfried's body is entombed, Kriemhild's serving-women, almost faceless and bodiless in their geometrically-patterned head-dresses and the vast folds of their heavy capes, surround their mistress in front of the sepulchre; their bent postures follow the curves of the vault, which forms a perfect semicircle, recalling an apse adorned with precious mosaics.

In order to land from the boat which has brought her to Worms, Brunhild walks along a pontoon composed of shields, which are held up horizontally by two rows of warriors standing in the water. The water comes up to their necks and their helmets are thus no more than the ornamental rim of this improvised gangway. Other figures make up a guard of honour on the bank, but their human appearance is likewise almost entirely suppressed: their silhouettes in outline against the horizon form a kind of wrought-iron screen.

The second part of *Die Nibelungen*, filmed a year after the first, displays a rather surprising change of style. *The Vengeance of Kriemhild* is less static; moreover the theme itself – more vehement, dynamic and colourful – necessitated more movement. The solemn, epic slowness of *Siegfried*, that melancholy *chanson de geste* lamenting the death inflicted on the fair-haired hero, has given way to an intense acceleration of destiny, a thundering

crescendo which sweeps those responsible for Siegfried's
death to their destruction.

This new pace loosens the decorative groupings,
brings the studied composition of the heraldic forma-
tions to life and makes them more flexible. Lang comes
back to studied compositions once the Huns give way to
the Burgundians (the coffin-like stiffness of the three
ceremonial beds stands out against a background of
sumptuously variegated hangings), but as the court at
Worms is gradually left behind the static element
diminishes in importance and only recurs from time to
time as a distant echo of lost grandeur, henceforth
unattainable. Even at Worms the monumental element is
occasionally humanized: Hagen, sitting on the drawbridge and swinging his legs with an ironical ease,
watching Kriemhild leave for her new kingdom, is
deprived of all sculptural solemnity, and no more than a
bantering spectator. Heine's 'towers of stone', throwing
themselves at each other's throats, have lost something

*The Vengeance of Kriemhild*

*Siegfried*

of their awkward weightiness, and these heroes appear
much less grandiloquent in their fight to the death than
when slowly making their way down the rows of warriors
to the dome at Worms.

Lang is wrongly accused of having depicted the Huns
as a mixture of cavemen, savages and redskins. They
never walk upright; they never lift their faces towards
the sky with the noble arrogance expected of the
Germanic hero: they slither like slimy reptiles or else
skip around, bent at the waist and knees, in a sort of
strange squatting posture. It is enough for a Hagen to
deploy his height to send these wretched offspring 'of an
inferior race' scuttling away like rats. It should be
obvious that Lang's intention was merely to vary his
characters and their attitudes in the name of a novel and
surprising dynamism. The racial implications were due
to Thea von Harbou and Ufa.

As his interest in stylized composition lessened, Lang
developed a fondness for the new colourful atmosphere

he discovered in folklore. The ornamental element gives way to an element of continually changing picturesqueness, and his style and lighting became more fluid and diffuse. His chiaroscuro comes to life, swaying and dipping; the movement becomes frantic; shadows infiltrate into the zones of light and the kaleidoscopic atmosphere; the immovable *Kolossal* is abandoned, and the pace becomes as panting and breathless as the heroes in their fight to the death. Horses gallop wildly across the vast steppes with their manes streaming in the wind; caverns gape in the earth, exposing the teeming life underground; demons cavort on the warpath in a dance of death. Ambushes, destruction, felony abound on all sides; at every step there are explosions of indescribable savagery, and the stench of blood leaps in the bitter air; weapons clash in clouds of dust, and wreaths of smoke wrap round the few survivors like snakes seeking to smother them to death.

Certain ornamental tendencies persist: the idealized, almost deified Kriemhild, a Germanic Electra-whom-her-mourning-becomes, sometimes (despite a certain resemblance detected by Georges Sadoul to the stylized Germania on old postage-stamps) has the inaccessible goddess-like bearing found in Theodora, Empress of Byzantium, in the Ravenna mosaics.

Eisenstein was struck by the ornamental effect of the square helmets like that worn by Rüdiger; he remembered their barbaric shape and used them for his Teutonic knights in *Alexander Nevski*.

Lang, one of the directors who, like Murnau, deliberately prolonged discussions on the *mise-en-scène* of the film, knew well what the contribution of his cameramen was. For example, in the programme notes to *Die Nibelungen*, in 1924, he distinguishes between the work of Carl Hoffmann and Rittau: 'What I dreamt up, as a painter wishing to evoke the plastic image, Carl Hoffmann accomplished, thanks to his effects of light and shade. . . . He knows the secret of how to photograph a woman. He can capture her face in such a way that not only the woman herself but all the psychical content of a scene is revealed – thanks to a glint in the corner of her eye, a shadow that passes over her forehead, or a highlight of her temple.' And Lang

169

writes of the second cameraman, Rittau, whose great capacity for tirelessly attempting new experiments he praises: 'He attacks the *plastique* of the film through mathematics.' To Rittau Lang owes some trick shots; it was thanks to Rittau that he was able to make the figures turn to stone in fulfilment of Alberich's curse as he is killed: 'What I made of stone must again become stone'.

'*Already in my first films I
chose "realistic" themes in
order to show that I was a
stylist. Realism is a method;
it isn't an end, it's a means.*'
G. W. Pabst, in an
interview: *Revue du
Cinéma*, No. 18, 1948.

## Der Schatz (The Treasure, 1923)

It must be said at once that *Der Schatz* abounds in
marvellous images, sculpted by light out of darkness.
Yet it is further from Reinhardt than Oswald's and
Buchovetzky's films from the same period. Pabst's model
was the 1920 *Golem*, and if his bell-founder has so great
a resemblance to Wegener's Rabbi it is not simply
because the two roles were played by the same actor,
Steinrück. It is characteristic of the period that a film
as advanced as *Warning Shadows* can exist side by side
with a film which still faithfully follows the precepts of
1920.

Pabst had the German taste for Expressionist ornament.
When the bell-founder's wife runs up carrying an
enormous tray she is nothing but a head set upon a
welter of puffy skirts which make her look like the
pot-bellied bells smelted by her husband. Or there is the
bole-like shaft of a pilaster over whose branchy fluting,
spanning the conjugal bed, the camera lingers inter-
minably.

That a director of Pabst's quality should have made
such a début gives one pause. It is astonishing enough to
find no trace of his strong personality: any Expressionist
director duly impressed by the beauty of chiaroscuro
could have made this film. But what is especially striking
is that Pabst, whose prime quality later was to be his
complete grasp of editing, has strung the shots together
end-to-end with a monotony and a lack of imagination
which cannot be ascribed solely to the clumsiness of a

beginner. The shots are long, heavy-handed, over-explicit or simply banal. Every psychical reaction in every character is shown for too long with too many close-ups. These psychological analyses which, contrary to all Expressionist precept, are handled quite natura-listically, foreshadow the technique which Pabst was to make his own later on. But we are still a long way from the judicious choice of angles and the psychological penetration of the Pabst of *Pandora's Box*.

In *Der Schatz* an occasional image foreshadows faintly the Pabst of the orgies in *The Love of Jeanne Ney*. The three characters who discover the treasure, already drunk with joy, start drinking, and Pabst details the situation voluptuously, revelling in it with all his taste for degradation. But the scene does not have the force or the authenticity which he was to succeed in giving to similar scenes later on. We can detect a rather curious stylized Naturalism and the use of certain models: his knotty, soft-nosed peasants with their faces apparently carved out of wood, and his drinking scenes, are in the manner of Teniers. Stroheim's *Greed* offers us much more striking and revealing aspects of concupiscence in a series of swift images showing a process of unre-mitting abasement.

Pabst shows more skill in another scene, that of the murder-attempt while the bell-metal is being smelted: the greedy founder and his jealous assistant spy their chance when the young goldsmith is almost swept away by the molten cast. But the least details are distilled with a grim, nerve-jarring slowness.

For this début Pabst used all the Expressionist para-phernalia: the bell-founder's house is squat, round, and bulging, with no apparent structure beneath its clayey masses; its ceilings are low and stifling, its main room is like a mysterious crypt. The main influence felt is that of *The Golem*: those thick, rough dilapidated walls, familiar to us already from many a German film, lurk like carnivorous plants ready to devour any mortal who comes close. There are staircases everywhere, and on all sides dark sunken corridors lead off with sudden steps and sharp curves. Here and there in the darkness we perceive a narrow window dimly lighting fragments of a human figure or a gloomy chamber. And then there is

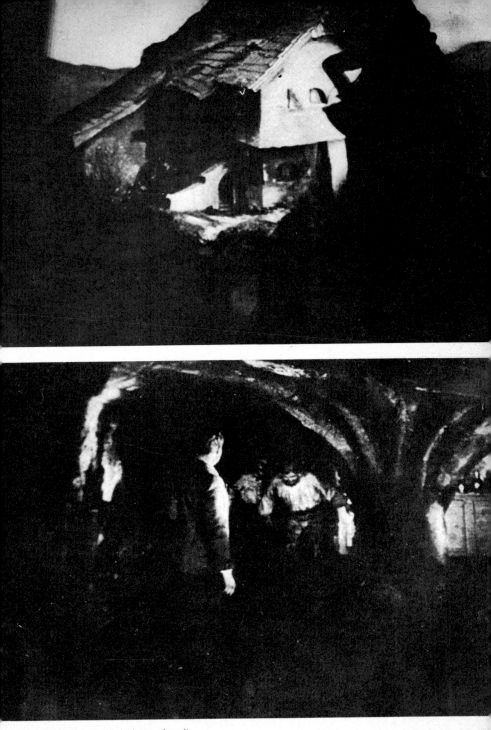

*Der Schatz*: all the Expressionist paraphernalia

*Der Schatz*: a stylized Naturalism

Werner Krauss, as the weird treasure-hunter, who goes off with a lantern hidden under his jacket, the stifled glow giving an uncanny transparency to his bloated, intent face. The furnace fire and the incandescent streams of molten metal add to the lighting effects; objects are wreathed in the mounting fumes, the chiaroscuro swells and glows and finally, at the end of the film, this Expressionist dwelling is consumed by an enormous conflagration.

There is a constant preoccupation with the picturesque qualities of light and gloom: the peasants sit at the inn-table in the dim light of the hanging lamp, recalling many similar *Stimmungsbilder*. When Krauss goes off into the dark to select a divining-rod it seems like the prelude to a scene in Murnau's *Faust*: through the harshly lit brambles beneath the glinting disc of a studio moon the undergrowth appears like the bones of a skeleton.

Several times over, and at length, Pabst shows the solitary shadow Krauss casts on the wall as he crawls along holding his divining-rod in search of the coveted treasure. Or else the young goldsmith appears in silhouette, framed in a doorway, before the door closes on the two lovers embracing in the vines. In short, all the elements of the classic German film are present, but there is nothing as yet to make us anticipate with any confidence the quality of the films Pabst was later to make.

*Backstairs:* intimate cinema

*'Carl Mayer gives his film* Sylvester *the sub-title of* "ein Lichtspiel", *"a light-play". This is certainly not a mere allusion to the technique which makes use of the transformations and movements of light. What he meant was the chiaroscuro in man, in his soul, the eternal ebb and flow of shadow and light which affect psychical relations. This is how I understood this sub-title.'* Lupu Pick: Preface to the scenario *Sylvester* by Carl Mayer, 1924.

Histories of the cinema tell us that the suppression of titles is one of the main characteristics of the *Kammerspielfilm*. But what of its origins and significance?

Once again we need to turn to the teachings of Max Reinhardt for an answer. One day, while rehearsing a very subtle play in which the characters' psychical relationships had to be brought out discreetly, Reinhardt sighed: 'Of course, I saw your gesture and understood your look. But I'm on the stage. Will the spectators in the back rows and, above all, those in the gods be able to do the same?'

This was why he finally created an intimate theatre, the Kammerspiele, with dim lights and warm-toned wood panelling, in which an élite (not more than 300 spectators) could feel all the significance of a smile, a hesitation, or an eloquent silence. Heinz Herald, one of his collaborators, to whom we are indebted for this anecdote, says: 'If an actor needs to lift his whole arm at the Grosses Schauspielhaus, he need only move his hand at the Deutsches Theater; and at the Kammerspiele it's enough if he moves a finger.'

## Hintertreppe (Backstairs, 1921)

*Hintertreppe*, a film by the stage-director Leopold Jessner, is a *Kammerspielfilm* before its time. Paul Leni worked on the art-direction with him, and Leni's talent went into creating a mood which, with the help of the sets, is spell-binding. The famous yard in *The Last Laugh* seems tame compared with this one by the backstairs, which

177

serves as a framework for the pitiful drama of the maid whose letters from her lover are intercepted by the postman, himself in love with her, and who concludes she has been abandoned.

This intimist drama moves at a very slow and heavy pace, in a very German, over-insistent style, and this despite the use of certain ellipses drawn from the theatre. For instance, we are not shown the murder scene; all we see when the bolted door has finally given way is a sort of tableau: against the wall the murderer is caught in an oblique attitude – the Expressionist attitude *par excellence* – still brandishing his axe over his victim.

What shocks us today in this film is the violent break in tone between the styles used. Already the main staircase, heavily overladen with ornaments in a lower-middle-class style, jars with the Expressionistic rendering of the shabby, equivocal back-stairs. Similarly the postman's sordid basement contrasts with the drawing-room furnished with plush emporium armchairs and artificial palms.

The acting reflects this contrast. Henny Porten, brimming with sentimentality and far too fat, plays naturalistically, as if this were a film by Carl Froelich. On the other hand, Wilhelm Dieterle, vastly different from the young over-fed baker he played in *Waxworks*, is here enigmatic, rather restrained, in every way Expressionistic. He follows the rules to the letter and his movements are mechanical and jerky. As for Fritz Kortner, a better actor than Dieterle, he manages to adapt the rules to his role. Everything is motivated: the slow reactions of a poor indecisive man scared of love, the hesitations of an outcast of fortune who, having won his happiness by dint of guile, stops wanting to believe in it. Clutching his wine-jug tenaciously, he succeeds in making his stiff attitude plausible. This instinctively Expressionistic actor blends into the setting.

Middle-class characters with coarse make-up loom up to witness the drama with mechanical, robot-like gestures.

Another ellipse: we first see the maid on the roof in despair, then the neighbours, in a very 'naturalistic' gesture of pity, suddenly lean out over the pavement, and we guess at the dislocated form of the suicide below.

Probably it is on account of a fundamental opposition between the Kammerspiele – intimist, psychological – and the techniques of Expressionism that this work, overrated by the cinema-histories (in which everybody copies everybody else's opinions), today appears rather disappointing.

Paul Leni is in no way to blame. We only need to see his other films to realize how little he had to do with this one, made as it was by the man of the theatre, Jessner.

## Scherben (Shattered, 1921)

The *Kammerspielfilm*, as it was conceived in *Scherben* (1921) by Lupu Pick, is the psychological film *par excellence*; it was to comprise a limited number of characters living in an everyday ambience. Thus Pick deliberately went counter to all the Expressionist principles; and he persisted in this anti-Expressionist attitude long after Expressionism had died out. During the sound era, reminiscing about a film by the rather commercial director Carl Boese, *Die letzte Droschke von Berlin*, in which he played a sentimental cabman in arms against progress in the shape of the motor-car, Pick said that this film was 'a naturalist slap in the face for the Expressionist snobs'.

The scenarist of *Scherben*, Carl Mayer, who wrote the scenario of *Caligari* with Janowitz, brought something new to it: wishing to have an élite of spectators capable of guessing what was happening in the characters' minds, he suppressed the titles.*

Lupu Pick's interview with a journalist from *Ciné monde* in 1930 was significant: he pointed out that he had always been prone to go against the fashion of his day, first of all in *Scherben*, 'unloosing the avalanche of psychological films', and then in *Sylvester*, trying to 'go beyond psychology and reach metaphysics'.

*Scherben* is the simpler film. Pick, extremely sensitive to atmosphere, contrives to give some relief to this melodrama of a railwayman's daughter seduced by an inspector. The father avenges the outrage by killing his superior. For the naturally hierarchically-minded German that he is, this is more than daring, it is real heroism.

Compared with the more complicated and complex *Sylvester*, *Scherben* is stark and contains few symbols. It

* At any rate, this is what Lupu Pick always claimed, but *Backstairs*, also written by Mayer, is likewise without titles, and seems a little earlier than Pick's film. Only a few film-makers realized all that the pace, optical fluidity and dramatic tension of a narrative had to gain from his technique. Robison, for example, used no titles in *Warning Shadows*; those seen in today's prints were added by a zealous distributor. For other films, of course, titles constitute essential rhythmical pauses, but this is not the case with films whose psychological tensions and peripetias occur on the intimate scale of the Kammerspiele.

Lupu Pick as the sentimental cabman in *Der letzte Droschke von Berlin; Scherben*

is life as it is lived, simple, dull, in a harsh and bitter countryside: railway tracks at night, scattered drifts of snow, dark pine-trees; the signal-levers, words tapping out on the telegraph; the trudge across the rails for the round of inspection with the heavy lamp casting a few inches of light in the darkness; no sun, nothing but long winter evenings and nights when the wind blusters and meals are taken in silence.

And for the women: solitude, washing that will not dry, the eternal round of meals to prepare. Perennial chiaroscuro, heavy, dense, stifling: the pale glow through the window from the snow outside; the lamp, when lighted, shutting in one end of the room behind a wall of gloom.

Then the storm, howling, buffeting the door, smashing a window-pane. The only concession to symbol so far: the fragments of glass, the *Scherben*, which the girl picks up indifferently and throws into a bucket.

Nothing but railway lines in a melancholy grisaille landscape. The express, which usually thunders through at full speed, stops – but only to bring a stiff and indifferent inspector. Not too indifferent, however, to notice the girl scrubbing the stairs. During a decisive moment we see nothing but a pair of polished jackboots pausing on the stairs. The seduction sequence can have no place at all in this drudgery; it is passed over in a matter of seconds. We see no tenderness, just the discovery of guilt. The mother wakes up and smashes down the bolted door with an axe; the inspector appears on the doorstep, stiff and haughty, the girl huddles in the bed trembling with shame.

And then immediately the mother is running desperately away across the snowy paths and collapsing at the foot of the wayside cross.

Though neither film has titles, the skilful ellipses Mayer and Pick managed in *Scherben* contrast with the prolixity of *Sylvester*. The mother's death from exposure is passed over, in the same way as the seduction scene. That she has not come home is revealed by the world of objects: the enormous back of the alarm-clock in close-up as it rings insistently next to an empty bed. In this silent film, in which the image has to interpret sound, the point is made by returning to the vibrating hammer several times over. A similar close-up of the back of a hammering alarm-clock interpreting sound in visual terms is found at the beginning of *Backstairs*; but there the sense is humorous – Henny Porten is unwilling to get up – and does not have the same tragic insistence. Here the object becomes the poignant symbol of death, of a desolate emptiness, and the symbol is both meaningful and motivated, like the scrawny branches of a shrub beating against a window or the useless wind-beaten scarecrow in front of the house before the mother discovers the inspector with her daughter.

Then we see the railwayman bringing home the stiff body of his wife and laying it on her bed. There are no exteriorized signs of sorrow. Later, in a heavy stupor, he transports the meagre coffin on a wheelbarrow across the sad grey countryside to the cemetery.

What interests the two authors of this intransigently absolute *Kammerspielfilm* are the slow, heavy reactions. Many moments pass while the old man stares at the empty bed; many moments also while the girl spies on him in the narrow corridor. Every emotional reaction becomes significantly ponderous, as if these characters were not accustomed to expressing themselves.

The acting is curious, half Expressionist, half naturalist. Only Werner Krauss, as the old father, succeeds in giving depth to his clumsy stupefaction at the tragic events which transform his routine world. The two women (the daughter is played by Edith Posca, Lupu Pick's wife) have sudden convulsive movements of mind and body, and writhe in their despair.

Nevertheless Mayer and Pick succeed in creating a *Stimmung* vibrant with wild poetry, the intensity of which appears to vary proportionately with the ill-fortune falling upon the characters.

The daughter, after vainly begging the passing lover to take her away with him and after being rejected, incites her father to act: it is a murder without grandiloquence. Then the old man trudges off to wave down the express with his lamp and give himself up. We know that this image was tinted red in contemporary prints, and the title – the only one in the film – wording the confession makes the screen almost burst.

Here Mayer and Pick give a free rein to their liking

182

for symbols: the anonymous, unfeeling passengers in the restaurant-car are seen dining gaily and with appetite. This intentional contrast between the idle class and the very poor is presented insistently and at length, as it was to be for the shabby suicide and the indifferent crowd of revellers in *Sylvester*.

Then, another emphatic symbol: the camera slowly focuses on to the fragments of glass in the bucket – the debris of three destinies.

### Sylvester (1923)

Although he professed indifference to fashion, the Rumanian Lupu Pick whole-heartedly embraced the spirit of the German *Weltanschauung*. 'When I read the scenario of *Sylvester*', he said in his preface to the published version of 1924, 'I was struck by the motif's *eternal* aspect. And I intended to transmit to the spectator the feelings I experienced while reading it. But in the course of filming, new perspectives opened up. I realized that I had to do with a subject as vast and eternal as the world, masterfully condensed into the events of an hour (the last hour of the year, as it happened) which, instead of being used for reflection, for withdrawal into oneself, is merely the occasion for festivities and noisy joy.'

Mayer's aim in choosing this time-setting was purely symbolic, and this was what stirred Pick's enthusiasm. New Year's Eve and the ambiguity of the hour between eleven and midnight, when the old year gives way to the new and the *Sein* (being) collides with the *Werden* (becoming), had already attracted the Romantics. 'For New Year's Eve', writes Hoffmann, 'the Devil always keeps some particular windfall in reserve for me. He is skilled in plunging his steely claw into my breast at the right moment, and with frightful irony, in order to feast his eyes on the blood spouting from my heart.' It was this irony of an absurd destiny that Mayer and Pick set out to underline.

One may ask what the aim of these artistic German directors was. 'This book', says Pick, 'fulfils the conditions of a scenario because, when we read it, it suggests feelings which move us and is not composed of merely

Hanging lamps: *Sylvester* and *Die Strasse*

visual elements. *Seeing* the three characters confined within a narrow framework and tearing each other apart, we *experience* with each of them the particular sorrow which results from the fact that they want to show kindness to each other and cannot. *Seeing* this drinking, this explosion of joy, this celebration of the *Umwelt* (the world around them), we *feel* all these creatures so remote from each other rush forward, fail to make the human contact they seek, then lose their way in life. In short, we *feel* the curse which weighs upon humanity: to be subject to the condition of the beast and yet to be capable of thought. We become conscious of this if we wish to *feel* and not merely to *see*.'

Carl Mayer adds in his foreword that, apart from the kitchen, the dining-room and the tavern, all the other scenes and places are merely *Umwelt*. This *Umwelt*, imbued with a kind of magic, takes on a particular meaning. Pick says: 'The composition of this "lightplay" seems to me to be novel because it encloses the action within a limited framework, giving a major role to the *Umwelt* without involving it in the action proper, which would be banal. The *Umwelt* must constitute the base and symphonic background of a particular destiny, and thus become the emblem of a principal idea.'

A number of shots of this *Umwelt* have disappeared from modern prints: the eternal, infinite sea, the limitless sky, a cemetery in which skeletal branches and harshly lit crosses stand out against a black sky, a vast deserted heath stretching as far as the eye can see, a forest in which the bole of every tree looms up as a black shadow in the stifling gloom; and all this seems to become still more limitless when the camera tracks back to reveal the whole landscape.

This *Umwelt* participates 'symphonically' in the action: a storm breaks, the sea crashes against the cliffs in gigantic waves, the trees bend. And at the end, after the banal suicide of a human being whom nature does not even deign to notice, everything returns to normal, everything quietens down, everything comes back to the equilibrium of the eternal elements.

'The *Umwelt*, varied by a simple incident,' says the editor of the scenario, Ernst Angel, 'is interpolated not

Hanging lamps: *Destiny* and *Torgus*

as accessory action or reaction, but as accessory rhythm, in or out of tempo, as a symbol reinforcing and amplifying the given facts of the drama: it is introduced in such a manner that in places, at certain decisive moments, the action is apparently halted and can only continue passively, almost secretly, by means of an intensification of the *Umwelt*, which is not really independent but disinterested, so to speak, and which withdraws as the action is taken up again.'

Carl Mayer's scenario is worth analysing in depth because it contains an abundance of other elements which help us to understand the classical German film. In the fifty-four 'images' which comprise the scenario there is virtually none in which Mayer does not define very precisely the lighting intended to create mood. From the beginning, with the fade-in of the tavern, we find the instruction: 'The tavern. Small, low-ceilinged. Full of *thick smoke*. And! In *the wavering light*: tables!' Then at the end of this 'image' in which a guest teases the young woman: 'She laughs more and more. And everybody starts laughing again with her. In *the smoke, the light and the hazy glow*.' Describing the movements of his characters, Mayer frequently interjects such short phrases as: 'While all this *Betrieb* (coming and going) takes place in a *smoky atmosphere*' or 'The man. He is busy. In the wavering *Betrieb of a hazy lamp*.'

Every presentation of the tavern has the same indications: '*Tavern. Gloom. Smoke. Dim lighting*', while the elegant night-club opposite, its counterpoint, has: '*Smoke. Dancing. Music. Lights*' and opens '*in Glanz und Licht*', shimmering with splendour and light. The presentation of the smoky tavern is much better done than that of the elegant night-club. Mme de Staël had already noted: 'Stoves, beer and tobacco-smoke form around the German common people a kind of warm heavy atmosphere which they are reluctant to leave.'

The kitchen in which they prepare the traditional New Year's Eve punch is described as 'full of harsh gaslight'. The dining-room is gloomy because the gas has been turned down, or on another occasion the hanging lamp is dim because the young woman has masked it with a sheet of paper to stop it disturbing the child sleeping in its pram. This room is to have a door with a

188

frosted-glass panel, through which the light can be diffused into the kitchen. When the two women start fighting, we wonder as Mayer does, 'Has the light in there gone out? It seems so . . .' The glass door also enables him to show the silhouettes of the two figures crushed against its diaphanous surface, which they then smash in their fury. The man's first gesture when he comes in to intervene is to go up to the lamp 'so that light is cast once more'.

We have the same play of light for the façades. The tavern frontage is 'nocturnal and black', while 'a warm dim light' can be perceived swirling behind the frosty window-panes. The night-club's frontage is shown in a panning shot: the tall windows are brilliantly lit and the revolving door 'keeps turning in the light'. The camera follows the movement of the revolving door, through which we can perceive a 'lighted' hall. The tall mirrors of the cloakroom reflect the elegant clients '*in Glanz*' (brilliant light), and another glazed door suggests a room 'full of chandeliers and lights'.

We find the same kind of appearance in the street, which assumes the 'metaphysical function' also assumed by Grune's street in *Die Strasse* (*The Street*, 1923). Mayer's instructions on this subject hold good for all those films in which the street plays an active – and often tragic – part. 'A square looms up. Like a shadow! In the glow of many lights. And traffic! Motor-cars! Trams! Carriages! Men! Electric signs! Motor-cars! A single entangled mass. Whose elements are barely distinguishable.' On this square glows the illuminated dial of a huge clock which, beneath the camera which moves forward, is finally to become, a few minutes before midnight, 'as large as Fate' and almost burst the limits of the screen. (The same 'dramatic function' is given to a clock in the hanged man's bedroom, beating with an uncanny artificial life-rhythm, its pendulum swinging and its hammer striking the twelve definitive strokes.)

Crescendo of light-effects as midnight approaches. The crowd thickens in the square, fireworks explode, all the windows suddenly fill with light and we see silhouettes clinking glasses. In a symmetry which is itself symbolic the lighting diminishes after midnight, after the suicide. The heath again, with a solitary flickering

*Die Strasse; The Hands of Orlac*

lantern; another image shows the storm at sea slowly dying down. On the street and the now gloomy square the traffic thins, then disappears; a few lights go out one after the other. In the shadows, the revolving door has stopped turning. A faint light filters from the tall windows of the night-club, showing the tables and chairs piled up inside. In the tavern one dim flame is still left burning behind the façade.

Then, in the square, the last lights go out. The street and square are in darkness, the only light comes from the dial of the clock: the camera tracks back and the clock-face dwindles to a mere point of light in the darkness.

Modern prints of this film have been shorn of so many shots of the *Umwelt* that we can now only get a clear idea of the function of the moving camera by turning to the scenario. It is full of such directions as: 'Tracking slowly back curving to the left, then panning back' or 'Tracking forward at an angle'. These directions are usually kept for the *Umwelt*, more conventional shots being used for the main action. For Mayer, this mobility of the camera-unit ought to heighten the impression the spectator gets of the *Umwelt*, for it tells him that he is being shown a particular world. Mayer adds that the movements of the camera, by a continual shift in depth and height around the events taking place, should convey the vertigo human beings experience when trying to come to terms with their environment.

Mayer's notes and the illustration of a dual camera dolly made specially for this film argue that Pick was the first to use the *entfesselte Kamera*, the 'unchained' (mobile) camera, in a German studio. (But Boese affirms that Wegener had already used a mobile camera for the ghosts in *Der Golem*; see page 70.)

In *The Last Laugh*, Murnau was to use Carl Mayer's directions more skilfully than Lupu Pick. They were to be the very basis of his optical prowess and his penetrating explorations in the visual field. For Murnau the camera moving on a dolly was no longer enough: he tied it to his cameraman's chest and made him follow Jannings step by step, bending, leaning, and twisting in order to shoot from the most complicated of angles.

Yet Pick had grasped the implications of his author's

technical notes perfectly well. He says: 'The new camera movements are rich in significance and inseparable from the scenario. Film being essentially image in movement, the author's suggestions are such that the action appears to be bathed in the *Umwelt* like an island in the middle of the sea.' It was Pick's attachment to symbol rather than to image which prevented him from equalling Murnau in the handling of the mobile camera.

Carl Mayer's short, unfinished, often choppy phrases are constructed Expressionistically with inverted verbs and punctuated with unexpected caesuras. Words such as 'And!', 'Now!', 'Thus!', scattered between the phrases and sometimes isolated on a line, repeated to quicken or slow down the action, reveal Mayer's acute sense of rhythm.

In his *Expressionismus und Film* Kurtz called attention to the divergence of two stylistic aims: an Expressionist poet cannot agree with a director seeking (even stylized) psychological developments in a middle-class atmosphere without accepting certain modifications to his personal style.

Kurtz added that Mayer attempts to minimize the everyday attitudes of his heroes and turn them into Expressionistic 'elements of composition'. Pick only goes half-way in this direction.

It is not merely Mayer's language which makes this film much less remote from the Expressionist ideology than Lupu Pick thought. When Expressionism tries to avoid the snares and pitfalls of naturalistic 'detail' it falls under the ascendancy of the object. The meticulous-minded Germans have always been fond of stressing details. We need only remember in this connection the verbose digressions of their authors, from Jean Paul via Theodor Fontane to Thomas Mann: detail for its own sake, not the authenticity-increasing detail of a Stendhal. The immediate predecessors of Max Reinhardt pin-pointed the realistic detail in the plays of Gerhart Hauptmann or Sudermann, lavish exponents of 'local colour' like the Duke of Meiningen, in his historical dramas, before them. Thus we frequently find in Mayer and Pick the exaggeration of the fateful object: in *Sylvester*, for example, emphasis is placed on the table laid with its narrow cloth and only two places. When Lang cuts rapidly, in *M*, to the unoccupied chair and empty plate of the murdered little girl, the shock hits the spectator immediately. In Pick's film the technique requires much greater watchfulness on the part of the spectator: he is supposed, like the young woman (warned of her mother-in-law's imminent intrusion by the shadow profiled on the frosted window), to stare at the table where two people's intimacy is going to be ruined. Then the young woman unwillingly sets a third place at the other side of the table where there is no cloth. Mayer and Pick take their time, the young woman comes and goes. Finally, after inserts of detailed shots of the *Umwelt*, including the tavern, we are shown the two women's temporary reconciliation, as they exaggerate their brisk pleasure in laying the table, this time for three.

Along with Mayer, Pick explores the byways of the soul. While her daughter-in-law is asleep, the little old woman, with nothing to do, starts fidgeting between the pram which she does not dare touch, and the stove, which she pokes timidly. Pick goes through whole lengths of film before revealing the climax of this lower-middle-class tragedy: two family portraits – one the photo of the unmarried son beside his proud mother, the other showing the son and his bride, who has contrived to snatch him from his mother's devotion – prompt a scene of jealousy between the two women. Finally, torn between them, besotted with punch, the man is pushed to suicide.

Throughout this film objects are all-important. The stove to which the old mother clings when the son sees himself obliged to send her away becomes the very emblem of the familial hearth. Her mechanical wheeling of the orphan's pram round the dining-room, where the gap left by the dead man can already be felt, becomes unbearably 'significant'. The streamers which are trampled underfoot and swept up in the streets in the early hours of morning, or which hang intertwined and torn on the tables and chairs of the empty tavern; the last leaf of a calendar which, before the customers leave, a drunk stares at over his big cardboard nose and which he finally decides to tear off and crumple (a scene not in Mayer's scenario) – all this belongs to Lupu Pick's scheme of the symbolism of 'psychical relationships'.

The gay street scenes, the lush night-club with its elegant guests, the noisy carousing at the tavern, the drunken revellers in fancy dress invading the hanged man's bedroom, the belated night prowler vainly knocking at the locked door of the gloomy tavern – all these passages, dominated by the trivial event of a shabby suicide, are juxtaposed, and reveal an Expressionistic taste for violent contrast. The extremely pared-down treatment of the main characters, around whom the extras in the brief, hour-long tragedy shade into the background, conforms to the Expressionist ruling which lays down that characters must only embody 'principles'.

For Mayer talks about *Gestalten*, shapes, and gives the direction 'The man, *his* wife, *his* mother', depriving the two women of all individual existence by means of this possessive pronoun. Then again, he directs that only these principal figures are to appear in medium shots, 'since the general atmosphere of celebration merely constitutes the background against which the action is set'. The rooms and kitchen are to be small and low-ceilinged so that, even taken in their totality, the figures fill space 'intensely'.

It is worth pointing out that the Expressionism in this film serves to conceal a curious return to Naturalism. The acting of Klöpfer as the man is most revealing. He has a way of throwing back the upper part of his body into a slanting posture. When he is struggling to decide between the two women he loves, his crazy laugh, his tall figure, at once flabby and stiff, foreshadow his later appearance after the hanging, when his rigid, bloated expression in death resembles that of a drowned man.

The insinuating manner of the Kammerspiele intensifies the weight of the action and increases its ponderous slowness. It is plausible when the wife sees her mother-in-law at the window and hesitates before informing her husband; but when the latter, sluggish though he may be, lets so many interminable minutes pass before letting his mother in from the cold, it is not very convincing.

One lesson Pick learnt from the Kammerspiele was to prove useful to other film-makers. His characters, whose intensity of expression comes close to pantomime, stop

moving their lips; those silent dialogues, whose purport had been conveyed, however inadequately, by the titles, were now quite pointless. On those rare occasions at which, in their despair, the characters in the *Kammerspiel-film* appear to moan and let incoherent sounds escape from their lips, the spectator's emotion is at its height.

Lupu Pick with his everyday tragedies did not give realism to the German cinema. Though he complicates the action by elaborating his own brand of depth-psychology, his characters still have at least some of the nebulous abstraction found in figures stemming from the Expressionist ideology. And the genuine beggars he outlines here and there, after duly making them up to resemble Peachum's fakes in *Der Dreigroschenoper*, lose, in a cloud of crudely sentimental symbols, all social significance they might have had. Was it on account of what Pick calls 'the *eternal* aspect of the motifs', with added elements of *Weltanschauung* and *pittoresque*, that German realism has always been bound to undergo the

195

*Nju:* Elisabeth Bergner

artistic adulteration of a more or less extreme stylization?

There is one passage in *Sylvester* – that of the revolving door in the night-club – which, though rather insignificant in itself, is worthy of note because it anticipates some scenes in *The Last Laugh*. Carl Mayer, the scenarist of both films, had no doubt foreseen what could be gained from this revolving door, but the less subtle and inventive Lupu Pick had not. If the visual effects of this passage are compared with Murnau's shots through the revolving door or the doors of the restaurant and hall, it is impossible to believe that Pick, the first choice as director of *The Last Laugh*, could have achieved as much. Pick was undoubtedly sincere, but he was no genius.

## Paul Czinner

Paul Czinner is a much better exponent of the ambiguity of the Kammerspiele, to which his wife Elisabeth Bergner, an astonishingly gifted actress, was so well adapted. In *Nju* (1924) he depicted two characters facing each other, in silence, and the very air was full of this silence. Czinner's subtlety was to develop still further in his last silent films, when in a novel, though now to us familiar, fashion he interpreted latent mood with close-ups of faces in which the passage of an emotion was reflected like a cloud crossing a limpid sky.

Or again, as in *Der Geiger von Florenz*, he uses slow motion, and here Bergner, holding her violin, glides across the drawing-room as in a dream, a chord about to fade away.

## Elisabeth Bergner

Vibrant, sensitive, an actress of great nervous intellectuality, Elisabeth Bergner had as it were taken up the mantle of Asta Nielsen in the second half of the twenties. Up to the advent of Hitler, she embodied the spirit of an age which was ardent, anguished, intensely spiritual and still very close to the expansive ecstasy of the immediate post-war years.

Elisabeth Bergner came to the fore with Reinhardt when, as a child-woman full of fragile charm, she played the young heroines of Shakespeare; her slim ephebic

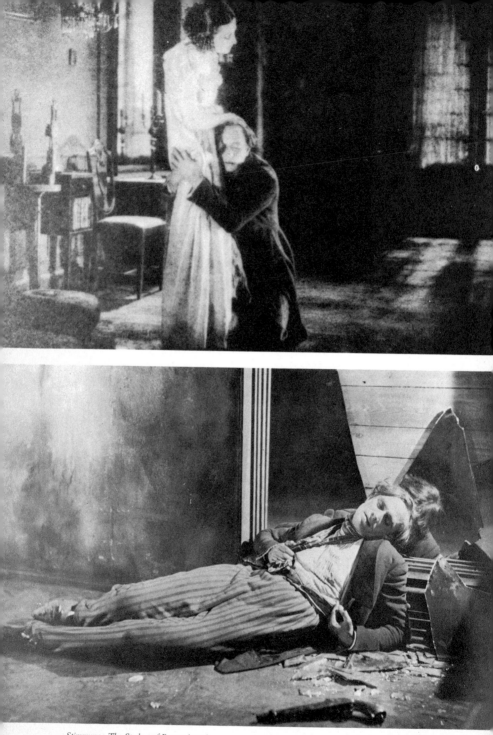

*Stimmung: The Student of Prague* (1926)

figure was dressed in Reinhardt's favourite Quattrocento costume; her shoulders were hunched slightly. Like Asta Nielsen, she could wear a youth's clothing without the disguise ever becoming vulgar; she played Rosalind without betraying her femininity.

No one was her equal, a few years later in O'Neill's *Strange Interlude*, for expressing asides, thoughts from the unconscious, with her slightly hoarse yet supple voice distinguishing them from the dialogue of reality.

In her, Paul Czinner found the ideal executant for his *Kammerspielfilme*. Her bearing and appearance already seemed to contain all the quintessence of the Kammerspiele. In *Nju* she appears even more frail, confronted by Emil Jannings as a robust and uncomprehending husband. Thanks to her, Czinner succeeded in expressing all the subtle nuances of mood, above all when next to her he placed the perennially demoniac Conrad Veidt. The pauses evoke tension, and the silence of the silent film becomes eloquent. When at the end she throws herself over a cliff, dragged down by the folds of her wide skirt, it is the climax of Kammerspiele.

Yet one has reservations about Czinner's and Bergner's talent. In *Liebe* (1927), for example, Bergner, very nervous and often tense, becomes embarrassing, particularly when she tries to convey gaiety; she has no sense of playfulness.★ And as for Czinner, as soon as he emerged from the spell of the Kammerspiele, he turned out to be rather mediocre.

## Stimmung

In any German film the preoccupation with rendering *Stimmung* ('mood') by suggesting the 'vibrations of the soul' is linked to the use of light. In fact this *Stimmung* hovers around objects as well as people: it is a 'metaphysical' accord, a mystical and singular harmony amid the chaos of things, a kind of sorrowful nostalgia which, for the German, is mixed with well-being, an imprecise nuance of nostalgia, languor coloured with desire, lust of body and soul.

This *Stimmung* is most often diffused by a 'veiled', melancholy landscape, or by an interior in which the etiolated glow of a hanging lamp, an oil lamp, a chandelier,

★ *Liebe* showed that it was not necessary for a *Kammerspielfilm* to have a limited number of characters, nor for the characters to belong to a simple everyday milieu. Here the silence and reserve characteristic of Balzac's two farouche lovers (the film was based on *La Duchesse de Langeais*) are worthy of note.

*Stimmung:* Conrad Veidt's *Wahnsinn*

or even a sunbeam shining through a window, creates penumbra. This is how Lang seeks to suggest the uncertain chiaroscuro atmosphere in the old people's home in *Destiny*; in *M* he uses cigarette smoke floating in the glow of a hanging lamp. In *The Last Laugh* Murnau creates the stifling atmosphere by accumulating the reflections of objects shining in the steam in the lavatory mirrors: the electric lights, the dark shimmering battens of a kind of pergola in the neighbouring street. Arthur von Gerlach, in *Die Chronik von Grieshuus*, intensifies the atmosphere with the use of veiled lights, the reflections playing on the pleats of a velvet garment, and the suggestion of a superimposed spectral apparition.

Thoughts whose presence is almost tangible seem to lurk everywhere like dead souls deprived of rest; they are the 'distant memories' we find in Novalis, 'youthful desires, childhood dreams, all the brief joys and vain hopes of a lifetime, approaching robed in grey like the evening mist'. (The poet also remarks that the notion of

*Stimmung: Alraune* (1928); *The Hands of Orlac*

*Stimmung: Variety*

*Stimmung* alludes to 'musical conditions of the soul' and that it is bound up with 'psychical acoustics and a harmony of vibrations'.)

There may still be a few people who remember a fine passage in Murnau's lost film *Der Brennende Acker* (*The Burning Earth*). Coming from the back right, two long streams of daylight penetrate into a gloomy room and stop short of two human forms, a man and a woman, also on the right, dressed in black and almost merging into the half-light: one of the streams of light passes quite close to the man's foot, uncannily increasing the dramatic, mysterious silence.

Or again, a wavering trellis-work of hazy light is diffused through the slits of a venetian blind on to the parquet floor where the Student of Prague, in a moment of bliss, kneels at the feet of the woman he loves; the shimmer of the mullioned window is reflected in the tall mirror which, a few moments later, will betray his dark secret.

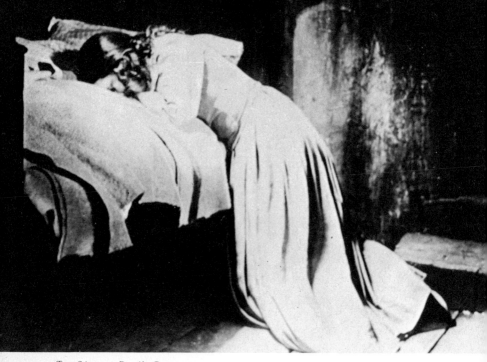

True *Stimmung: Das Alte Gesetz*

The final touch of *Stimmung*: after firing at his double, the Student of Prague lies on the floor in front of his smashed mirror. In the half-light is suspended an aura of peace regained.

To explore by such means the levels of the soul, to evoke mood by playing on the references to feelings, is very Germanic. Lang had already adopted this style for the famous scene in *Die Nibelungen* in which Kriemhild and Siegfried walk towards each other very slowly in a typical moment of solemnity, of the intensified acting which the Germans find so rapturous. Kriemhild bears the cup of welcome, which she offers to Siegfried as if it were the Holy Grail. Neither Kriemhild nor Siegfried bend from their hieratic rigidity. This is Kammerspiele transformed into Wagnerian opera. The heraldic group formed by Gunther and Siegfried drinking the cup of blood brotherhood is presented with less religiosity than this first meeting of the two lovers.

The *Stimmung* sometimes inclines, without the least

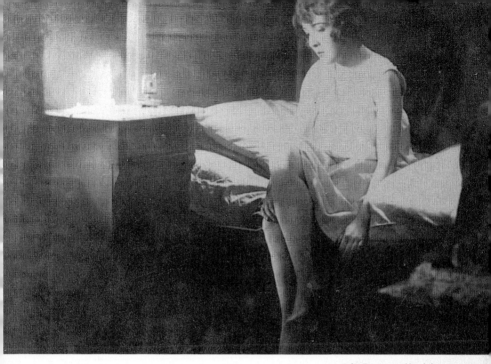

False *Stimmung: Heimkehr*

transition, towards terror. When the storm breaks in *The Student of Prague*, the clouds lacerate the sky, the trees shake and the branches bend in an extremely violent accompaniment orchestrating the hero's interior struggle. The despair of Faust as he summons up the demon is associated with flashes of lightning. And the fragile form of Nju, straying off towards a lonely suicide, a small pathetic figure swept along by the wind buffeting the folds of her dress, is accentuated by a shower spattering on the gaunt white branches of bare trees outlined in the darkness.

The Germanic soul can go blithely from the sublime to the ridiculous. If certain passages in German films make us smile today, if their rhythm sometimes seems intolerably slow to non-German spectators, the reason is that German film-makers generally apply themselves to exhausting all the *Stimmung* in a situation, and to searching the furthest recesses of the soul.

'The Germans', Mme de Staël says in connection with

the German theatre, 'ask nothing better than to settle down in the auditorium and give the author all the time he wants to prepare the action and develop his characters: French impatience will not tolerate this slowness.'

It is the weight of these silent dialogues of the soul, this claustral atmosphere of the Kammerspiele, which today we find so stifling.

'*When as a child I passed near you*
*You would surge with infinite assurance from the doorway*
*Your three-cornered hat seemed to reach the emblems of the stars*
*All-powerful your beard spread out,*
*O man with the sceptre-stick!*'
Werfel: 'The Divine Doorman' from the cycle of poems *Wir Sind,* 1913.

'*A revolving door. Which turns perpetually in the light. And in front of it: A Doorman! Tall. Stiff as a lackey.*'
Carl Mayer: Scenario of *Sylvester,* 1924.

* Fritz Lang has pointed out to me that this tragedy could never have occurred, as no doorman would ever stoop to doing the job of the luggage-porters or valets.

## Der Letzte Mann (The Last Laugh, 1924)

A disagreement between Pick and Mayer put an end to their plan for a trilogy of *Kammerspielfilme,* a kind of triptych with *Scherben* and *Sylvester* as the flanking panels for *The Last Laugh.*

Again, as in *Sylvester* and *Scherben,* the absence of titles gives rise to a succession of shots in which the action progresses by purely visual means. Again, and even more so, *The Last Laugh* goes against Expressionist precept. Surely Edschmid had violently denounced the drama of social ambition and the petty tragedies stemming from the wearing of uniform?

Mayer and Murnau tackle the tragi-comedy inherent in the destiny of a hotel doorman, proud of his braided livery, admired by his family and neighbours, the general of his own back yard. Having grown too old to carry the heavy luggage,* he is retired and put in charge of the gentlemen's lavatories where he has to exchange his dress uniform for a simple white jacket. His family feel dishonoured and he becomes the laughing-stock of the neighbours, who in this way take their revenge for the adulation they have previously lavished on him. This is pre-eminently a German tragedy, and can only be understood in a country where uniform is King, not to say God. A non-German mind will have difficulty in comprehending all its tragic implications.

Murnau's imaginative power overlaps the framework of the *Kammerspielfilm,* and this is not solely because *The Last Laugh* contains more characters than is usual

207

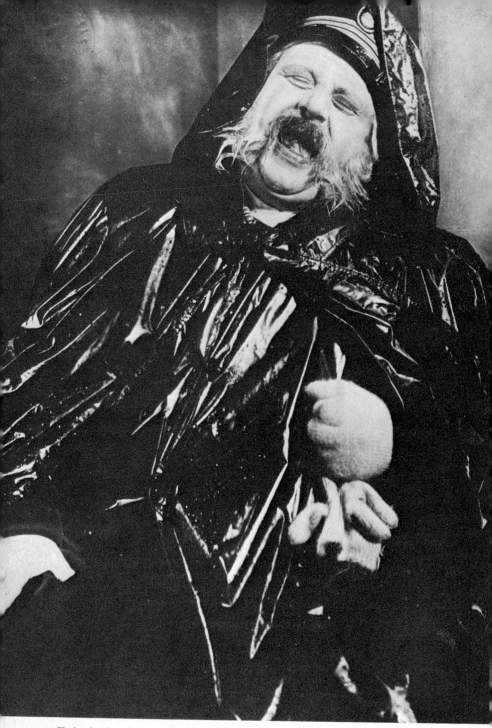
*The Last Laugh:* Emil Jannings

in the genre. Apart from the protagonist, who was to have been played by Lupu Pick himself and is played here by Jannings with an appropriate pompous aplomb, the other characters display a singular lack of depth: they only seem to be there at all to give this pathetic hotel doorman his cue. This is perhaps a remnant of the Expressionist doctrine that denies a personal life to all the characters with whom the hero is in conflict. A contemporary dramatic critic, referring to Hasenclever's Expressionist drama *Der Sohn*, called such characters 'die Ausstrahlungen seiner Innerlichkeit', the radiations of the hero's inner essence. Vague puppets like the anonymous guests at the hotel, the neighbours of 'the last of men', exist only in the way they react to the hero, and only come to life when he appears. Once he has gone up to his room they can turn out the gaslights on the stairs. And when all the inhabitants of this microcosm busy themselves at their windows and on their balconies every morning, airing sheets and beating eiderdowns, their gestures seem to serve no other purpose but that of a modest, quasi-mechanical accompaniment to the main action, the brushing of the sacred uniform.

Murnau deliberately emphasizes this effect: the doorman going off to work in his gold-braided splendour is filmed in such a way that he seems much taller than the people he meets; during the wedding scene he appears at the centre of the image with more depth, sharpness and height than the guests around him, who remain blurred.

Nevertheless Expressionist techniques have but little place in this film. If Murnau uses them for the dream passages, it is only because this style has a capacity for fantasy which he can draw upon for the effects he judges necessary at this point. Of course, having, like all his compatriots, a weakness for symbols, he never tires – and Carl Mayer eggs him on – of bringing out, as soon as the opportunity arises, the 'metaphysical' meaning of an object. The porter's umbrella becomes as it were his sceptre, and he only gives it up to one of the hotel pages on rare occasions, with a heavily underlined magnanimity. The button torn from the doorman's livery as he is stripped of his uniform is filmed in its fall, a detail which makes the stripping the equivalent of

*The Last Laugh:* where uniform is King

a military degradation. Yet symbol in a work by Murnau never has the false profundity beneath which so many Germans conceal a solemn void. In the hands of Murnau and Mayer symbols relate to the action; the absence of this button, for example, constrains the doorman to remember, despite himself, the humiliation which preceded his dream of triumph. At the same time, the symbol takes on the implacable character of Destiny: when the doorman goes down towards the lavatory, it is the descent into Hell, and inexorably the leaves of the door swing to behind him. Lubitsch, whose taste for vaudeville delights in artificial double meanings, also uses incessantly opening and closing doors, but they are far from assuming the significance they take on in Murnau. In *Nosferatu* the closing of the gate by invisible hands emphasizes the fact that the young man will from now on be incapable of freeing himself from the doom which is about to overtake an entire town.

The merry-go-round of the revolving door, whose movements the doorman is so proud of controlling, becomes the whirlpool of life itself. Once again the inorganic world, the object absolutely necessary to the action, is invested with a transcendental meaning which is solemnly insisted upon in the German manner. But Murnau, unlike Pick, who easily lapses into an arid symbolism, succeeds in bringing his revolving door to life.

Objects can also determine or accelerate the peripetias of the tragedy: the movement of the door leading to the lavatory betrays the doorman's downfall to a women neighbour. The door swings again when the rich client, outraged at not being attended to immediately, sweeps past in search of the manager; the camera seizes upon this movement, which alternately reveals and conceals the slumped form of 'the last of men'. And the obstinate swinging of this door recalls the swinging of the light cast by the invisible lamp in the deserted cabin of the phantom ship in *Nosferatu*.

Murnau elaborates and counterpoints his symbols in the slow manner of his compatriots, and it is in this field that the influence of Carl Mayer is most felt. In the cloakroom the well-to-do client twirls his proud moustache, brushes his hair around a brilliantined parting, and performs exactly the same fatuous gestures as the doorman in his days of glory. Or the tension in the atmosphere corresponds once again to a state of mind: the despairing doorman goes home to his empty room in which the objects convey all the desolation of a morning after the night before, windows ajar with their meagre curtains fluttering, overturned chairs and dirty glasses littering the disorder, leftovers from the feast which are but the visible reflection of his spiritual despair. (Pabst used a similar effect, though more elliptically, in *The Love of Jeanne Ney*: the young couple who had watched a wealthy wedding with envy are shown the other side of the events; they see, again through the window, the sadness of the next day.)

Murnau gives dimension to his symbols by varying the shooting angles. The doorman, resplendent in his uniform and puffed up with fatuity, is filmed from below, flaunting his belly, an enormous, ridiculous and cumbersome mass, like a Tsarist general or a capitalist in a Soviet film. After his disgrace, however, in the

*The Last Laugh*: the courtyard

lavatory he is filmed from above, crushed by his downfall.

## The mobile camera

Karl Freund's camera tirelessly details the doorman's mortifications, going everywhere with him, rushing with him down the hotel corridors, playing with the beams of the nightwatchman's torch, which moves forward, flashes around, then moves forward again. German film-makers were always fond of the effects of light slipping along walls, giving depth to two-dimensional space.

The best-known instance of this kind occurs in *Metropolis* when the black-gloved hand of the inventor Rothwang, holding a torch, bears down upon the exhausted Maria.

In *The Love of Jeanne Ney* the wavering electric torch guiding the murderer in the dark reveals for us at every step the wretched furniture and sordid surroundings the detective has lived in. Finally, in *Der Blaue Engel* (*The Blue Angel*, 1930), the circle of light from the janitor's lantern slowly searches a dark staircase.

Under Murnau, the moving camera is never used merely decoratively or symbolically. Consequently every movement, even when his joy at having 'unchained' the camera is apparent, has a precise, clearly-defined aim. Thus, in *Tabu*, he showed each of the native canoes dashing out to meet a sailing ship; the camera shots are varied and inventive, and he cuts rapidly between the different canoes, making them cross each other and even sending the hero back to the shore to fetch his little brother, who has arrived too late; Murnau takes every opportunity to play on the ebb and flow of the narrow canoes slipping swiftly through the limpid water.

The success of the admirable opening of *The Last Laugh* is entirely due to the handling of the camera. Through the windows of the lift as it goes down we see at a single glance the entire hall of the hotel and the revolving door beyond, and we perceive the particular atmosphere created by the uninterrupted flow of visitors entering and leaving beneath the vibrant lights; in a series of breathtaking jumps outlines break and immediately reform.

Murnau's camera exploits all possible visual resources. It bares – slowly, skilfully, by degrees – the pitiful state of the doorman whom we could still see, a few moments before, safe and sound in the sumptuous security of his heavy livery: it pitilessly reveals the crumpled neck of a shabby jacket, the worn patches on a woollen cardigan, and moves steadily – for nothing must escape us – along his legs huddled in a pair of baggy wrinkled trousers.

Murnau likes to join mobile camera effects to the effects of shots through a pane of glass, just as at the opening he filmed the hall of the hotel from the lift. The scene of the turning-point – the manager informing the doorman of his appointment to a more modest function – is seen from a distance through a glass panel. The mobile camera moves in and focuses on the doorman's dismay and the manager's indifferent back. Through another glass wall we see the housekeeper charged with leading Jannings to his new post moving towards him with all the rigidity of Inexorable Fate, while the lost uniform glows in symbolic splendour from the wardrobe. Pabst was to follow the same technique in *Diary of a Lost Girl* when he showed the decisive scene between Louise Brooks and Fritz Rasp, her seducer, through a glass door, and in *Die Dreigroschenoper* when Mackie Messer is discovered asking Polly Peachum to go away with him.

The smooth surfaces of windows, which in German films so frequently replace that other smooth surface, the mirror, give Murnau special pleasure. His camera delights in opalescent surfaces streaming with reflections, rain, or light: car windows, the glazed leaves of the revolving door reflecting the silhouette of the doorman dressed in a gleaming black waterproof, the dark mass of houses with lighted windows, wet pavements and shimmering puddles. It is an almost Impressionistic way of evoking atmosphere: his camera captures the filtered half-light falling from the street-lamps, rays which the movement of the camera transforms into pulsing grooves of light; it seizes the reflections of toilet articles seen in the lavatory mirrors, and the slanting shadow of street railings through the basement window.

The doorman's drunken dream is the direct result of all the impressions he has received in the course of his conscious life. The leaves of the revolving door, now gigantic and Expressionistically distorted, collide with the sleeping man's brain and split it in two: a precise image of the schizoid nature of all dreams. The outline of the leaves is accentuated in proportion as their real form becomes indistinct: soon there is only the wooden frame left, then suddenly nothing but the corners whirling round and round. Are these corners the graphic representation of the ideal revolving door? Or are they intended to mean the flapping door of the cloakroom, which is at times superimposed on the spinning of the revolving door? Murnau's artistry shuffles, blends and overlaps the ingredient impressions of an entire destiny, just as, in the hotel hall of the dream, he uses hazy superimposed images – the ghostly lift going up and down – to condense impressions of haste, impersonality, incessant change and transitoriness. The meaning of the

214

*The Last Laugh:* reflections in the mirrors, shadows from the street

blurred anonymity of the extras around the doorman, who is presented in relief, finally appears to us in all its clarity: his tragedy is shown to us as it occurs within himself.

Murnau had shown the doorman in the manager's office, at a critical moment, failing to haul an excessively heavy valise on to his shoulders, and the swift cut had enabled us to perceive almost simultaneously the lively new doorman casually manoeuvring a huge trunk. Now, in his *Wunschtraum* (compensatory dream), a rejuvenated Jannings juggles triumphantly with an enormous trunk which a whole team of flunkeys have failed to lift. The Expressionist character of all this is obvious. The circle of hotel servants, larvae with identical livid expressions and shaved heads, who flock round the trunk which they are too puny to cope with, comes closer to the aim of 'the most expressive expression' than many thoroughbred Expressionist creations.

The 'unchained' camera totally dominates this drunken

dream: movement and vision unite into a single dramatic factor giving driving force to the action which, outside the dream, remains static. In the passage which indicates the beginning of the doorman's drunkenness, when he can no longer tell whether the chair he is sitting on has suddenly whirled into space or whether it is the room that has started turning around him, the counterpoint of movements is composed in a masterly manner: the camera follows the stunning slide of the chair and films the distortion of objects as the doorman sees them. It is true that all Murnau's films exploit the possibilities of panning, tracking, and high-angle shots to the full, but here the 'subjective' camera becomes the point of departure for an extraordinary vortex of visions without the composition of the image ever suffering from it in the least. He dovetails his shots, leaves one direction for another in his montage, juggles with proportions until the hero's vertigo takes hold of us in our turn and we find ourselves being swept away in the movement. Never has the unconscious been evoked with such constructive violence. What, by comparison, are the walls splitting around the wax effigy of Jack the Ripper in *Waxworks*? Even the superimpositions of the psychoanalytic dream in *Secrets of a Soul*, with their barriers and scaffoldings, symbolizing the obstacles desire comes up against, lack this dramatic power.

Murnau had already attempted to capture what Balázs calls 'the reality submerged by the dream' in his film *Phantom*: in a chaos of objects, a table starts turning, streets pass 'in a staggering daylight', swept along in a fantastic maelstrom, steps go up and down beneath feet which, even when they do not move, seem to be unstable.

Certain passages in the film other than in the dream bear the trace of an evolved Expressionism. Murnau's audiences were still used to the trances and frenzies of the ecstatic theatre; to make them understand the despair of 'the last of men' he shows him about to run away with his livery, momentarily petrified, listing to one side like a sinking ship. His tragic silhouette slants across the screen, against the wall he used to pass in front of every day in his puffed-up, uniformed complacency.

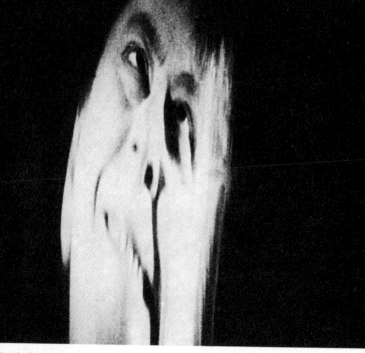

*The Last Laugh:* distortion

The Expressionists had already exploited this oblique body-attitude to emphasize exalted dynamism and its associated frenzy of gesture. It was thus that Wiene showed his diabolical doctor, full of excited emotion at the book revealing the secret of hypnosis: a trick shot makes the now gigantic Caligari rear up obliquely, petrified in the kind of paroxysm frequently found in the acting of stage-actors directed by Karl Heinz Martin, Jürgen Fehling, or even Piscator. Nosferatu is also shown in this attitude at the moment of giving up his last breath. We recall Kurtz's statement that the diagonal, with its expressive violence, sets up an unexpected reaction in the spectator's soul; Hans Richter also claims that a diagonal can in itself express extreme degrees of emotion.

Another Expressionistic device is the effect of gargantuan laughter – enormous gaping mouths, immense black cavities twisted in infernal mirth – which seems to engulf the 'last of men's' back yard. The scene, after the dream, of a woman neighbour's face anamorphosed in a distorting mirror, is another Expressionistic effect, and was adopted by Metzner for his *Überfall*. In the laughter-scene in the back yard the misogynistic Murnau spares no detail of the frightful bosomy women. Ufa did not miss the implications of this mass mirth; they were to use its effects with many variations, down to showing, on a single image, a dozen people telephoning at the same time. In *Metropolis* the covetousness of the spectators watching the robot's dance is expressed by a row of lustful eyes.

These days people criticize *The Last Laugh* for its slowness of pace. But Murnau's fondness for developing each detail, amplifying the least gesture or suggesting his hero's every changing expression with excessive minuteness, is due, all allowance made for Janning's over-acting, to the fact that the *Stimmung* of the *Kammerspielfilm* requires proper pauses. It is also due – however contradictory this may seem – to the fact that the use of

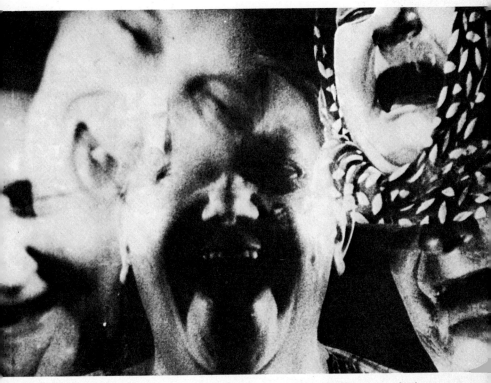

*The Last Laugh:* gargantuan laughter

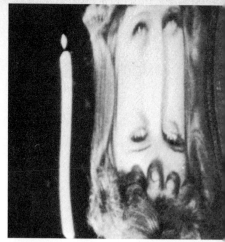
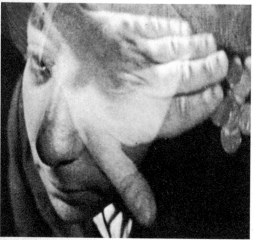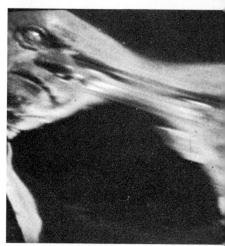
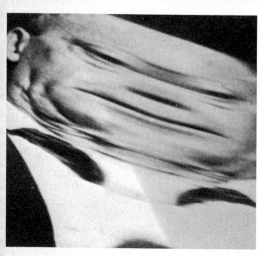

the mobile camera, conferring greater fluidity on the title-free narrative, permits him to explore characters and objects at length. What is more, the narrative itself – a trivial anecdote of human vanity, a banal event deeply rooted in a Germanic world – demands this ponderous rhythm, this weighty immobility which can alone give it meaning.

*Metropolis:* the handling of crowds

*'Faustian culture is a culture of the Will. . . . It is the 'I' rising up in Gothic architecture; the pinnacles and buttresses are 'Me's and the entire Faustian ethos is an ascension.'*
Oswald Spengler: *Decline of the West.*

## Metropolis (1926): the influence of the Expressionist choruses and Piscator

These days many passages in *Metropolis* seem old-fashioned and even vaguely ridiculous, especially those in which the *Kolossal* is overlarded with sentiment. Lang had not yet attained the simplicity of *M*, in which reality is made to resound quite naturally with overtones of the weird.

To detect the beauty of the light and shapes in *Metropolis*, as in many other German films, we need to go beneath the surface.

The deliberate symmetry of *Siegfried* conveys a slow, inexorable rhythm like that of the destiny brooding over the epic. But in the crowd scenes in *Metropolis* the rhythm becomes dynamic. In addition to having an observant mind, Lang has the gift of assimilating in a very personal manner what he has seen, whether it be Max Reinhardt directing his army of extras on the vast arena at the Grosses Schauspielhaus, or the theatrical discoveries made by the Expressionists and by the stage-director Erwin Piscator – the *Ballung* (agglomeration of human figures) of the *Sprechchöre* (speaking chorus), and the deployment of massed extras over the innumerable scaffoldings on stage.

In the *Sprechchöre* the crowd became a compact sombre mass, often almost amorphous, subject to a heavy machine-like movement from which, at rhythmical intervals, a single character, a leader of the chorus, detached himself. For Piscator, who was greatly

223

influenced by Russian stage production, the Expressionistic Anonymous Man belonged to a collectivity, and his body expressed either forward-bounding or restrained Will. Piscator was the perfect interpreter, in terms of the theatre, of an age pledged to technology and an essentially constructive *Weltanschauung*. He even contrived to transform extras into architectural elements, which he then projected forward again in swift, preferably wedge-shaped movements, either singly or in groups. He excelled in making the isolated extra lean to one side while maintaining an attitude of exalted tension similar to that sought after by the Expressionist directors, from whom Piscator differed principally in that he did not altogether proscribe transitional movements.★

His film *Revolt of the Fishermen* (1934), made in the USSR, still has a few traces of this expressive method. For example, the main character, going down a gangway accompanied by a shift of workers coming out on strike, stops for a moment, pulling up his shoulders, throwing out his chest and straddling his legs in a heroic stand-at-ease which can still be seen in German advertisements for products promising vigour to neurasthenics. Kurtz had had a word for it: the figures in German films are always 'in geistiger Fechterstellung', spiritually poised like a fencer.

Insofar as crowd-directing for the screen is concerned Lang had had a predecessor, Otto Rippert, who directed the remarkable film *Homunculus* in 1916. Those people for whom the German film begins with *Caligari* should see an episode of this extraordinary film, which has passed almost unnoticed. It contains, in addition to the chiaroscuro, all the elements of what the German cinema was to stand for during the next fifteen years. The attitudes of Olaf Fønss as Homunculus, his brusque gestures and grimacing mien, anticipate the style of acting adopted by Kortner in *Backstairs* or *Warning Shadows* and that of Klein-Rogge in *Metropolis*. But the influence of *Homunculus* on *Metropolis* is especially apparent in certain mass movements which exactly recall the excited rabble roused against Homunculus ranging themselves in a triangle in a rush for the stairs. These similarities between Rippert and

★ Lang owed little, however, to Karl Heinz Martin, whose explosive *mise-en-scène* used clashing lighting effects to create violent movement and dramatic vertiginous sets. In choosing sets of monumental proportions for *Siegfried* Lang was mainly influenced by Leopold Jessner, who was fond of co-ordinating or subordinating the different parts of a scene in a restrained symmetry on a stage with matching flights of steps. See page 121.

Lang are obvious; moreover, Lang worked for some time with Rippert, as a scenarist.

To describe the mass of inhabitants in the underground town in *Metropolis* Lang used Expressionistic stylization to great effect: impersonal, hunched, servile, spiritless, slavish beings dressed in costumes of no known historical period. The stylization is extreme during the change of shift when the two columns meet, marching with rhythmic, jerky steps, and when the solid block of workers is heaped into the lifts, heads bowed, completely lacking individual existence.

The cubes of the houses placed corner to corner, the uniform rows of windows, or the few slanting doors all with the same number of steps, reinforce the monotony of the underground town; the barrack-like tenements compose an appropriate background for the mechanical distribution of the impersonal masses. The cameras of Freund or Rittau record them as they cross the yard in which the famous flood scene will later take

*Homunculus*

*Metropolis*: the bowed workers

place. And here the masses deploy in an echelon movement, as practised by the Expressionist choruses, moving
in several rectangular or rhomboidal divisions, whose
absolute sharpness of outline is never broken by an
individual movement.

The procession of the Moloch's victims moves with
this same mechanical perfection; the great facade of the
machine-room is transformed into the face of the
devouring god (reminiscence of Pastrone's *Cabiria*); the
file of rectangular, equally-spaced divisions sweeps
towards the voracious mouth. We have already noted
the symmetrical arrangement of the warriors in *Siegfried*
and one finds the pattern repeated later in Leni Riefenstahl's *Triumph of the Will* (1935) about a Nazi rally
at Nuremberg.

The inhabitants of the underground town are more
like automatons than the robot created by the inventor
Rotwang. Their entire person is geared to the rhythm
of the complicated machines: their arms become the

226

*Metropolis:* the powerhouse

spokes of an immense wheel, their bodies set into recesses on the façade of the machine-house represent the hands of a gigantic clock. The human element is stylized into a mechanical element: in the recesses between the two levels the diagonal of each figure points in an opposite direction to its neighbour's. Kurtz decreed that the laws of the 'formation of space' apply also to the human body, for the human body imposes its dimensions on the scenic structure.

The Germans do not use exaggeration to create a type, they use stylization to create a stereotype. In this they differ from the more restrained Soviet directors.

Apart from these machine-men, Lang seeks more and more to make his groups of extras fall into a geometrical pattern. In *Siegfried* the human body was often used as a scenic element. But in *Metropolis* it becomes a basic factor of the architecture itself, immobilized with other bodies into triangles, ellipses or semicircles.

Yet in spite of this geometrical stylization, the last vestige of the Expressionist aesthetic, Lang never becomes trite. Even when his crowd is 'architecturalized' it remains alive, as in the pyramid of arms which rise in supplication during the flood – the cluster of children clinging to Maria's body on the last little island of concrete. Lang sometimes replaces this pyramidal grouping (which is also found in the studied mêlée of avid hands stretching out towards the bogus Maria appearing on the apocalyptic beast, and in the robot's auto-da-fé) by a triangular grouping whose apex is elongated by a perspective effect, as was done in the rebellion scene in *Homunculus*. Lang used this effect several times: for instance, the children flocking towards the little island or the workers rushing to destroy the machine-house and capture the robot. Also worthy of note is the procession of workmen marching towards the cathedral doors, headed at the apex of the triangle by the foreman played by Heinrich George.

The semicircle of rebelling workers around the smoking ruins of the machines is part of the action; the high-angle shot of the square in which the workmen encircle the anguished father, the rigid figure of Rasp rearing up like an anonymous accuser, is conceived in a more formal, deliberate manner. The borrowing from *Caligari* should

229

*Metropolis:* Lang organizing his 'architecturalized crowd'

be noted: like Cesare, Rotwang goes mad and bears Maria off across the rooftops.

At times the tight stylization of the groupings is slightly relaxed: the workers listening to the bogus Maria in the catacombs take on a more individualized appearance for the first time, despite the Expressionistic distortion of their faces. At other times, crystallized groups can come to life and form an integral part of the action, as in the scene in which the workers from the Tower of Babel move forward in five converging files. In the same sequence the view of the rebels rushing up the staircase towards the Chosen One who lifts his arms ecstatically heavenwards recalls Piscator's handling of the clash of masses.

The geometric handling of crowds is sometimes sustained by a quasi-similarity of gesture picked up by the editing. Maria trying to force a skylight is counterpointed with Freder hammering at the door of the mysterious house in which Maria is held prisoner. In

*Metropolis:* the skylight

*Waxworks* the movement of the Vizier's gesture as he sharpens his scimitar is continued by that of the baker kneading his dough. In *The Last Laugh* the movement the fiancée makes to sugar the cake is associated with that of the doorman brushing his hair.

The scenes set in the immense office, with a few actors lost in the vastness, are less forceful than those with the crowds of workers. The mawkish garden where the children of the rich are sent out to play and the Nazi-style sports stadium in which these gilded youths are trained in athletics, together with the pleasure-house ruled by the bogus Maria, all contrast with the gauntness of the underground town. Similarly, the horny-handed worker's superficial reconciliation with his boorish boss, arranged by his son with the slogan 'the heart mediating between the directing brain and the toiling hands', comes straight from Ufa and Thea von Harbou, then Lang's collaborator. Her sentimentalism and her deplorable taste for false grandeur were to make

232

her lapse rapidly into the darkness of Nazi ideology.

In *Metropolis*, as in all his films, Lang handles lighting admirably: the futuristic city appears as a superb pyramidal accumulation of shimmering sky-scrapers. By means of trick shots and hyper-elaborate lighting, illuminated windows and stretches of dark wall stand out like the white and black squares of a chess-board; the light seems to explode, spreading a luminous mist, falling as iridiscent rain. The models of the city, with its streets and jutting bridges, seem huge. With the aid of Schüfftan's *Spiegeltechnik* (later known as the Shuftan technique) the façades of the workers' houses, of which only part of the total height was actually built in the studio, are magnified.

Light can even create the impression of sound: the scream of the factory whistle is represented by a shriek of light from four spotlights. Light also plays a major role in the creation of the robot, as it had done in the symphony of the machines derived from the abstract

*Metropolis:* the Chosen One

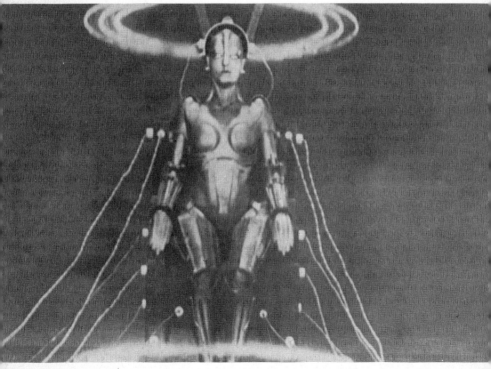

*Metropolis:* lighting

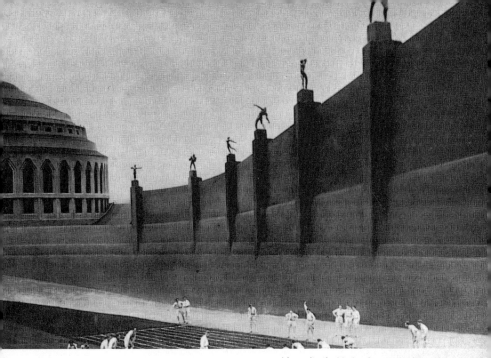

*Metropolis:* the Nazi-style sports stadium

films of Léger and Ruttmann. In this 'féerie de laboratoire' chemical retorts fill with a fluorescent light, coils
of glass piping suddenly start to glow, zigzag flashes and
sparks explode, rings of fire rise in the air. Lighting and
superimpositions make the swirling mass of machines
and ghostly elongated sky-scrapers sweep Fröhlich-
Freder into a feverish nightmare, and he loses conscious-
ness.

On the rare occasions when Lang relaxes his hold on
the lighting effects, we suddenly notice that the
machines have practically no *raison d'être*: they do no
more than compose a kind of moving background, an
accompaniment, a sort of noises-off; in the noisy visual
orchestration of *Metropolis* – a silent film – we can almost
hear them, like the factory whistle.

The luminous smoke rising from the pyre; the steam
from the destroyed machines; the spouts and cascades
of water steeped in light beneath the iron struts; the
misty vapours from the factory masking the outlines of

the workers; the mother-of-pearl whiteness of the candles around the crucifixes bristling in the gloom of the underground church; the dim vault of the catacombs in which the inventor's electric torch pursues the fleeing silhouette of Maria while, here and there, a white skull grimaces at the cone of light: Lang uses all this to increase the intensity of the atmosphere, achieving a genuinely dramatic crescendo.

# 14   The Fritz Lang Thriller

*'When the detective film dropped the style of the penny-dreadful it had to find a formula which would have a chance of pleasing a cultivated audience as well as spectators attracted merely by the excitement of the action. This is how criminal psychology came to be introduced into the detective film.'*
Fritz Lang, quoted by Luc Moullet.

## Die Spinnen (The Spiders, 1919)

In *Die Spinnen* Lang reveals another aspect of his genius. This unfinished serial – only two episodes were filmed – has a profusion of varied incidents which overflow their framework, complicating the action; these colourful, multiple adventures, overlapping or interlinked, now defy all understanding. In the existing copy, the titles judged necessary for it to be understood at the time are unreadable, which does not make matters easier.

It is surprising that a young director in his third film (the first two have been lost) should show such mastery in directing certain sequences. The scenes actually filmed in a train without back-projection, the chases in which every detail of suspense is calculated and placed with the logic and precision we admire in his later works, the atmosphere created by skilful lighting and sets – all these proofs of Lang's talent are already there to be seen for those who can *see*.

It is easy these days to notice nothing but the old-fashioned, even ridiculous aspects of some of the situations or the stiff, mannered acting of the corpulent Ressel Orla. She makes us regret the boyish Pearl White or the frailer Musidora of *Les Vampires*. Yet certain bit players, such as the little bell-boy in the train greedily devouring a banana, are given presence by the few sure strokes that were to become Fritz Lang's trademark.

Though his comedy is still too emphatic – the butler and servants sampling the wine before serving the guests – he was later to evolve appreciably. One recalls

237

in this connection the heavy-handed, very German joke of the butler and the little pig in Murnau's *Sunrise*.

Sometimes the comedy takes an almost fantastic turn. The odd little professor the hero goes to see for a translation of the Inca script, anticipates the mad professor in *Die Frau im Mond* (*The Woman in the Moon*), and the lair in which he lives with his talking magpie foreshadows the mysterious laboratory of the little apothecary in *Destiny*.

We find a taste for fantastic decoration in the apparition of the black-hooded silhouettes in the hero's sumptuously exotic hall, which, multiplying and intermingling, seem to issue from the mouldings of the wrought-iron banisters.

Behind the multiple bronze arms of a Hindu goddess lurks a hood whose slits reveal two strange glittering eyes similar to those of the robot in *Metropolis*. The second after we notice it, Lang deliberately cuts short this ornamental effect: the hood is pulled off, and reveals the snub-nosed face of Georg John, the leader of the Spiders.

These hooded figures – direct borrowings from Feuillade's *Vampires*, though Feuillade used them with restraint, preoccupied as he was with the documentary notion of 'life as it is' – thus have a double role: they belong both to the action and to the setting. Lang has yet to attain the perfection of the 'warrior-pillars' in *Die Nibelungen*.

As in the first *Mabuse*, hypnosis plays a major role; the appearance of an emaciated fakir in a luxuriously oriental setting recalls Paul Wegener's *Der Yogi*. All is grist to Lang's mill; as in Feuillade, as in all the serials ever made, the kidnappers carry off their victim trussed up elaborately.

At one stage the film turns into a western, and the hero seems to borrow the impassive features of William S. Hart. In the attack on the log-cabin he hauls himself on to the roof, jumps on to a horse and, chased by the Spiders, makes a last-minute grab at a rope slung from the providential balloon.

The secret trapdoors, the complicated lifts guarded by a Chinaman with a cutlass, the ground caving in, the terrifying underground chambers in which sinister

238

gentlemen in top hats hold secret meetings, the armour-plated vaults, the sliding partitions, the cellars filled with poison gas – all these accessories, of course, Lang drew from the common stock of the suspense film.

Lang succeeds in using them to good effect, and since nothing goes to waste in this 'conscious and conscientious' director, for whom 'all films, whatever they be, demand much care and reflection'* he was to use them again in his later films.

Thus the mirror in *Die Spinnen* which 'televises' scenes before the beautiful vamp Lio Shah anticipates the multiple television screens in *Die Tausend Augen des Dr Mabuse* (*The 1000 Eyes of Dr Mabuse*, 1960). There is also a parallel in *Metropolis* when the master learns about the riot from his foreman, whom he can see and talk to through a sort of television screen in his study.

The Spiders' raid on the bank foreshadows in part the burgling of the office block in *M*, even down to the nightwatchman trying to untie himself.

For an instant the form of a man in a vast cloak and a large soft hat stands out against the light on the sailing vessel in *Die Spinnen*, and this extra, who plays no part in the action, is a rough draft for the appearance of 'weary Death' in *Destiny*.

In the second *Mabuse*, in the scene where the two young lovers are threatened with drowning, Lang was to repeat, with refinements, the *Spinnen* scene in which the cellar where the hero is imprisoned is flooded with water.

Lang has always had a taste, almost amounting to an obsession, for fantastic caves deep in the bowels of the earth. The opening in the rock leading to the fabulous town of the last Incas (a paralleling, with its carefully reconstructed temples, of the grandiose buildings in Joe May's 1920 version of *Indische Grabmal*, for which Lang wrote the scenario), and the stalactited caverns in the pirate episode, anticipate Alberich's luminous treasure-cave in *Die Nibelungen* or the lunar cavern discovered by the mad professor in *The Woman in the Moon*. This cavern is as it were echoed by the one in which Debra Paget dances in the 1958 version of *Indische Grabmal*, and by the gloomy underground passages from which the terrible flood of lepers streams.

* Taken from an interview with (or an article by) Fritz Lang, published in 1946 and quoted in Luc Moullet's book on Lang, Editions Seghers 1963, with no other indication as to its source.

239

Thus the Inca city in *Spinnen* is also a draft for the underground cathedral in *Metropolis*. And when the hero of *Die Spinnen* goes down through the trapdoor into the cellars of Chinatown, one is not astonished when he finds there the tiger of Echnapor.

## Dr Mabuse, der Spieler (Dr Mabuse the Gambler, 1922)

Lio Shah, the enigmatic vamp, weaves the spider's web of her multiple crimes, the motive for which remains unknown. Adventure? Or profit?

In *Mabuse der Spieler* Lang already brings in a few psychological traits; he attempts to give some depth to this 'master-mind of crime' *à la* Edgar Wallace, whose tremendously popular detective novels were being devoured by everybody at that time, Brecht included.

Dr Mabuse suffers a nervous breakdown every time he loses at the tables; he gets drunk when he thinks he is winning. In a word, he is a human being and not a monster. He is subject to sudden changes of mood and consumed by the desire to rule by money (whereas Dr Caligari's thirst for power always remained abstract).

Yet it goes even deeper than this. The Berlin critics, more sagacious than we today, saw in this film, which to us seems to fall half way between reality and fantasy, something quite different. For Lang had given the first part the sub-title 'Image of our Times' and the second part – *Inferno* – the sub-title 'Men of our Times'. And the critics of 1922 recognized the unflattering but authentic reflection of their own day, of the inflation of the mad lost years when every vice and passion was rife.

So we find this film going beyond what we took to be simple adventure and becoming a kind of document on the early twenties when people tried at all costs to forget the disasters of the war and the poverty of the immediate post-war period.

Thus Mabuse, less of a superman than a product of the inflationary period, a kind of tireless Proteus, constantly changes his appearance.

Lang uses his wealth of contemporary settings quite differently from the settings of *Die Spinnen*: they heighten and also explain the atmosphere, practically joining in the action; they are much more than a back-

*Dr Mabuse der Spieler*: image of its time

ground. But this setting, despite certain features which recall Expressionism, especially in the tavern sequences, was not created in that style, the only suggestions of which come from occasional harsh lighting effects. Otto Hunte and Stahl–Urach, the designers,★ patterned their settings on the Munich *Kunstgewerbe*, a development from *art nouveau*.

Present-day copies of the first *Mabuse* have been taken directly from the original negative, with all the subtle tones and luminous modelling which that implies. (Copies of *Die Spinnen*, on the other hand, have to be obtained from another positive.) As had already happened in *Destiny*, the settings create the atmosphere, heighten it, and make the spell-binding chiaroscuro of the *Stimmung* pulse with life. For example, Mabuse meditating in front of a blazing hearth with the immense portrait of a gigantic Lucifer, which resembles himself, standing out in a curious light above his head. Or the vast hall in the sumptuous mansion of the Count –

★ Hermann Warm also claims to have designed sets for this film.

241

*Dr Mabuse der Spieler*

Alfred Abel – who wanders around at night, despairing, drunk, holding a candlestick, among his accumulation of works of art. Here and there the *objets d'art* shine out insistently, Expressionistically, as if they are infused with an insidious latent life. An enormous, primitive, fluorescent statue catches the eye, the crystal of a chandelier sparkles, an immense mask seems to split the screen. All these precious objects are no longer elements of the setting, as they were in *Die Spinnen*, and even less the ornamental arabesques on a kind of back-cloth. Their luminous presence makes the silence more and more oppressive, and they are as it were the hieroglyphs of an ineffable solitude and despair.

The Lang of *Destiny* had already learnt how to control the suggestive power of superimpositions. In the first *Mabuse* he used them to create chimeric visions like that of the Count under hypnosis, rehearsing – accompanied by his own phantoms – the wretched gestures of the cheat he is forced to be.

*Dr Mabuse der Spieler*

In Lang the real world is never far removed from
fantasy. Mabuse sees his victims arising from the depths
of the delirium into which he is foundering; the complicated mechanism of a printing-press changes into monstrous steel claws. One is reminded of the transformation
of the powerhouse façade in *Metropolis*.

Other influences from which the young director draws
novel effects in a masterly manner are worthy of note.
When Mabuse disguised as an old man flees from the
gambling-hell because von Wenck, the Procurator,
resists his hypnotic powers, Lang films him from behind
as Wiene had filmed Dr Caligari, dresses him in a cape
like Caligari's and has him walk with the same jerky
step.

When Mabuse hypnotizes the audience at a public
lecture, a desert, complete with oasis and caravan,
appears, curiously recalling the one conjured up by the
Rabbi Loew in the second *Golem*. And when Mabuse,
disguised as a worker, incites the crowd to attack the

243

*Dr Mabuse der Spieler*

police convoy, Lang is remembering a similar sequence in *Homunculus*.

The appearance of a dancer on the immense gaming table which fills the whole of the orchestra stalls anticipates the dance of the robot at the home of the inventor Rotwang in *Metropolis*.

As in his previous films, Lang multiplies the small comic touches which give depth to his characters. The harridan in the disreputable back-alley scratching her greasy hair with her knitting-needles; the enthusiastic old man bombarding the dancer on the stage with flowers, even borrowing others from a lady beside him; the odd, degenerate, drugged secretary shaking with tics; the little bourgeois with a hangover in Room 112; the fat lady at the gaming tables with her gigolo; even a character we just catch a glimpse of in the great hall of the hotel, the husband faltering under the weight of his wife's parcels – all these people are the creations of an extremely inventive imagination.

*Spione*

Lang is concerned with every detail: he shows us, quite a long time after the explosion of the infernal machine at von Wenck's, his office ceiling still propped up with scaffolding. And his precision, his taste for detail and his desire for rigorous authenticity are apparent from the very first sequences. An example is the attack on the man bearing the contract in the train. On three occasions three characters consult their watches in three different places. Step by step, with a meticulous inventiveness, the intrigue moves remorselessly forward, and the editing emphasizes the quasi-simultaneity of the events. If an audience these days can sit through the four hours of *Mabuse* without tiring (the two episodes were formerly shown in two sittings) it is thanks to the precision of the editing. As a young man Eisenstein was dazzled by this film; he obtained a copy, analysed it, dismantled it and reassembled it in various ways to see how it worked.

The fact is that everything is provided for in the

245

ingenious editing of *Mabuse*; one image leads into another, giving its pith and meaning to the only shot which can possibly follow. In this way the succession of adventures is given a controlled force which carries the suspense to its climax.

## Spione (Spies, 1928); Die Frau im Mond (The Woman in the Moon, 1929)

After the first *Mabuse* a film like *Spione* (*Spies*) is disappointing. It lacks the rigour one admires so much in the two episodes of *Mabuse*. The fault may be Lang's for having tried to introduce too many small traits of character. More plausibly, it may be attributed to Thea von Harbou and her taste for pompous melodrama. Thea von Harbou always dwells excessively on the feelings and reactions of her characters. The action gets clogged, and Lang's vigorous editing suffers accordingly.

Lang has challenged the legitimacy of these accusations. 'You have to think that the times themselves were effusive and inordinately sentimental. What is more, the silent film had to express itself in mime. What else could we do when, for example, Gerda Maurus in *Die Frau im Mond* had to express her love, but fall back on certain gestures which these days seem ridiculous, such as when she touches her heart and her lips and blows a kiss to the man she loves?'*

But Lang's explanations are not very convincing. Moreover Gerda Maurus, despite her feline eyes, is a rather poor actress, and Willy Fritsch is even more insipid than Gustav Fröhlich.

Even Rudolf Klein-Rogge, Lang's favourite actor for the criminal superman roles, is less impressive in *Spione*. Lang only retrieves his visual power in the apparition of the three emissaries killed in the course of their dangerous mission, who loom up, surrounded by an Expressionistic halo effect, like a spectre of remorse come to haunt the flouted Japanese diplomat (played by Lupu Pick), whose hara-kiri Lang later portrays with convincing power.

Other scenes of pure Lang occur when the shadows, anticipating the real action, invade the screen on several

* Talking to the author.

246

*Spione*

Building the sets for *Die Frau im Mond*

occasions in a kind of black magic, or again when he depicts the methodical progress of the police with his usual concern for authenticity. Certain passages, such as the accident in the train, also recall the suspense of the first *Mabuse*.

The influence of Thea von Harbou is obvious in *Die Frau im Mond*. In the vast expanses of white sand in the lunar landscapes the falsity of the turgid sentiments is especially jarring: the grandiosity of the fantasy often becomes plain bathos. From one end of this sentimental piece to the other, Fritz Lang's genius only comes through in the rocket-launching scenes, which are exact in their prediction of the future. Good examples are the scenes before the take-off, where the newsreel tone is even more convincing than the science-fiction inventions.

Sketch by Alfred Kubin (1877–1959)

## 15    Tragedies of the Street

*What need is there for romantic treatment? Real life is too romantic, too ghostly.'*
G. W. Pabst, in an interview: *Close Up*, December 1927.

The metaphysical vision of German-speaking artists, whether they be Ludwig Tieck, Kubin, or Meyrink, creates streets crammed with snares and pitfalls, which appear to have no relation with reality. In German films the street represents the call of Destiny – especially at night, with its deserted, treacherous corners, its thundering traffic, its spluttering gaslights, its electric signs, its car headlights, its asphalt gleaming with rain, the lighted windows of its mysterious houses, and the smile of its painted prostitutes; it is the lure and enticement of all poor devils who, tired of their dull homes and monotonous lives, are out for adventure and escape.

For Kurtz the street can as easily be a completely flat surface as a dark stain with jagged edges vibrating with a 'frenzied' light in which blurred spectral figures can be perceived. He says that it is also possible to single out a sector from one of these non-existent streets and bathe it in dazzling light and sharp shadows which make it loom up out of the darkness; it is equally possible by the use of lighting – of a harsh kind – to bring out the outlines of the street in a foreshortened network.

Of a painting by Umberto Boccioni, *The Power of the Street*, in which the street's suggestive power is symbolized by light-rays and triangles, the German writer Sörgel says (in his book *Im Banne des Expressionismus*, 1925) that Boccioni's intention was not to paint the street itself, but its *Kraftlinien*, the force-lines irradiated by objects. And the man in his street is inescapably caught up in this network of *Kraftlinien*. German films seem to follow the same precepts.

251

The back yard in *Backstairs* answers fairly well to this description, although here the vision is accentuated by the intrusion of novel architectural notions. Moreover Kurtz was well aware that though the setting of this film was not altogether Expressionist it could never have been what it was if Expressionism had not already prepared the ground for it. The construction of space by abrupt contrasts of shadow and light, by tonality decomposing or unifying certain architectural elements, had no other origin. This method of juxtaposition also operates in the interiors: a shot in *Backstairs* shows, below, in shadow, the despairing maid (played by the sentimental Henny Porten, the idol of the German public), while above, harshly lit, the ladies of the house berate her with virtuous cant.

## Die Strasse (The Street, 1923)

In the film entitled *Die Strasse*, by Karl Grune, the street plays a more complex role, and it enters directly into the action. We first see it as a luminous temptation from a middle-class dining-room, an invitation cast through the window by the lurid life outside, in the form of light-rays wavering in the gloom and printing a furtive lace-pattern on the ceiling, provoking longings in Eugen Klöpfer, the meticulous bourgeois.

Then outside, the giddying swirl of impressions makes hesitant feet unsteady, rather as in Murnau's *Phantom*; adventure slips from one's clumsy grasp. The fascination of the object comes into play: an optician's sign is transformed into the eyes of an enormous demon. A shop-front is a mirage that reflects at the same time an ocean liner promising escape and the equally promising silhouette of an enigmatic young woman. This perpetual mirroring on glass of desired objects or persons is also found in Fritz Lang's *M* and *The Woman in the Window* (1944) and Pabst's *Die Dreigroschenoper*.

Kurtz says that Ludwig Meidner's sets for *Die Strasse* transpose the brutal dynamism of a city high street into a vision of light emphasized by occasional picturesque details. The architecture is subordinated to the chiaroscuro: the space is filled by the balls of light of the arc lamps, shapes evolve, the jagged outline of a

*The Street*; sketch by Otto Hasler for *M*

*The Street*

staircase is seen, doors move mysteriously. Grune creates the 'dynamism of space eaten into by movement', his 'constructive Will' forges 'the spirit' of a glittering city. This 'spirit', Kurtz says, cannot be captured by the camera-lens if the image is not fashioned by the 'constructive Will'. So Expressionism was to be used not just for effects proposed by the real object as it presents itself to the physical eye, but also for effects needing to be experienced intellectually.

Yet Kurtz had not realized that the vision of the street in this film is not always exclusively Expressionistic, and that what we sometimes find is an Expressionism which has evolved and been transposed and which uses quasi-Impressionistic elements to render atmosphere. The Expressionism has retained more of its purity in the interiors: a gloomy drawing-room in which the bright hanging lamp merely lights the forms of the central characters, or the shot of one of the (by now) classical staircases in which the spectral glow of a gaslamp

Poster for Conrad Veidt's *Wahnsinn*

suspended from a vaulted roof creates the typical ambiguity which Pabst was to use for his version of the chiaroscuro staircase in *Die Freudlose Gasse* (*The Joyless Street*).

The bourgeois with the traditional umbrella – played by the pompous, endomorphic Klöpfer – goes off into the street, confusedly hoping that it will deliver him from the uneventful honesty of married life. 'This morning I went out in search of the unknown', says the cashier in Georg Kaiser's play *Von Morgens bis Mitternachts*. 'Something was driving me on. . . .' For a German this 'something' is always Destiny.

The cashier's escapade is irrevocable, whereas the kindly bourgeois in *Die Strasse* finally emerges from the fallacy of adventure which, ultimately, can only lead to humiliation and murder. He goes back home to his dreary wife and the daily round; the street by night, with all its glitter, is left behind him. The tragedy here is not total, Destiny does not have the last laugh after all. This is surely a sign that the obsession with Expressionism is beginning to lose its hold.

## Die Freudlose Gasse (The Joyless Street, 1925)

Pabst's *The Joyless Street* epitomizes the Germanic visions of the street and the obsession with dimly lit staircases and corridors; it is also the definitive consecration of the ersatz studio architecture deriving from Expressionism. In the scenes of misery in *The Joyless Street* the cliché is dominant – everything is too studied, too arranged, too emphatic. The back-alleys are too disreputable, the staircase too enigmatic, the counterpoints of shadow and lights too discordant and too obvious. The face of Werner Krauss (the butcher with the twirly moustache) is too prominent, the parting in his hair too oily and his brutality excessive. The prostitutes on the alley-corner, the nobly fallen bourgeois, and the insinuating madam all look too much like a Victorian print entitled 'Poverty and Human Depravity'. The picturesque triumphs over the tragic, and this is why many passages in this film are now disappointing; it is rarely possible to feel involved in the emotional turmoil of the film's period.

Another film depicted the disasters of the post-war

Griffith's *Isn't Life Wonderful?* (1924); *The Joyless Street*

years with much more restraint and humanity: *Isn't Life Wonderful?*, in which Griffith succeeded in producing an epic of despair and hunger without ever lapsing into facile sentiment. The sad queues of city-folk pushed by poverty into buying and buying before the goods run out and the value of the mark goes down still further, jostling, pushing, shoving, envying those in front, and keeping a wary eye for queue-jumpers are much more forceful than Pabst's decorative queues of self-consciously symbolic extras.

Nevertheless, forcing the picturesque to the extreme, Pabst occasionally achieves poignant effects like the hand of the stunned butcher rising up against the window and clenching in the air. This shot is more convincing than the one in which we see his face covered with blood, a reminiscence of the previous passage in which his complacent lustful face loomed up at this same window before he opened the door to the women prepared to trade themselves for a little food.

During the rather theatrical riot scenes the contrast between the shots of the mob rushing towards the bawdy-house and those in which the black marketeers run for the exit in terror of their lives reveals the skilful techniques characteristic of Pabst's films from then on. In an often-quoted interview for *Close Up* in 1927, Pabst said in connection with *The Love of Jeanne Ney*: 'Every shot is made on some movement. At the end of one cut somebody is moving, at the beginning of the next the movement is continued. The eye is thus so occupied in following these movements that it misses the cuts.' His intention was to avoid breaks in the narrative so as to achieve a perfect fluidity of action. His method was completely opposite to that of the Soviet directors who deliberately went after shock cuts and dialectic juxtaposition.

One is occasionally struck by a revealing shot fore-shadowing what the mature Pabst was to be capable of: for instance the overhead shot of Werner Krauss, the butcher, in the bawdy-house, showing us his brilliantined head in all its hideousness, with his bull-neck thrown into relief and his shoulders hunched; the camera follows his attitudes, his rigid way of sitting down, carefully lifting the flaps of his frock-coat, his gloved hand grasping a piece of sticky cake which leaves bits of sugar on the leather – all the vanity of the newly-rich, ill at ease in his Sunday best.

Pabst still uses the rather threadbare techniques of Expressionist symbolism: the glazier's enormous, super-imposed hand stretches out to claim his due from a swooning Garbo, who has only a derisory sum of money left. Or Garbo's half-length figure is left blurred under the gaze of the butcher in his Sunday suit, and this blurring conveys that his natural inclination towards more rounded women saves her from him. And there is the very brief shot of two coats hanging on neighbouring pegs – the one poor and threadbare, the other a dainty grey fur which will have to be paid for in kind.

Pabst, who was later to pursue realistic objectivity, frequently made known his satisfaction with having here presented the murder of the beautiful adulteress as a newspaper item: the corpse remains imprecise and hence becomes something anonymous, impersonal and very remote in the diffused light falling from the half-closed venetian blinds. This particular atmosphere was to recur in the scene where the fleeing heroine in *Pandora's Box* comes momentarily into the deserted flat of the husband she has murdered.

Like so many German directors Pabst is fond of filming mirror-reflections: the madam's assistant forces Garbo to dress in an evening gown which leaves her almost entirely naked. We see the girl standing in front of a mirror which only reflects the image of the woman badgering her. (Note also the particular use of a hand-mirror, when the jeweller puts the necklace round the neck of the immobile, entirely passive Asta Nielsen; she raises the mirror with a mechanical gesture and the circle of light projected by the glass appears twice over her face.) Then Garbo, dressed in this gown, is reflected in a three-faced mirror in which there appears the silhouette of a drunken man, also three-fold; his real presence is revealed solely by a lustful hand stretching towards the girl. Pabst is fond of this enormous hand at the edge of the screen: the rich profiteer approaching poor Asta Nielsen is also announced by a large hand. When Asta Nielsen tries to explain the murder-scene to the bewildered profiteer, Pabst shows nothing but the movements of her aristocratic, emaciated hands. The same murder related to the policeman is once more evoked merely by Asta Nielsen's hands, fluttering like frightened birds.

For *The Love of Jeanne Ney* Pabst invents more refined mirror effects, for example the mirror in which the Russian officers' orgy is momentarily reflected and which, smashed by a bottle, still reflects the huddle of bodies in one of its fragments. And the scene in which the lovers decide to spend the night at the hotel is shown reflected in the window of the car which they have stopped and which goes off empty.

*The Joyless Street* already reveals that Pabst uses actresses to better effect than actors. It is true that for this film he had two exceptional women at his disposal, one of whom was Greta Garbo who, though very young and inexperienced, had just played unforgettably the part of the Countess in Stiller's *Gösta Berlings Saga*. The camera-lens captures the perfect sweep of her face with its gentle expression of timid sadness, and on the rare occasions when she risks a faint smile for the American officer she is infinitely more captivating than the 'Garbo who laughs' launched in *Ninotchka*. These hesitations, partly due to stage fright, are all to the good. They harmonize with the consummate artistry of Asta Nielsen, whom we first see, before the murder, submissive and almost childlike, with just a poor little wish for happiness; but gradually her passivity is infused with sorrow and her expression of a dying Pierrot takes on extraordinary power. The closing of her eyes, as with Eleonora Duse, is a weary gesture of experience; her hands seem to have some wound which we cannot see; her pathetic fate cuts us to the heart. Her infinitely weary walk is clumsy, as if her legs were made of wood; she seems defeated beforehand, the chosen victim of all earthly misfortune. Many scenes in this film which are mere commonplaces of human suffering come alive through her presence.

## Asta Nielsen

*'Dip the flags before her', Béla Balázs wrote after seeing Asta Nielsen play the death of Hamlet, 'dip the flags before her, for she is unique.'*

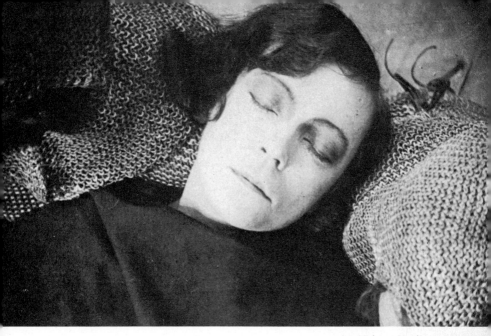

Asta Nielsen as Hamlet

*People nowadays cannot understand what that pale mask, with its immense blazing eyes, meant for the nineteen-tens and twenties. Others wore this smooth straight fringe of dark hair, but only she and perhaps Louise Brooks seemed inseparable from this stylized adornment. A hypercultivated, unstable, sophisticated period had found its ideal, an intellectual of great refinement. Who better than she could play Hedda Gabler, at once passively frigid and devoured by passion?*

*But Asta Nielsen was more than what a generation cultivating the linear and the arabesque was in search of. It was impossible to put a label on this great actress: she was neither 'modernistic' nor 'Expressionistic'. Her warm humanity, full of the breath of life and presence, refuted both abstraction and the abruptness of Expressionist art. She could transform herself, in* Engelein *or* Das Liebes A-B-C, *into a mischievous girl, and her great tragedian's eyes would suddenly shine with petulance. Never did she stoop to mawkishness, never did her travesty shock. She could play in trousers without ambiguity. For Asta Nielsen's eroticism was without equivocation; her passion was always authentic.*

261

Asta Nielsen in *The Joyless Street*

*Her fringe hairstyle sometimes led her to play vamps, but there was nothing calculating about her. She made audiences feel the fire which was to destroy not only men but also herself.*

*In every film this woman who seems the quintessence, the epitome of her era, renews herself. In* Hamlet *she is as vibrant as a Damascus sabre, the Danish Joan of Arc. What could be more Stendhalian than her* Vanina?

*No one has ever been able to schematize Asta Nielsen, and it is characteristic that it is because she managed to be herself and keep her own face that she was never engaged by Hollywood, which could not transform her.*

*She is typically Nordic, issuing from the savage legends of the* Edda, *and even if she hardly ever filmed in her native land, Denmark, she remains a figure apart in German films, and not only because Danish directors, Urban Gad and Sven Gade, her two successive husbands, directed most of her films. This complex aura persists around her when she films with such German directors as Pabst or Bruno Rahn.*

262

In sum, Pabst was much more skilful in depicting the hideous world born of the inflation and the desire for facile pleasure, the world of the pimps and profiteers, than in making a viable cinematic description of the dull grisaille of poverty. He was always to yield to the temptation of giving it a gloss, of glamorizing it with some picturesque touch.

Nevertheless, he did manage later on to break away from this pasteboard architecture, this commitment to artificial settings and sentiments, when he came to film a few scenes of *The Love of Jeanne Ney* in Paris. Even though he returned to the studio for the London of *Pandora's Box*, what he had learnt while making *The Love of Jeanne Ney* had left its mark. As in Ford's later *The Informer*, an entire town is built out of fog, and the evocative power of Andreiev's settings is such that the absence of reality is no longer felt at all; what one notices is a willed, soberly accepted renunciation of the artificial.

But can one really call Pabst a 'realist'? Iris Barry★ seems to me to have struck the right note by saying that Pabst organized his different shots in such a way that their order reinforced 'the illusion of reality': for Pabst, reality was simply another convention.

Nevertheless, even if Pabst wanted us to say 'how true' rather than 'how beautiful', he never managed to reject a shot which was both forceful and picturesque.

## Dirnentragödie (Tragedy of a Street, 1927)

*Dirnentragödie* was filmed by Bruno Rahn, a very erratic director who made rather commercial films about 'vice' (*Sittenfilme*) before suddenly achieving this bitter and violent work. It is undeniable that this film's extraordinary quality is principally due to the presence of Asta Nielsen. Her expression when she looks at the man who has done her so much harm is unforgettable, like her weary gesture as she paints her face in the hope of winning him back, though knowing that she stands no chance against the youth of her rival. This was to be Rahn's only film of any value, and that is what is tragic about it. Thwarted in his ambitions and wounded in his pride, he died young.

★ Iris Barry, *Program Notes* (Museum of Modern Art, New York), Series III, program 3.

263

He worked in the days of the 'féerie de laboratoire'. The light of a gaslamp explores the nooks and crannies of an alleyway, slipping across the irregular cobblestones and creeping into the vestibule of a house of ill fame, while in the chiaroscuro of a disreputable café prostitutes display their charms in the light of a hanging lamp and the white blob of a face belonging to one of them shouts from the darkness; as in *Die Strasse*, their bare arms are seen through the man's eyes as silvery tentacles.

But what has been termed 'le fantastique social' – a more exact term would be 'le social décoratif' – has lost its pre-eminence. Here the street is merely a fragment of irregular paving on which innumerable feet, mincing on heels which are too high and rather worn, slopping in shabby slippers, or stamping in boots, follow one another, stop, and continue, representing cheap seduction, the pimp, and the weary wait of a whore strolling up and down. This street devoured its souls long since; it cannot be evoked by faces and bodies, only by the movements of legs and feet, which Rahn follows for yards and yards of film, along the pavements and up the soiled steps of a staircase, drawing from their anonymity a surprising eloquence.

Even when the Germans had gone beyond Expressionistic abstraction they were to keep their fondness for animating impersonal elements and making symbols and principles act rather than human beings. And when we do find these anonymous feet adapting themselves to a specific body or face, their owner never departs from a certain automatism.


## The Absolute film

In these passages Rahn was possibly influenced by the *absoluter Film*, the German avant-garde. *Berlin, die Symphonie der Grosstadt* by Walter Ruttmann, *Inflation* and *Vormittagsspuk* by Hans Richter date from the same year as *Dirnentragödie*.

And Joe May may have been recalling this passage of Rahn's when he presented soldiers' boots dragging along endlessly in a snowy plain in *Heimkehr*.

A few words are necessary on this film-genre of the

Darkness and light: shooting *Voruntersuchung* (Robert Siodmak, 1931)

German avant-garde, this 'absolute' film which the French call 'le film abstrait', half way between the 'new objectivity' and fantasy.

For Victor Eggeling, who drew the first German absolute film, it was at the outset merely a matter of transposing his abstract-figured plates onto spools in order to gain storage space. On the other hand he was already interested in the behaviour of certain form-elements among themselves, in their force of adhesion and repulsion, in their contrast and analogy. This is how we need to understand the variation and evolution of his forms in *Diagonal-Symphonie*.

Hans Richter went further and conducted research into a law which he believed governs the avant-garde. He attempted to decipher problems of time, space, colour and light. By capturing plastic forms in movement he tried to account for their dynamism and simultaneity, postulating that an object's rhythm should be brought out in terms of time and space. Kurtz could legitimately say that Richter sought 'the primordial rhythmic function of movement'.

Whereas several people even then criticized Ruttmann for his 'feuilletoniste' manner, Richter himself stressed that Ruttmann merely sought 'improvizations of forms' and that any interconnecting rhythms between them were purely fortuitous and gratuitous.

In Ruttmann's figures Kurtz saw 'surging impulsions'; he had the impression of contemplating undulating forms which devour each other in a bitter struggle, or which embrace each other lovingly. As the direct antithesis of this, Richter insisted that Eggeling's forms and his own testified to a profound transcendental meaning.

However, because Ruttmann brought to the absolute film these elements of sensibility and organic life, he was able to create Kriemhild's dream for *Die Nibelungen* without the least hesitation or break in style.

## Asphalt (1928)

The influence of these avant-garde film-makers is undeniably present in *Asphalt*, which was made the year after *Dirnentragödie* by the skilful director Joe May. It is a cogent example of the use that Ufa commercial films made of the results of artistic research. May uses everything. The suggestive chiaroscuro of the early hours while the workmen lay the asphalt, and the shots of legs, feet, and tools pounding the still-liquid mass, could come from some artistically made documentary. The climbing smoke, the gear-wheels of a steam-roller as it lumbers forward, and the various overprinted details of wheels owe their origin to the symphony of the machines in *Metropolis*. We also have tangled visions of simultaneous criss-crossing superimpositions, mingling, linking, and complementing each other as in Ruttmann's *Berlin* or Richter's *Rennsymphonie*, which attempted to capture the street's meaning with an abstract, quintessential turmoil of traffic. May, wishing as he did to create the Song of Songs of the indifferent street, where tragic liaisons and fatal encounters are shaped unbeknown to the traffic which crushes the budding illusion of tenderness, interposed such shots on several occasions. Unhappily this deployment of abstract art remains external to the luxurious studio street *à la* Ufa, who were never ones to hesitate over a few extra buses and another hundred or so extras. So this self-styled 'daring' is not an integral part of the action, which is a wholly conventional love story.

Within this insipid plot Joe May occasionally remembers his artistic ambitions. Then we get the high-angle shot of the street where the young Fröhlich, the Führer of the crossroads, on duty as a policeman, dominates the traffic – a shot in which the German taste for ordered ornamentation comes through yet again. A similar shot of a policeman had already appeared in Carl Mayer's scenario for *Sylvester*:

> 'Like shadows: Traffic. Motor-cars.
> Passers-by. Carriages. Motor-cars.
> And
> A policeman who
> rears up as if made of brass. Often whistling. And still
> directing. Raising his arms. Thus ordering the traffic.
> Which divides one way and the other'.

In order to portray Fröhlich's embarrassment in the flighty woman's drawing-room, Joe May just shows two straddled legs clad in thick leather gaiters above a pair of enormous boots. But the hesitant movements of the camera are incapable of creating atmosphere and describing the mawkish elegance of the drawing-room. The shot of a strip of luxurious carpet before the couple's entrance ought to have informed us of the kind of life led there, but it falls completely flat.

The rest is a mixture of the successes of previous films. In the Paris slum the gentleman-burglar suddenly changing into a gasworker is shown as a gigantic shadow on the wall. We get another facile play on shadows in the staircase when the young policeman staggers home after the unintentional murder; and the murder itself is well within the tradition of German cinema – it is seen in a mirror.

In the end, all that Joe May's pretentions to avant-garde artistry and his skilful imitation lead to is an image which is highly symbolic of his own insignificance. A bird sits in its cage, and four superimposed trams bear down on it from the four corners of the screen. Here May seems to have been outclassed by techniques whose potency exceeded his own small talent. We need only recall Stroheim's use of the birdcage motif in *Greed*, as he plays with cruel insistence on this emblem of family peace and bourgeois solidity.

# 16 The Evolution of the Costume Film

*'Art – authentic art – is simple. But simplicity demands the maximum of artistry. The camera is the director's pencil. It should have the greatest possible mobility in order to record the most fleeting harmony of atmosphere. It is important that the mechanical factor should not stand between the spectator and the film.'*
F. W. Murnau, quoted by Ludwig Gesek.

## Tartüff (Tartuffe, 1925)

This version of Molière's comedy may shock non-German audiences. Dorine, the soubrette, all light and skipping and very French as we had always imagined her, takes us by surprise when she comes sailing in as the imposingly plump Lucie Höflich, whose heavy build would be more appropriate to Lessing's Minna von Barnhelm, a role she often played for Reinhardt.

The moralizing prologue and epilogue tacked on to the scenario are faintly ridiculous: they portray a hypocritical housekeeper ill-using a poor dotard with an eye to his inheritance. The old man's nephew makes him realize her hypocrisy by showing him the film of Molière's play. This utterly pointless framing story is redeemed by some marvellous shots. For Murnau, as later for the Pabst of *Pandora's Box*, the actor's face becomes a kind of landscape, which the inquisitive eye of the lens explores indefatigably down to its most hidden recesses, incessantly discovering new and unexpected angles and new surfaces to illuminate. He gets Karl Freund's camera to explore all the crevices of the faces, every wrinkle, every twitch, every blink, each hidden flaw of freckles or bad teeth: mountains and abysses, pits and peaks are modelled on the facial surface by effects of shade and light.

Later, interviewed for *Close Up* in 1929, Karl Freund said: '*Tartuffe*, photographically, was quite interesting. The beginning and the end I took in the modern style, allowing the artists no make–up, and using 'angles';

while the middle section is soft-focus, gauzed and artificial.'*

This anticipates certain out-of-focus shots in *Faust* (made immediately afterwards), in which Murnau was to develop the facial shapes discovered during the making of the *Tartuffe* prologue and epilogue.

It is worth noting the mobility of the camera as it follows a character in the main action. Tartuffe's back is seen moving slowly towards the background, getting broader, filling the doorway and becoming gigantic as it crosses the threshold. The encounter between Tartuffe and Orgon on the stairs is also striking. The camera places the two movements in opposition, and then lets them collide. The sequence starts with two parallel shots. Tartuffe spies on Orgon, who does not notice him. Then a close-up of Tartuffe's enormous face suddenly rears up at Orgon and the spectator. We see Orgon shrink back and then there is a cut to a back-view of Tartuffe moving towards Orgon, who backs gradually away. These two shots (the shot-and-reverse-shot technique) constitute a remarkably powerful visual cue: the ascendancy that the 'hypocrite' wields over the credulous Orgon becomes immediately clear, and is confirmed by the last close-up of the immense face of Tartuffe slanting across the screen and leaning over Orgon who, utterly submissive, is seen in profile, to one side. Every shot and every arrangement of shooting angles is planned with a view to its effective participation in the action, the first close-up being a kind of initial contact and the second its conclusion.

A single close-up reveals the character's abjection: the camera shows the man's ignominious hypocrisy, a few slicked-down strands of hair on his egg-shaped head.

The elegant contours of the simple, restrained architecture are well adapted to the movement of the camera. The delicate curves of the fluting, the graceful sweep of a pilaster, and the filigree ironwork of a Louis XV balustrade contribute a freshness which is full of charm. Murnau seeks the contrasts infused by the different shades of black, grey and pure white. Every element of the set plays a predetermined role in the action: an enormous candlestick set against a pale, smooth wall-

* In his article 'A Film Artist', in *A Tribute to Carl Mayer*, Memorial Programme, Scala Theatre, London, 1947, Freund says: '. . . It was in the modern sequences of *Tartuffe* that sets, for the first time, were lifted from the floor and ramped for the sake of the camera.'

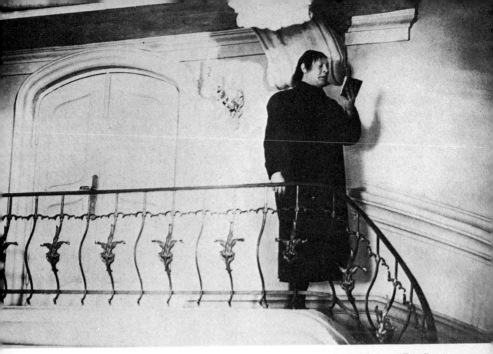

surface becomes the counterpart of the huge black silhouette of Tartuffe as he comes and goes in front of this wall; the cast of the banisters supports the relief of a crinoline brushing over the volutes of the stairs. Murnau had these sets, designed by Herlth and Röhrig, constructed with extreme care. The mouldings of the ornaments were made by hand, and the iron balustrade was wrought by smiths in the traditional manner.

The camera lingers momentarily over the elegant architecture on each of the three floors; on the last one a door opens and Tartuffe appears and dashes down to the ground floor. Immediately another door opens, Dorine comes out, the camera leans with her, and we see through the balustrade the black and white tiled floor below, with a furtive strip of light shining at the foot of a door standing slightly ajar. This is all that Mayer and Murnau show us to make us realize that Tartuffe has fallen into the trap and gone into Elmire's

*Tartuffe; Manon Lescaut* (Arthur Robison, 1925/26)

bedroom. Then Dorine goes downstairs in her turn, holding a candle whose uncertain light flickers on the staircase walls; she runs to warn Orgon, and Carl Mayer and Murnau open another door into a brightly lit room. This brief passage constitutes a real symphony of lighting effects, and brings out the concise structure of the film: the allegretto of the hurriedly opening and closing doors; the andantino of the comings and goings on the staircase; and the glissando of transparent blinds and curtains which alternately reveal and conceal the characters of the play.

Seen in this light, Molière's *Tartuffe* dressed up as Minna von Barnhelm takes on overtones of a Mozartian intermezzo, and the plump Prussian Dorine seems somehow less hefty, with something of the charm of a figure by Chardin.

Murnau succeeds admirably in harmonizing his costumed characters with their setting. We sometimes see the black figure of Tartuffe or the gleam of a lace-trimmed taffeta gown moving against vast smooth backgrounds. Again, we have the richly-folding velvet of the curtains, or the filigree of a coverlet bearing the glint of a tender silk déshabillé. The charm of all this is even more effective when Tartuffe (Emil Jannings) snorts around in it insulting its fragility. All the contrasts resulting from this usurpation of privacy are skilfully exploited: slim and haughty, the beautiful Elmire (Lil Dagover) rebels at the rustic mirth of Tartuffe sprawling on her bed of lace.

All Murnau's enthusiasm goes into rendering the voluptuous pallor of a woman's décolleté, or the nuances of a silk gown in a profusion of darks and lights – a distant recollection of Watteau. This gift developed in him during the evolution of the chiaroscuro. The costume film is free of the naturalism that marked certain films in other genres. In *Manon Lescaut* and *Der Verlorene Schuh* (*Cinderella*) Robison and Ludwig Berger portray the etiolated glow of velvets and the streaming crackle of silks: Lubitsch, from his very early days onwards, never let slip the opportunity of giving a shimmer to silks or deploying dazzling draperies. German film-makers, haunted by the desire to break beyond the shallow dimensions of their art and of human existence through the manipulation of shadows, did succeed in infusing life into surfaces.

In *Tartuffe* we also observe a play on intermingling forms, for example when the hypocrite alone with Elmire notices the distorted face of Orgon reflected in the round teapot as Orgon lifts the curtain behind which he is hiding. (Here Murnau the art-historian is again recalling a painting: Krauss's face peering round the curtain resembles that of a character hiding in the same way in Hieronymus Bosch's hell.) We find a similar passage in Ernö Metzner's *Überfall*, and its quality enables us all the better to measure the difference in style and conception. Like Gance in *La Folie du Dr Tube*, Metzner is merely after uncanny distortion effects, whereas for Murnau the least reflecting surface is likely to be used for Impressionistic play with anamorphic forms.

German transpositions of Molière's comedies give odd results. Heinrich von Kleist left the trace of his own personality on his adaption of *Amphitryon*: the witty comedy of a divine adultery becomes the disturbing, almost tragic story of a woman torn between two loves and a god who is basically very poor and miserable; his longing for human existence leads him to envy Amphitryon, the deceived, but in no wise ridiculous, husband.

The same thing happens in *Tartuffe*. But though it is true that the film is more heavy-handed than the original, we do detect in addition a strange uneasiness, and we feel that even without Tartuffe things would not go better between Orgon and Elmire. There is, in fact, no happy ending in Murnau's tragi-comedy.

The German writer Grabbe called one of his plays *Ironie, Scherz und Tiefere Bedeutung* (*Irony, Joke, and Deeper Meaning*). *Tiefere Bedeutung* could be the title of more than one German work, whether by poets such as Kleist, or film-makers such as Murnau; for it is always the other side of things which haunts their despair.

## 17 The Eye of the Camera in E. A. Dupont

'The spectators – those successive streams of people knowing nothing of one another – were now seated in the circus, each wedged into the absolute sphere of astonishment. . . .
'The excited hands clenched on the backs of the front of the circle produced the effect of decorative motifs, and the arc-lamps swung their pails of energetic milk. . . .'
Carl Einstein: Bebuquin oder die Dilettanten des Wunders (Expressionist novel).

When Dupont's talkies started coming out with *Atlantic*, many people were disappointed, and justifiably so. The sound film affected Dupont much more than it did other film-makers because, though he knew how to place his actors, he did not know how to get them fully to express themselves. His strength lay elsewhere.

### Das Alte Gesetz (The Ancient Law, 1923)

An old copy of *Das Alte Gesetz* luckily recovered by the Cinémathèque Française enables us to appreciate the real qualities of Dupont, who succeeded· in giving exquisite subtleties to his images and whose range was capable of infinite variations. His aim was not the Germanic immobility of ornamental form, or decorative stylization, but the matching of tones. Using here a checked jacket or a piece of striped trimming, there a vase of flowers or a strip of tapestry, he seeks to capture the fleeting quality of the chiaroscuro. He makes the interiors vibrate with the atmosphere appropriate to each situation, marrying the velvet of the darks to the tender silk of the lights. Without taking the premeditation too far, he places his actors with infinite elegance and sensibility, as when, for example, the girl in love with Baruch hides her head in despair on her bed in an attitude which brings out her fragility beneath the heavy folds of her dress. Again, Dupont composes an authentic *Kammerspiele* scene between Henny Porten and Ernst Deutsch, with the dull glow of a taffeta gown blending into the half-light of the silent drawing-room reflected in the window behind them.

275

*Stimmung: Das Alte Gesetz*, Froelich's *Mutter und Kind*

Here the period costumes stop looking like fancy dress.
These are daguerreotypes which come to life; the
crinolines swirl across the parquet floors and sway over
the freshness of the grass. The richness of the light in the
blending impressions is magical.

And even in the scenes of the dark-toned peasant
ghetto, with what artistry he succeeds in avoiding
brusque contrasts and forced highlights, maintaining,
with the help of his cameraman, Theodor Sparkuhl, the
vigour and *sfumato* of an etching of the school of
Rembrandt! One need only compare these passages with
scenes in Pabst's *Prozess*, a film which is also set in a
Jewish orthodox milieu, in order to appreciate the full
extent of Dupont's tact and extraordinary good taste.

The famous scene between the young actor Baruch
and Heinrich Laube, the rough-mannered theatre director
with the traditional heart of gold, reveals Dupont's
limitations. It is true that it was quite novel for its day.
Baruch is seen very briefly at the start of his audition,

277

then the camera focuses on the indifferent director, intent on his dinner. At this point Dupont gives a very elliptical clue to the young man's great talent by having the director suddenly stop eating and watch intently, while Baruch himself stays off-screen. Yet this device needs to be seen for what it is: artificial.

## Varieté (Variety, 1925)

In *Varieté* (*Variety*) Dupont's purely aesthetic intuition was to go even further. He can use the last vestiges of Expressionism very adroitly, as he proves with the high-angle shot of a prison yard with dark oblique walls which are more oppressive than those in *Metropolis*, forming a kind of pit at the foot of which the white circle of prisoners going round and round stands out against a black background. This is of course an Expressionistic device, but it derives from a painting by Van Gogh.

Another example is the impersonal back of a convict, whose entire existence is limited to the number 28. This back fills almost the whole of the screen, while – very remote, even blurred out at one point – we see the small luminous form of the white-bearded governor, a cross between Father Christmas and God the Father. Then all that remains on the screen is the abstract circle of the enormous number 28. Dupont varies this device when he gets Karl Freund's camera to film Jannings's revenge: all he shows is a back-view of a hefty shoulder and a hat, with the routed seducer, trembling, drunk, and afraid, seen over the shoulder. Faced with the elementary passion of the avenger, the rival, though quite tall and made to look even taller by his slim build, appears small and puny from this unfavourable angle when he bends down to grab at the knife he will be forced to use in the unequal fight.

Dupont has enough tact not to show this fight. The camera lingers for a brief, unemphatic moment on the bed to which the girl had willingly repaired, and then we just see the end of the fight: a raised arm brandishes the knife, then the hand opens limply and drops the weapon.

Pabst has the same thing in *Pandora's* Box: all we see of Louise Brooks's death is her hand slipping limply

from beneath the murderous embrace of Jack the Ripper.

The critics of the day made much of the convincing manner in which Jannings 'acted with his back'. But although Jannings plays the acrobat deceived by the vamp with remarkable restraint, considering his naturalistic talent, the spectator soon tires of this over-frequent 'back-acting': Jannings back by back with a warder going down one of the famous German crepuscular corridors just before the great back scene in the governor's office; or the hefty back of the acrobat among the innumerable ropes and guy-lines of a fairground; or Jannings's back seen after the famous scene with Lya de Putti, the beautiful intruder, as he moves heavily towards the curtains of the matrimonial bed, already half aware that he is in love. The camera returns to Jannings's back as he stares at the caricature on the café table with his hands painfully clenched. And finally Jannings is seen in a back view after the murder, going away across a hotel corridor, dragging towards the

Variety

staircase the vamp who clings to him. These shots of backs filmed in a great variety of situations ultimately erode the visual power of the image. (It is eventually much less effective than in Murnau's *Tartuffe*, where Jannings's back is seen but seldom.)

Dupont attempts to graft a *Kammerspiele* atmosphere on to the charm of the fairground milieu. When Jannings broods in the glow of a lamp in his dressing-room, or sits at a café table, the light wavers over the glass surfaces. Or a tap drips with monotonous regularity. But whereas in Pudovkin's *Mother* this dripping in itself stands for all the dull despair of a flat existence, Dupont spoils his symbol: he presents it with a comic echo in the form of drops running from under the baby's cradle.

In common with many of his compatriots Dupont has a weakness for contrasted symbolic images. For instance, Jannings gloats at Lya de Putti's back as she dances, then turns with distaste towards his wife stooping at the piano. He similarly compares the voluptuously silk-sheathed legs of the dancer with the darned and wrinkled woollen stockings beneath the tasteless dress of his wife.

The vamp's first entry is also a symbol, the symbol of destiny: climbing the caravan steps Lya de Putti is seen as a forehead and a pair of immense eyes, then slowly, like a sunrise, her entire face appears, and the mundane fairground seems to be transformed into a metaphysical parable.

Sometimes the symbolism is a little more discreet: the seducer, waiting for the arrival of the woman he desires, opens the window to create a draught and give him an excuse for closing the door. Sure of his success, he lowers the venetian blinds and – the counterpoint is brief, but eloquent – raises them again after the fatal scene.

If we compare the amusement-park atmosphere in *Variety* with that found in *Caligari* or the even more artificial version in *Waxworks*, we at last discern the secret of Dupont's talent: he has the gift of capturing and fixing fluctuating forms which vary incessantly under the effect of light and movement. His objective is always and everywhere the ebb and flow of light, which he accentuates, showing the circus artistes' lively party through the turning of an electric fan, or, briefly,

Jannings's face behind the movement of the napkin with which he fans his out-of-breath partner.

There can be no doubt that we have here an 'Impressionism' which bears traces of having passed through Expressionist abstraction: this is striking when, for instance, Dupont shows, beneath the grotesquely fore-shortened body of an acrobat huddling on his trapeze, the crowd as he sees it in his swing – a motley of innumerable floating blobs; other shots present the geometrical distribution of the mass as a mosaic, varying with the swing of the trapeze. The vulgar star-spangled ceiling of the Berlin Wintergarten music-hall is depicted as a shower of sparks. One shot shows us all these impressions blending and whirling around Jannings who, standing on his trapeze, is seized by vertigo at the sight of his rival's happiness.

Dupont was also to use swirls of visions to depict his protagonist's emotions. When Jannings discovers the caricature on the marble-topped table, he stays rooted in the same position while the world falls around him and images whirl past his (our) distraught eyes in a rapid, blurred panning shot.

All these 'Impressionistic' visual effects derive from the traditional chaos of an absolute Expressionism; they have gained in vigour and freed themselves from a purely Expressionsitic schematism. The impression of one of the music-hall exits in the night streets is fascinating and even more hallucinating than the harshly-contrasted transpositions found in previous films. Here, the traffic, the flashing electric signs, and the gaslamps whose refracting glow pulses in the darkness, have nothing in common with the abstract labyrinth of luminous geometric lines opposed to dark cubic forms. Similarly, the ambience of the amusement-park – the pegs and posts, struts and strings of fairy-lights – keeps the 'Impressionistic' fluidity conferred by rapid transitions.

This is why Dupont's black and white has such visual intensity and a vivacity so close to colour. In the huge music-hall the white figures of the three acrobats pass in front of the heaving, glowing sea of the dense rows of spectators. Their bodies are moulded against the dark background by a spotlight beam, which is joined by others to follow them as they climb. The camera is momentarily stationed under one of these bodies and follows its every movement lovingly, capturing the contracted form in a fantastic foreshortened view which finally makes it look like some purely ornamental white crab.

Dupont finds remarkable visual equivalents for the tension latent in a circus atmosphere. The images in these scenes are felt to pulse with the collective madness which takes hold of an arena at the moment of truth. In its blind frenzy the crowd becomes a thousand-headed monster lusting for blood. But as soon as the audience is seen as individuals the hallucination of this music-hall gives way to an altogether run-of-the-mill naturalistic caricature.

At one moment the crowd suggests a whole succession of comparisons: it is caught in the net of a shower of sparks, it evokes the ebb and flow of a sticky tide of innumerable eyes, it is a kind of slimy mud-pit with bubbles rising as from a lava-field. Here again Dupont's

*Variety:* the music-hall

concern is with capturing movement, whereas Lang, using similar methods, was to give a more static presentation of the dozens of lustful eyes ogling at the apparition of the bogus Maria in *Metropolis*.

The camera, operated by the great Karl Freund, voluptuously follows the agile forms as they leap forward and fly through space, turning over and over in daring somersaults or suddenly plunging earthwards in an almost certain fall, then gliding up again in the network of cables and rigging. Even the circus acts in *The Four Devils*, a film Murnau made in America in 1928, cannot equal this visual excitement.

In this ebb and flow of light and movement, that of love interest has only secondary importance: it is the old recipe of the eternal triangle spiced with a dash of melodrama in the form of 'the daring young man on the flying trapeze'.

Dupont tried several times to repeat the success of *Variety*. *Moulin Rouge*, made in England in 1927, is usually considered a disappointment, and the story is certainly banal, but in it Dupont used form and movement with almost baroque elation; and the film is remarkable, too, for the subtlety of its black-and-white photography, the range of its greys from velvety shadow to tender highlight, and the impression it gives of innumerable tints. The movements of the crowds, and the dense, voluptuous music-hall atmosphere, are lovingly conveyed. And in the film he made in the following year, *Piccadilly*, the night street-scenes have something of the effervescence of *Variety*. More interesting, though, is his later German film, *Salto Mortale* (1931), which in some of its long shots and tracking shots seems to stand as a direct forerunner to Max Ophuls's last great ornamental film, *Lola Montès*.

## Murnau's Faust (1926)

'It is sufficiently alarming and
rash to engage in a joust with
such a poet, even on an equal
footing; more perilous still is
the undertaking if the weapons
are unequal. The glorious
master had all the arsenal of
words on his side. . . . I have
written a mere slim libretto in
which I indicate as summarily
as possible the dancers' mime,
together with the music and
settings more or less as my
mind imagines them.
Indisposed and even really ill
as I have been, I have dared
to wrestle with the great
Wolfgang Goethe, who had
all the advantage of freshness
on his side. I have been
obliged, most reluctantly,
without doubt, to respect the
exigencies of my frame-
work. . . .'
Heine, in a letter referring
to his ballet Dr Faust.

This film starts with the most remarkable and poignant
images the German chiaroscuro ever created. The
chaotic density of the opening shots, the light dawning
in the mists, the rays beaming through the opaque air,
and the visual fugue which diapasons round the heavens,
are breathtaking.

The highlighted, slightly puzzling figure of an arch-
angel is contrasted with the demon, whose contours,
in spite of the darkness, have a grandiose relief. Jannings,
as the demon, temporarily renounces his over-acting and
for once is out-acted by his role; the demon appears
really primordial, a creature from the first age of the
world. (Though this was not to stop Jannings from
flaunting his usual fatuity once the demon descends to
earth, and exasperating the non-German spectator as much
as ever.)

No other director, not even Lang, ever succeeded in
conjuring up the supernatural as masterfully as this.
The entire town seems to be covered by the vast folds of
a demon's cloak (or is it a gigantic, lowering cloud?) as
the demoniac forces of darkness prepare to devour the
powers of light.

Carl Hoffmann's camera gives the terrestrial part of
this film extraordinary modelling and has the power
of impregnating everything, down to the cloth of a
garment, with diabolism. Before transforming his
Mephisto into a Spanish caballero, wearing elaborate
silks, Murnau subtly confronts him, dressed in a puckered

smock like some medieval villein, with the wealthy burgher Faust, in his rich, sweeping, velvet cloak. At times Mephisto's smock is gnawed by the shadows into depriving him of all resemblance to a human being. Like Scapinelli in *The Student of Prague* this little peasant suddenly appears to be a creature of Hell.

Murnau has Paul Wegener's and Arthur von Gerlach's gift for lighting costumes (though one may except the instance of the rejuvenated Faust, overdressed and a trifle androgynous, and that obsequious caballero Jannings at the fancy-dress ball).

In Faust's study the nebulous wavering light of the opening scenes persists. There are none of the arbitrary contrasts, over-accentuated contours, or artificially serrated shadows found in so many German films. The forms come through the misty light gently, opalescent. If Murnau is recalling the light-quality in Rembrandt's Faust etching, he interprets its function in his own fashion. Here the imprecise contours take up the super-natural theme of the opening, its resonance developing as if controlled by the pedals of an invisible pianist. In the auditorium the aged Faust rears up, immense, in front of the semicircle of disciples: here the masses and values balance each other in a perpetual shifting of tonality, as forms shade out, a beard crossed by trembling rays of light turns into moss, and the alchemical retorts shimmer in the *sfumato*.

Even the movement of a cheerless fair is merely blocked out in its main masses of flattened tone. Not a ray of sunlight filters through the fairground booths, and the capers and somersaults of the sideshow per-former are purely mechanical. Everything exists merely as the prelude to the imminent disaster. Suddenly panic breaks out: the plague sweeps away all these people and the storm overturns scaffoldings and rips apart the wretched booths. The huddled corpse of the juggler slants across the field of vision parallel to a shred of canvas straining against the tempest. Murnau's particular rhythm so dominates the film that the elaboration of this composition avoids the heaviness found, for example, in the scene with the young woman in *Torgus*. This is still more apparent in the passage where the monk attempts to halt the stream of revellers lusting after

286

Rembrandt's Faust

their last pleasures, and falls down. Decorative arabesque is replaced by incident, the dynamic of which increases the intensity of the action.

Throughout the film we meet with the richly subtle modelling deriving from Murnau's peculiar fascination with visual effects: e.g. the vision of plague-victims' corpses, the dead mother's pathetic marble features, or the monk standing waving his cross in front of the revelling mob. In the group surrounding Gretchen's pillory it is impossible to forget the heavy features of a slowly chewing rustic or the expressions of the choir-boys, open-mouthed, innocent, unaware, like the beautiful ambiguous angels in Botticelli; Dreyer, close to Murnau in many respects, recalled these images in his *Vredens Dag* (*Day of Wrath*). Contrasting with this circle of faces in high relief is that of Gretchen, strangely empty, stung by the snow, and this image recalls Lillian Gish, more moving, however, in *Way Down East*.

The light can waver over faces (the fleeing shadows of

*Faust:* Gretchen, children, and wax flowers

the unseen mob cast across the features of the dying monk) or stream in from all sides (Faust burning dusty tomes, Mephisto's blackened phantom conjuring the flames). The two effects are combined at the misty crossroads where Faust invokes the demon: a rising chain of circles of light casts a wavering glow over his face. Fiery letters flame across the screen, promising Faust – as Dr Caligari before him – power and greatness. From inside a church waves of gentle light rising towards the vaulted roof with the hymn-singing spill out through the open door and condense into a kind of wall with which the creatures of darkness collide. These subtleties of lighting participate in the action, like the torchglow weaving through the town at night when the enlarged form of the once more demoniac Mephisto rears up crying murder, or like Gretchen on the pyre when she recognizes Faust beneath his aged features and leans towards him imploringly; the flames leap towards the sky and a globe of light hangs there as the symbol of eternal grace, the apotheosis of a fulfilled redemption.

The movement of the mobile camera is less easy to follow than in *The Last Laugh*. In the two-year interval Murnau had learnt to gauge the depth of his tracking shots and the range of his pans, and to subordinate his enthusiasm to the rhythm of the film as a whole. The hilly terrain of his medieval town particularly lends itself to high-angle shots, but he contrives not to use them too often. If Carl Hoffmann's camera exploits the deep gash of a sharply-inclined stepped street it is because Gretchen's tragic destiny, embodied in her lover and his counsellor the devil, will stem from between these sharp-eaved roofs. Though Murnau obviously takes great visual pleasure in the famous panoramic shot during Faust's journey, this trip through the air does have a precise aim. But we may prefer the tracking shot of superimposed hills and valleys representing an anguished cry from Gretchen's open mouth – a cry thrown at Faust from the depths of her misery.

Histories of the cinema never tire of telling us that Dupont was the only director capable of filming a scene as seen by the actor, quoting the instance of the scenes filmed over an actor's shoulder in *Variety*. But Murnau had nothing to learn from Dupont. In *Nosferatu* the camera (the spectator) sees the small forms gesticulating in the alleyway through the eyes of the madman clinging to the roof. In *Faust* Murnau's technique is wrapped in such discretion that it almost passes unnoticed; nevertheless an American critic has singled out the scene in which the perspective of Faust pursuing Gretchen is centred on Mephisto who, by the mere fact of being invisible, manifests the sarcasm with which he greets these first steps towards her downfall.

The movement of images is complemented by counterpoints of rhythm: the pale-toned procession of children slowly climbing the steps towards the cathedral, holding taper-like white lilies, contrasts with the crowd of pikemen bristling with staves and flags as they advance towards the doorway.*

Murnau varies the shots of the stepped streets with great artistry: hooded men carry up coffins through the evil night, crowds bring up those stricken with the

* The technique is the same as for the meeting of Tartuffe and Orgon. In another sequence the device is used to show the opposition between the mob and the monk trying to halt it.

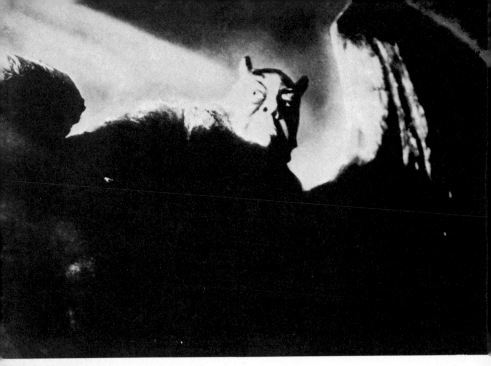

*Faust*

plague. If we watch this incessant fluctuation of masses
attentively, we immediately realize to what an extent
Lubitsch mechanized his crowd movements; here the
massed bodies are given a tirelessly regular, pulsing
*organic* movement towards the figure of Faust, healer
by the grace of Satan.

The steeply-pitched roofs ornamented with tiles seem
to be the only remaining elements of a semi-abstract
architecture created for Murnau by Herlth and Röhrig,
the designers of *Destiny*. This architecture is at a far
remove from the authentic town we see in *Nosferatu*
and closer, despite the precision of the line, to the
setting Poelzig designed for *The Golem*. If the steeply-
pitched roofs leading to Gretchen's house suggest many
an instance of Expressionist architecture, the evolution
it has undergone is shown by the duel scene in the little
square, where the impression of enclosed space is reinforced by the corbelled upper storey jutting into the
night. Here nothing is excessive, neither the shadows

gnawing at the façade nor the doorway, which seems to become the entrance to some mysterious cavern; however slow Murnau's rhythm may be, the fascinating fluidity that he obtains from the camera cancels out any static ornamental heaviness the settings might have had.

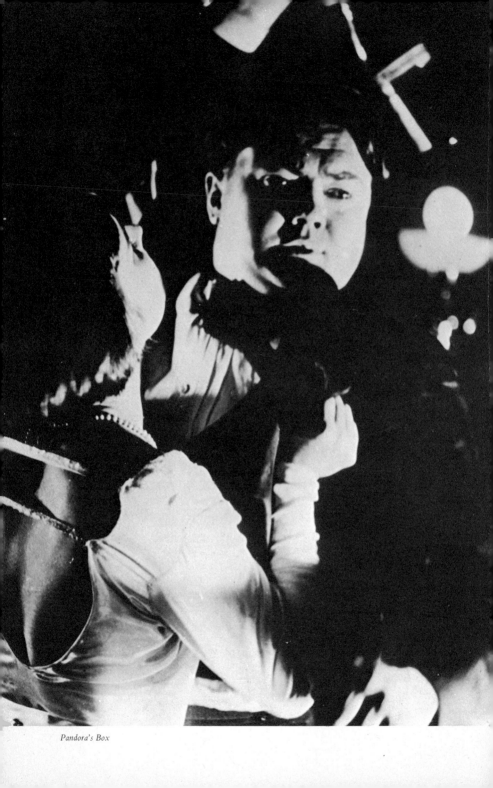

*Pandora's Box*

# 19 Pabst and the Miracle of Louise Brooks

*'The prime intention behind my presentation of Lulu was to depict a woman's body through the words she speaks. At each of my phrases for her I asked myself whether it was the phrase of a beautiful young woman.'*
Frank Wedekind: Preface to his play *Die Büchse der Pandora*.

*'Despite the rise of the "talkie" I remain convinced that in the cinema the text itself counts for very little. What counts is the image. So I would still claim that the creator of a film is much more the director than the author of the scenario or the actors.'*
G. W. Pabst: *Le Rôle Intellectuel du Cinéma*, 1937.

Pabst's case is extremely curious: he is both remarkable and disappointing; we wonder how the author of *Pandora's Box* or *Der Dreigroschenoper* could ever have made so painful a film as *Prozess*.

He is full of contradictions; the critics of the day had singled them out well before 1930. Some of them praise his intuition, his insight, and his perfect psychological awareness enabling him to use the camera as if it were an X-ray. Others see him as a passionate scrutinizer of the human soul, deeply involved in his discoveries. And others still, Pasinetti for example, see him as a coldly calculating observer.

Potamkin for his part regrets that Pabst never got to the root of the problems inherent in his art, but merely skimmed over the surface of his subjects. We may ask ourselves what foundation there is for such widely differing assertions.

In an issue of the Italian review *Cinema* in 1937, a critic declares that Pabst always translates his fondness for psychological subjects into the most popular idiom possible. If this is correct, and I think it is, it explains the apparently facile treatment of the inflationary period and its middle-class disasters in *The Joyless Street*, and the superficial use of psychoanalysis in *Secrets of a Soul* – and this in spite of great visual gifts.

## Die Büchse der Pandora (Pandora's Box, 1928)

What, then, was the intervening factor between these films and *The Love of Jeanne Ney* and the mastery we admire in *Pandora's Box*? In the English review *Close Up*, which so ardently championed Pabst's films in the thirties, a critic claimed that 'Pabst finds the other side of each woman'. This is obviously true in the case of Brigitte Helm, for example, frigid as the two Marias in Lang's *Metropolis* and so moving in Pabst's *Love of Jeanne Ney*. But how was it that for *Abwege* or *Herrin von Atlantis* Pabst failed to warm the impenetrable beauty of this actress, who is as insensitive in these two films as in the title role in both versions of *Alraune*?

But in *Pandora's Box* and *Diary of a Lost Girl* we have the miracle of Louise Brooks. Her gifts of profound intuition may seem purely passive to an inexperienced audience, yet she succeeded in stimulating an otherwise unequal director's talent to the extreme. Pabst's remarkable evolution must thus be seen as an encounter with an actress who needed no directing, but could move across the screen causing the work of art to be born by her mere presence. Louise Brooks, always enigmatically impassive, overwhelmingly *exists* throughout these two films. We now know that Louise Brooks is a remarkable actress endowed with uncommon intelligence, and not merely a dazzlingly beautiful woman.

*Pandora's Box* is a silent film. As such it does very well without the words which Wedekind – the author of the two plays *Erdgeist* and *Die Büchse der Pandora*, which Pabst condensed into one film – deemed indispensable to bring out the erotic power of this singular 'earthly being' endowed with animal beauty, but lacking all moral sense, and doing evil unconsciously.

In *The Love of Jeanne Ney*, Pabst's camera slowly explores the scene, starting with the toe-caps of the character played by Rasp and then climbing his legs and revealing the immediate surroundings – a mess of newspapers and cigarette-ends, all the sordid disorder of a scruffy hotel bedroom – in such a way that the wretched existence of a small-time crook is gradually revealed.

For his subsequent films, particularly *Diary of a Lost Girl*, Pabst invented a more direct method which provided him with more violent accents: for example, he concentrates the attention of the camera on the hard, suspicious, spiteful face of the new housekeeper deter-

*The Love of Jeanne Ney*

mined not to be seduced like the previous one; when he cuts to her fawning at her boss, the spectator knows her for what she is. Another example is the cruel face of Valeska Gert, as the reformatory wardress, whom we then see tapping a gong; the camera tracks back and shows the long table of inmates spooning their meagre soup in time with the gong.

The editing of *Pandora's Box* is more fluid, perhaps because Pabst's weakness for fluctuating atmosphere or violently-contrasted chiaroscuro (the lighted boat at night) comes to the fore. Despite this stylistic fluidity the fusion of two stage-plays leads to certain passages in the film standing out from the whole, as was noted by one of the *Close Up* critics. Each composes a drama in its own right, with its own peripetias, rhythm and style distinct from the rest. Such self-contained sequences are the Impressionistic glitter of the revue scenes, the Expressionistically lit gambling-hell on the boat, and the foggy images of London low-life.

Nobody has ever equalled Pabst's portrayal of the back-stage fever on the opening night of a big show, the hurrying and scurrying during the scene changes, the stage seen from the wings as the performers go on and off and bound forward to acknowledge their applause at the end of their act, the rivalry, complacency, and humour, the bewildering bustle of stage-hands and electricians – a stupendous whirl of artistic aspirations, colourful detail, and a facile eroticism. Even the famous *42nd Street* does not get across this dazzle and warmth, this sensuality swamped in the light shimmering on the lamé curtains and the helmets and suits of armour, and silvering the bodies of the all-but-naked women. Pabst directs all this turmoil with remarkable dexterity; everything has been worked out in advance; at precisely calculated intervals a few figures cross in front of or behind a main group, giving an impression of effervescence and dynamism. Lulu appears like some pagan idol, tempting, glittering with spangles, feathers, and frills, against a wavering, out-of-focus background.

She is the centre of attraction, and Pabst succeeds in devising an infinite variety of seduction scenes to show her to advantage, as when Dr Schön comes into the flat wondering how to tell his mistress that he is getting married. The camera catches his nervousness as he paces up and down the room; the ash from his cigarette burns a table-runner, and he fiddles with a bibelot, as Jannings had fidgeted with a liqueur glass in *Variety*. Then a skilful shot-and-reverse shot shows us Lulu observing him. She sinks back into the cushions, moves, lies on her front half-reared like a sphinx, while Schön goes up to her and sits down. The camera dives and scrutinizes Lulu's impassive features, lingering over the perfect sweep of her face, the pearl-like quality of her skin, the fringe of her lacquered hair, the sharp arch of her eyebrows, and the trembling shadow of her lashes.

Another passage offers a subtle variant: in the prop-room Lulu throws herself on to the divan, and the camera moves up to the white nape of her neck and slips along her legs as they kick with impatience. The two lovers wrestle and sink into a long embrace. These scenes are extremely erotic, but quite free from vulgarity.

Many times Pabst films Lulu's features on a slant. Her

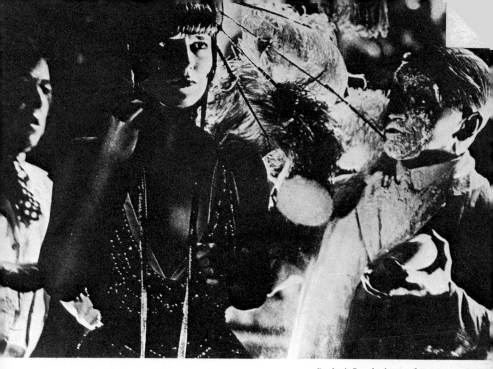

face is so voluptuously animal that it seems almost
deprived of individuality. In the scene with Jack the
Ripper, this face, a smooth mirror-like disc slanting
across the screen, is so shaded out and toned down that
the camera seems to be looking down at some lunar
landscape. (Is this still a human being – a woman – at
all? Is it not rather the flower of some poisonous plant?)
Or again Pabst just shows, at the edge of the screen, the
chin and a fragment of cheek belonging to the man next
to her, with whom the audience automatically identifies.

In the final episode, in her London slum, she uses the
reflector of the lamp as a mirror with which to apply
her lipstick. Jack the Ripper gets the idea of using the
bread-knife from seeing it glint in the light of this same
lamp. His face stands out from the half-light in full
relief, a tragic counterpoise to the smooth features of
the beloved Lulu. For a brief moment the haunted man
smiles and the veil of despair seems to lift from his

suddenly appeased features. Then the camera immediately reveals again each bump in the skin; each pore is visible, and the sweat over the contracted muscles.

It is the close-ups which determine the character of film; the flamboyant or phosphorescent atmosphere and the luminous mists of London remain throughout merely a kind of accompaniment to these close-ups, heightening their significance.

Pabst introduces a character with a single shot: scrutinizing the acrobat Rodrigo waiting in the street, the camera lingers over his square shoulders and barrel chest; in this shot his head has become a mere accessory, and we immediately realize that the man is brainless, nothing but physical strength.

As soon as Lulu's adoptive father makes his appearance on the landing Pabst shows us his hunched silhouette from behind, and this stresses the sordid aspect of the debauched old artiste's way of life.

Sometimes Pabst can indicate all the drama in a single shot: Lulu, wearing the wedding-dress, looks at herself in the mirror and then leans forward to put down her pearl necklace; while she does so, and her image leaves the mirror, the threatening figure of Dr Schön is framed in the glass. Lulu straightens up, and her image meets that of Dr Schön, who has decided to kill her. Pabst then cuts very briefly to the struggle for the revolver; Lulu is seen from behind, we perceive a puff of smoke and realize that the gun has gone off. Then we have all the details of Schön's death throes, shown from dramatic angles.

Pabst is a virtuoso of tilt shots, above all when he wants to portray the beauty of Lulu. Sometimes he films men's faces from below, thus enlarging the lower part of the face: the throat and chin bulge out and dominate the image. It is through such a shot that the face of the dying Dr Schön begins to take on a corpse-like quality, the impersonality of a thing. Pabst uses this angle to vary his actors' expressions: when Lulu's graceful form swings on Rodrigo's arm, the fatuity of the muscle-proud acrobat is made plain by this means, and he is shown from the same angle when he is drunk and raises a chair to hit Dr Schön. The same effect is also achieved at times by a high-angle shot: the features of the murdered

300

The death of Schön

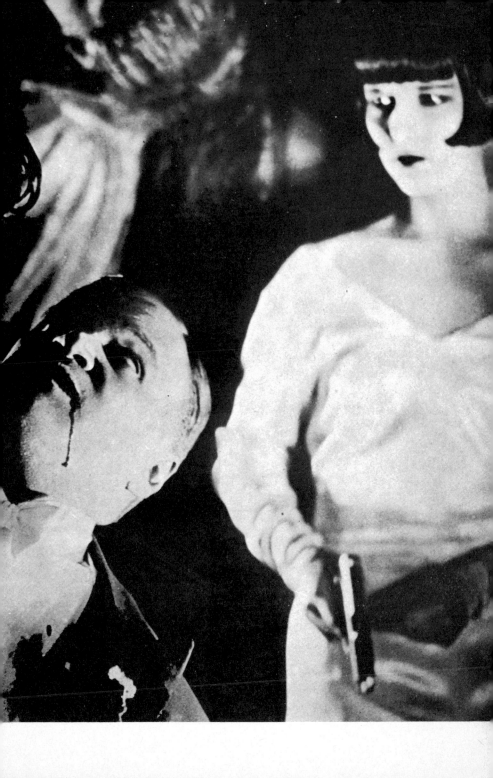

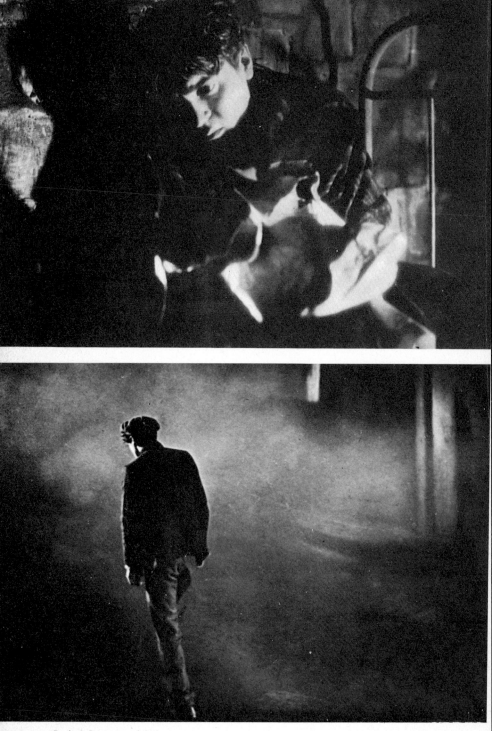

*Pandora's Box:* mist and shadow

Rodrigo become an amorphous glowing mass in the cabin where he is discovered by the police.

To sum up the elements of Pabst's technique: he seeks the 'psychological or dramatic angles' which reveal at a single glance character, psychical relationships, situations, tension, or the tragic moment. Most of the time he prefers this method of shooting to Murnau's technique of following a scene at length with a moving camera. So, for Pabst, the action is ultimately built up by the montage.

In *The Joyless Street* one was occasionally struck by a revealing angle or shot which foreshadowed Pabst's future capabilities. For example, he shows only the lower half of Werner Krauss's face in close-up together with the twirly moustache and the buttonhole into which the unseen madam's hand slips a carnation. But on the whole Pabst had not as yet learnt how to use a more advanced montage to integrate such shots into the action, as he was to do later in *Diary of a Lost Girl*.

## Tagebuch einer Verlorenen (Diary of a Lost Girl, 1929)

In *Diary of a Lost Girl* the technique is very different. Here and there we still see revealing, disturbing close-ups of Louise Brooks's face, for example when Rasp watches her while he makes a note of the fatal rendezvous in her brand-new diary. His face, shot in profile, is just perceptible at the extreme edge of the screen where, in the centre, the pure face of Louise Brooks offers itself like the petal of a flower.

The seduction of Thymiane (Louise Brooks) is seen from outside through the glazed door of the chemist's shop. Then, with his typically supple virtuosity, Pabst cuts to a reverse shot filmed inside the shop: the seducer (Rasp) jostling the girl up against the inside of the same door.

Symbols also come into play. On the bed where Thymiane yields uncomprehendingly, her inert feet inadvertently knock over a glass of red wine.

The film displays a new, almost documentary restraint. Pabst now seeks neither Expressionistic chiaroscuro nor Impressionistic glitter; and he seems less intoxicated than he was by the beauty of his actress.

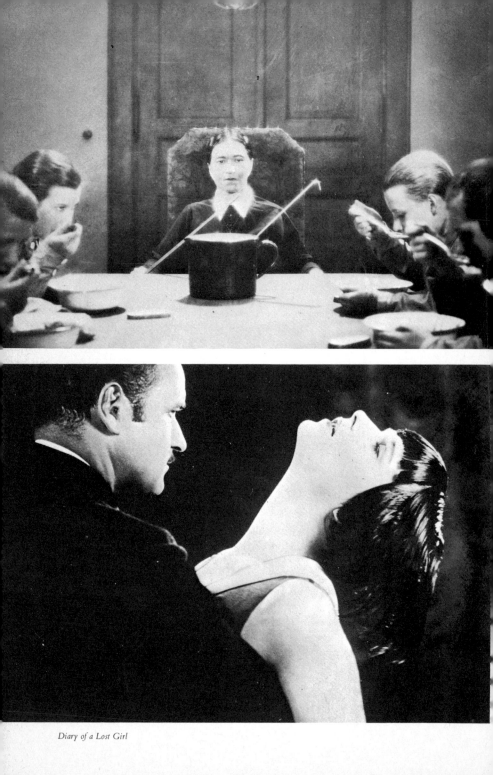

*Diary of a Lost Girl*

Louise Brooks in *Pandora's Box* (*above*) and *Diary of a Lost Girl* (*below*)

If the brothel scenes in *Diary of a Lost Girl* are compared with the scenes in the gambling-hell in *Pandora's Box*, Pabst's progress is clearly distinguishable, particularly in regard to local colour. All monotony has disappeared from the secondary scenes such as the dancers at the wedding in *Pandora's Box* or at the hotel in *The Joyless Street*. But *Diary of a Lost Girl* has lost the variety and the disturbing richness of atmosphere found in *Pandora's Box*. A new and more realistic Pabst is beginning to emerge.

## Censorship and Pabst's realism

Rudolf Leonhardt, the author of the scenario, wrote to me from East Berlin on 17 September 1953:

The German censor, who had blithely slept his way through the period of the dreams and fantasies, seems to have woken up at the *neue Sachlichkeit* (the 'new objectivity') and realism which emerged around 1927–28.

His attention turned against Pabst in particular. The French censor had already found it 'indecent' that father and son should love the same woman in *Pandora's Box*, so the titles and captions described Alva Schön as 'Alva, Dr Schön's secretary'. But this modification led into an even more equivocal situation: the paternal gestures of Dr Schön (Kortner) towards his son Alva Schön (Franz Lederer) are natural; but when the relationship becomes that of an employer and his secretary, the same gestures become tainted with homosexuality. But of this the French censor seemed to have no inkling.

Matters were worse still for *Diary of a Lost Girl*. Pabst's accommodating nature had already made him prepared to make two different endings – for vice, even involuntary vice, must not go rewarded.

Where the censors had not forbidden passages beforehand, entire filmed sequences were cut without mercy later on. In one version, if I remember rightly, they cut 450 metres, and in either this or another version they made 54 further cuts.

I get the feeling that the censor, like certain rather ingenuous girls, must think that you can catch a baby from a kiss. For one copy shows the chemist's assistant giving Thymiane a kiss, and in the next image she is seen cuddling a baby.

I had a very beautiful scene: the girl faints and the assistant chemist takes her in his arms and carries her into her bedroom, her feet slipping over the display table; he lays her on her bed and her feet knock over a glass of red wine which spills over the bedclothes – a symbol for those who understand, a *Stimmungsbild* for the others.

There is another scene which has disappeared: Thymiane's trudge from the rich quarter through progressively poorer and poorer quarters until she reaches the cemetery wall.

The film comes to an end shortly after the middle of our script, inconclusively and incomprehensibly. I once saw it myself at a cinema in Paris and stayed in my seat at the end because I thought the film had broken.

Broad farce: *Kohlhiesels Töchter* (Lubitsch, 1920).
Sentimentality: Leni Riefenstahl in *Die Weisse Hölle von Piz Palü* (1929)

'German youth is now in the
service of Power. The concern
for art can only come after the
concern for victory, it can only
come on the evening after
victory.'
Gottfried Benn: *Kunst und
Macht*, 1934.

## The coming of sound

The decadence of the German film, already foreshadowed
in the last years of the silent era, is confirmed in the
first years of the talkie, where films such as *Der Blaue
Engel, Die Dreigroschenoper, Mädchen in Uniform*, and *M*
are rare exceptions. Why this should be is not easy to
explain.

We cannot put all the blame on the intrusion of Hollywood interests and American capital coming in to float
Ufa. Even if the return gift (a number of major directors
such as Murnau, Dupont, Leni, were signed up to work
in America, where Lubitsch had been since 1923) represented a quite considerable loss for the German cinema,
directors of the class of Lang or Pabst, along with
Lamprecht, Froelich and Grune, carried on working in
their own country.

Non-Germans seldom realize that the films nowadays
denoted as German classics were in their day exceptional, and swamped by the spate of commercial films
on Heidelberg and the German Rhine, Vienna and the
Blue Danube, and all the patriotic films about Frederick
the Great, the Eleven Officers of Schill, the Grenadiers
of the King, or others recalling the exploits of the Great
War – not to mention all the barrack-room comedies and
the mass of *Aufklärungsfilme*, supposedly devoted to sex-
instruction but treating straightforward brothel stories
in a pseudo-scientific fashion.

If we consider that annual German film production

309

from 1926 to 1928 amounted to an average of about 210 films, and that the number of *acceptable* films rarely goes beyond ten or a dozen, we may admit the probability that the *quality* films of this period were limited to four or five – at the most – per year.

Some other facts are worth remembering. First, Reinhardt's and the Expressionists' legacy of chiaroscuro gives certain films a semblance of artistic value which is often due more to the designer's models and the skill of the cameraman than to any talent the director may have had. In the second place, many old films gain a kind of charm from what might be called their 'patina'. Finally, we should not lose sight of the fact that certain directors whose early films derived some value from the Expressionist style subsequently made nothing but works of distinctly poor quality. This is why nobody should be surprised at Robert Wiene making *The Duchess of the Folies Bergères*, at Richard Oswald actually enjoying directing *Wir Sind vom K. und K. Infanterie Regiment* (*We're the Men of the Infantry Regiment*) or at Zelnik, after a quite ambitious film *Die Weber*, filming *Die Schöne Blaue Donau* (*The Blue Danube*).

It also seems significant that the best German directors limited themselves to tragic films. Their comedies for the cinema never escape the charge of vulgarity and it is easy to understand why Lubitsch's films *Romeo und Julia im Schnee* or *Kohlhiesels Töchter* (both 1920) make non-German spectators feel violently indisposed. But Murnau's and Berger's occasional lapses into bad taste in *Die Finanzen des Grossherzogs* and *Walzertraum* are revealing. The German cinema has not produced a single comedy which might be described as classic, *Tartuffe* being a tragi-comedy and *Der Verlorene Schuh* (*Cinderella*) a fairy-tale. What is more, Lubitsch prepared his *Lady Windermere's Fan* in America, and deliberately changed his manner, saying 'Good-bye slapstick and Hello nonchalance'!

Before Hitler came to power the Germans liked to declare that their great poets, such as Goethe or Schiller, always emerged at times of national hardship. It is tempting to see a repetition of this phenomenon in the aftermath of 1918, this time in favour of the cinema. In Germany chaos and despair often seem propitious to creation. The flowering of the art of film after the Great War (limited, as we have seen, to a few exceptional works) was not repeated, however, after 1945.

It is not easy to find a dream again once the spell is broken. After 1925, when stabilization had brought a return to prosperity, Germany swiftly forgot her guilt-feelings and aspired to the possession of territory. In the world of heavy industry which had succeeded in getting the whip hand in cinema production, the lust for colonies again reared its head.

As early as 1926 the future of the German cinema seemed compromised, all the more so since commercially successful American cinema had begun to make the box-office paramount. 'Until now', said Kurtz in 1926, 'the essentials of the German film have been dramatic content and the development of strong characters and passionate actions; the scenario aimed at dramas whose peripetias, resolving in catastrophe, amplified the sentiments called into question. Abroad, when people define the German film, the word "analytic" recurs again and again. At the present time, contact between the American and German cinemas will enable the latter to extricate itself in the immediate future from its prestissimo [*sic*] of successions of events and establish more harmonious relationships between the action and the development of character.'

We may wonder whether this explains how the German artistic cinema came to renounce the very qualities which gave it its value.

During the closing years of the silent era the image still managed to succeed, following as it did the traditional conventions of the chiaroscuro. But the sound film betrayed with words the mystery of gestures, and cruelly showed up the mediocrity of the current output. The veil of *Stimmung* would seem to be rent without hope of repair.

If Galeen's silent *Alraune* of 1928 is so much superior to Richard Oswald's sound version of 1930, the reason is to be found not only in the greater talent of Galeen: the first *Alraune* has the benefit of silence to safeguard the tension inherent in an essentially fantastic subject. Even so, this film of Galeen's made during the period of decline lacks the quality of *The Student of Prague*, which the same director made in 1926 within the conventions of the Expressionist vision. By 1928 German film-makers seldom dared to indulge in fantasy as completely as before, and elements of the 'new objectivity' mar the unity of a film like *Alraune*.

But an impassable abyss seems to lie between the silent and sound versions of a like subject: even a director of Robison's quality ended up with a failure when he made the third *Student of Prague* in 1936.

The German talkie had to surmount purely technical difficulties which the cinema in the Latin countries had no need to take into account: the frequency of sibilants and double consonants gave rise to distortions which seemed, at the outset, insurmountable. When Dita Parlo pronounced the word 'Pferd' in *Melodie des Herzens*, an early talkie by Hanns Schwarz, the entire audience burst out laughing and the critics went home to write long articles declaring that the sound film had no future. And even when the first imperfections had been eliminated, the beautiful language of Hölderlin and Rilke still seemed harsh, and this effect could only be attenuated by South German dialects and the softer speech of the Austrians. The success of Viennese films abroad, where *Maskerade* (1934), *Episode* (1935), and *Operette* (1940) played to packed houses, not to mention the films of Viennese music such as *Leise Flehen meine Lieder* (1933) and *Dreimäderlhaus* (1936), was partly due to the softness of the Austrian dialect. In the German film, the deliberately emphatic pronunciation of the Nazi period accentuated the trenchant sonority of the words.

The post-synchronization of a silent film generally gives painful results: *Die Weisse Hölle von Piz Palü*, made in 1929 by Arnold Fanck in collaboration with G. W. Pabst and given a soundtrack in 1935, is an example. Yet the sound in this film is no more unexpected than in the 'mountain' films of the early days of sound. This is perhaps because a number of shots in these films were taken silent due to technical difficulties on location. One's impression that all is not well is perhaps aggravated by the fact that dialogue shows up more clearly than titles the discordances inherent in the conjunction of natural images and melodramatic plots, which is what we get in most of the mountain films, even when the author is of the quality of Béla Balázs, the scenarist of *Das Blaue Licht*. In this film, directed by Leni Riefenstahl in 1932, the sound often seems superimposed on the very fine shots by Fanck's former cameraman Schneeberger, and the bleating goats and sheep weaken the force of the image.

What is more, the same is true of Leni Riefenstahl's film as of all Fanck's mountain films: the freshness and spontaneity of the open-air shots are marred by the over-perfect, over-smooth shots they excelled in filming in the studio whenever the climbs were too difficult or the acrobatics too dangerous; they were made in landscapes of salt and white powder representing snow and ice. The cave in *Das Blaue Licht*, a reminiscence of a model in Fanck's *Heilige Berg* (1927), is difficult to justify in this film conceived for authentic exteriors (unlike the cavern of Alberich, for example, which was perfectly in place within the legendary framework of *Die Nibelungen*).

Nonetheless Fanck's mountain films are better than the one by Riefenstahl. Fanck never set out to 'illustrate' a drama with the beauty of nature. For him the action developed step by step through an abundance of images, and the image was the more important element. Thus in *Ewiger Traum* the visions of storm-swept mountains and snowy slopes are masterfully orchestrated by the vigour of his editing. Leni Riefenstahl was incapable of attaining such visual force, even though she usurped Fanck's cameramen.

Once German film-makers had got used to the miracle of sound they soon abandoned their experiments with sound effects. In 1929 Dupont attempted to 'concretize' the wreck of the liner in *Atlantic* by noises-off – screams in every language mingling with the wailing of the sirens, the background music and clanging of bells, while the noise of the engines suddenly stopped short. The same year Walter Ruttmann's *Melodie der Welt* attempted to heighten the image with sound, but this work is really just a silent film made into a sound version by the addition of Wolfgang Zeller's music and a few natural noises. (It is perhaps not generally known that during this period Ruttmann was dreaming up a 'film' composed solely of a montage of sounds, *without images*, and that he actually made it under the title of *Wochenende*.)

In 1931 Kurt Bernhardt's *Der Mann, der den Mord beging* presented a stretch of deserted street at night in which words exchanged by two people on a terrace mingled with the sound of footsteps and dwindled as the passer-by moved away. In the year before, in *Abschied*, Robert Siodmak showed the corner of a bedroom where the presence of an unseen couple enlaced on the bed was indicated merely by a few words of love.

Sternberg had made only one sound film before *Der Blaue Engel* (*The Blue Angel*), but his work in the American studios had taught him how to use sound more effectively than the German film-makers of his day. An example to note is the play on doors, from which snatches of laughter or singing escape as soon as they are opened. In these early days of the talkie he has still to learn how to lap-dissolve or fade out sound as doors or windows are closed. But Sternberg succeeds in associating a sparkling, dazzling 'Impressionism' with the German chiaroscuro; and this Impressionism is joined by a visual eroticism as soon as the footlights come on and Marlene Dietrich delivers her loaded, ambiguous songs.

This mixture of styles is nonetheless full of charm; the German designer Hunte created twisting alleyways and oblique, elongated, Expressionistically gabled houses; and this set harmonizes with the typically Sternbergian interiors dominated by a concern both for the pictorial and for the creation of a spell-binding mood.

Pabst, for his part, was too interested in the image to understand at first the essential role of sound. In *Westfront 1918* (1930) and *Kameradschaft* (1931), the frequently very fine camera-work is marred by extremely banal dialogue.

Yet in *Kameradschaft* the scenes down the mine – especially that in which a survivor taps a pipe with an iron bar and the sound echoes down the deserted galleries – have all the vigour of a newsreel or an unstaged documentary. The image that emerges from the darkness is at one with the sound, and this sequence vibrates with a new tension in Pabst's work, an atmosphere made dense by an extraordinary range of sounds.

314

A sketch by Otto Hunte for *The Blue Angel*; *Die Dreigroschenoper*

## Die Dreigroschenoper (The Threepenny Opera, 1931)

We have still to discuss the undeniable artistic success of Pabst's *Die Dreigroschenoper*. On the stage Brecht's play had already been admirably produced – not by Erich Engel as is generally thought (this stage-director subsequently made a few films of no interest whatsoever) but by Brecht himself, who gave it the harsh, uncompromising interpretation he had meant for it, retaining the trenchant phrases and very pure stylization of the Expressionist experiment.

In his adaptation for the cinema Pabst diluted the original by his attachment to chiaroscuro and *Stimmung* – and perhaps even more to please a very 'realistic' producer. This gave rise to a resounding lawsuit lodged by Brecht and Kurt Weill (an account of which is given in the appendix on pages 343–5). Yet the vigorous starkness of the original was not entirely lost, as some of

*Die Dreigroschenoper:* the brothel

the main actors in the play kept their parts in the film. The dialogues and the poignant rhythm of the songs created under Brecht's instructions are counterpointed by a visual theme which is not unworthy of it, for Pabst's talent is as remarkable here as it was during the silent era, and more particularly the period when he made *Pandora's Box*.

Andreiev's misty London for *Pandora* was a first version of his sets for *Die Dreigroschenoper*. Pabst and Andreiev contrived to clothe everything in chiaroscuro and mist, making the brick walls of the Thames-side docks and Soho slums both real and fantastic at the same time. Swirls of dust and smoke wreath the dwellings of the beggar king and cling to the bare walls, where the wretches' rags are like ornamental blobs of paint, and hover in the nuptial shed on the docks, softening the splendour of the tables brimming with fruit and silverware amid the reflections of the gentle candlelight, creating the still-life atmosphere also found in Jean Epstein's *L'Auberge Rouge*.

The encounter of the renaissance of 'Impressionism' and the waning of Expressionism is a happy one (it had already made itself felt in certain scenes in *Pandora's Box*). It is seen here in the gaudy shots of the brothel, with its Victorian lushness confined in plush and pelmets and its *fin-de-siècle* statue of a negress, the whole seeming to stifle bourgeois hypocrisy between over-embroidered cushions and over-opaque curtains. In this black-and-white film the provocative déshabillés with Edwardian-style corsets, Caligari-ish light-coloured gloves with black ribbing and bespatted boots, do even more to heighten the impression of colour.

Though Queen Victoria came to the throne in 1837, Brecht, who had already transplanted the eighteenth-century *Beggars' Opera* to a more recent period, again chose for his *mise-en-scène* the stiffened gowns, feathered hats, starched collars and stiff frock-coats of the end of the Victorian period because they accentuated the sham middle-class appearance of his low-life men and women. Pabst and his excellent cameraman, Fritz Arno Wagner, used sophisticated shooting angles with taste and evident pleasure. They gave to the film an impression of infinite liveliness and variety.

317

Mackie Messer, filmed through panes of glass, tries to seduce Polly and asks her to go away with him; we see him talking but can only guess what he is saying. The image gives the sound a background and this, at the beginning of the sound film, is captivating.

Yet the setting of the authentic *Dreigroschenoper* as originally presented in Berlin was more imaginative and more striking.

The success of Brecht's play perhaps stemmed from the contrast between the colourfulness of the milieu and costumes, and the set itself, which had been calculated mathematically after the theories of Stanislavsky and Taïroff. Projected on folding flats, Casper Neher's sharp, precise sets, austere yet complex at the same time, owed nothing to the new objectivity. Placards bearing captions in black on a white background gave the impression of immediacy. These placards, which displayed ironical and violent Brechtian maxims by way of commentary, had no tendency to create the atmosphere which Andreiev's maquettes set out to evoke. Instead they served to shock the audience into taking part and taking sides.

Kurt Weill's songs, based on a few notes whistled by Brecht, were the very pivots of the play, springing up in the constantly spontaneous dialogue, whereas in Pabst's film they are no more than pleasant embellishments. Their impact is deadened with atmosphere, and though made visual, much of their effect is blurred if not lost altogether. Yet the German version of the film retains something of Brecht's sharp diction and sarcasm, and certain actors from his troupe – Ernst Busch, extraordinary as the interpreter of Mackie Messer's lament; Lotte Lenya, Kurt Weill's wife, as Jenny; and Carola Neher, moving as Polly – had learnt the Brechtian singing technique from Brecht himself. In the French version, only Margo Lion has the necessary overwhelming presence (why did the French cinema neglect this remarkable *diseuse*, who deserved to take the place of Yvette Guilbert?) and she had lived in Berlin for quite some time. As the wife of Marcellus Schiffer, a talented young composer who died prematurely, she had learnt how to sing with a staccato lilt unknown to the Germans of today.

318

*Die Dreigroschenoper* on the Berlin stage

*M*

## M (1931)

Lang, immediately impressed by the expressive possibilities of sound, very naturally turned his hand to
contrasts between sound and the image. In *M* (1931), for
example, when Peter Lorre's shadow is cast across the
reward poster, we only hear his voice, while he himself
remains off-screen. The same effect is found in the thieves'
conference: only their shadows appear on the screen
as they pursue their conversation. In *Liliom*, made in
France in 1933, Lang likewise shows nothing but the
two partners' reflections in the water as they discuss their
crime.

 Lang's counterpointing of sound and image is done
with supreme mastery: the sound actually enhances the
image. When Elsie's mother leans over the desperately
empty staircase to call her name, the little girl's absence
is impressed upon us by the images – the table with a
place set before an empty chair – and the inexorable

ticking of the clock. The mother's calls ring out in the deserted attic. Then the murder is suggested elliptically by the ball rolling away and the balloon getting caught on the telegraph wire, while the mother's cry against these images rings on, and dies.

The sound occasionally precedes an image, or laps over into the following image, thus binding it even closer to the previous one. Overlapping allusions of sound and associations of ideas accelerate the rhythm of the action and give it its density.

Sound can intensify an image's significance; as Lorre is fleeing towards the building where he will go to earth, a fire-engine clangs noisily past. In the next shot the entry into the building is empty and silent.

Lang was the first to realize that, unlike the theatre, the sound film did not have to limit itself to a straight-forward narrative of events. Thus, while Inspector Lohmann is making his report other images flock in to give breadth to the narrative, and we see the broken-open

321

doors and the safes intact. Similarly, when the minister telephones the police superintendent and the latter gives a résumé of the measures being taken, Lang presents the various search-parties and teams of detectives conducting their enquiries in all manner of places.

Sound is used to prepare the discovery of the murderer: Lang shows us the blind balloon-seller in the bistro stopping his ears at a harsh, out-of-tune barrel-organ (just as the murderer does on a café terrace at the increasingly strident whistling of his leitmotiv, a theme from the trolls' dance by Grieg) and then sways in time delightedly when he hears a gentler, sweeter one. In this way the audience realizes that the whistling will later recall the encounter with Elsie to the blind man's acute hearing.

Gradually, sound leads to the murderer's discovery. It starts with the oppressed breathing of the hunted monster in the silence of the attics. When the night-watchman locks the door Lorre's knife snaps in his attempt to force the lock. Then the repeated blows he gives to straighten a nail he has torn from the wall betray his presence. Then the invasion: the doors are rattled and there is a banging on the partitions.

At the climax, when sound and image fuse together, Lorre's yell rings out at the jury of thieves: an invincible force, he says, drives him to kill.

## Das Testament des Dr Mabuse (The Testament of Dr Mabuse, 1933)

With his next film Lang's sound techniques continue to evolve.

In the forgers' factory the machines growl away and in the infernal din of bumping, shivering objects beneath the swinging of the lamp – the image thus quite naturally backing up the sound – Hofmeister, the ex-detective, is forced to plug his ears to avoid going mad. When the two employees discover the intruder's presence their whispers are lost in the noise.

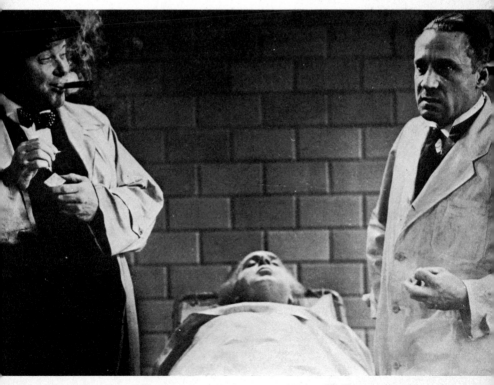

*The Testament of Dr Mabuse*

Similarly, when the young couple are locked into the curtained room we hear with them – and this heightens the tension of the scene – the unbearable din, the pulsing of the infernal machine.

As in *M*, Lang uses dialogue to link one shot to another. Very often he announces the scene: thus Lohmann, contemplating Hofmeister, who has gone mad, exclaims: 'I'd like to get my hands on the man responsible for this fellow's madness.' And the next image shows Mabuse at the asylum scribbling out his monstrous orders. Or again, just after the explosion of the bomb which misses Hofmeister, Lang cuts to Lohmann in his office, and the two shots are linked by the expression 'Feuerzauber', magic of fire, used by Lohmann talking about an opera by Wagner and knowing nothing, of course, of the murder attempt.

Elsewhere the acolytes discuss the organization and its mysterious chief and one of them says, 'Woe betide anybody who tried to rat on him'; the next image shows us Kent, desperate at being caught up in this situation, and Lang does not need to make him speak for us to understand.

At another juncture Lang has us contemplate Dr Baum's empty office for some time, then we hear the voices of Lohmann and his policeman behind the door, followed by the metallic 'I don't want to be disturbed' coming from inside the room. The voice is the same as that of the loudspeaker hidden behind the curtain, and Kent, who fails to recognize the doctor's real voice, recognizes the mechanical reproduction.

At the end of the film, the sound swells into a broad orchestration blending with the movements and lighting effects. To the crackling of the flames coming from the burning gasworks are added the wailing of sirens, the clanging of fire-engines, the rumbling of falling chimneys, the puffing of a locomotive, and the back-firing of motorcycles. Amid all this din spotlights scanning the bushes track down the villain, and headlights light up the vast thicket pierced by police whistles. A motorcar roars off. And the frantic chase begins.

The crazy careering of Von Wenck, hypnotized by the letters of fire in the first *Mabuse*, is nothing compared with this spectacular chase through the darkness, with spectral milestones looming up Expressionistically and lines flashing past in an irresistible movement which is the pure expression of speed: fleeting reflections of leaves caught in the car headlights flare in the mist, while the vault of trees flashes past overhead.

Lang tells me that these days he would not use the device of the superimposed apparitions of Mabuse's ghost, which he judges clumsy; he prefers a 'voice off' to guide the doctor's crazy careering, which ends, like Dr Caligari's before it, in front of the gates of the asylum.

Paul Czinner used dialogue in an attempt to intensify the atmosphere of the *Kammerspiele* in *Ariane* (1931) and *Der Träumende Mund* (1932). The words become subtle intermediaries between the long 'psychological' pauses which he had already used to good effect in his silent films.

## Mädchen in Uniform (1931)

*Mädchen in Uniform* was supervised by Carl Froelich, but the real credit for its quality must go to Leontine Sagan, whose feminine reading of the *Kammerspielfilm* led her to turn her back on the 'new objectivity' and concentrate on atmosphere.

Certain images, borrowed of course from the Soviet film but marvellously adapted to a Prussian ambience, stand at the beginning of this film to bring out the situation clearly and precisely. We see the Potsdam Stadtschloss, which has now been destroyed; and enormous stone grenadiers, as stiff as pikestaffs *à la* Friedrich Wilhelm I, make a droll contrast with plump little eighteenth-century putti. Goose-stepping recruits march past; then we see a parallel parade of the girls 'in uniform' – striped convict-dress – followed by a shot of the hems of long cumbersome skirts and coarse shoes.

This film is the last word on the slavery and starvation to which the aristocracy subjected its daughters, whose headmistress says, 'Wir Preussen haben uns gross gehungert' – 'We Prussians became great by starving'.

Humour has its part to play. Of course these future mothers of glorious soldiers sigh after the *Delikatessen* of their ancestral farms – while in an enormous low-angle close-up the ominous form of the scarecrow head-mistress looms like a personified *Verboten*. Hitler's coming to power was only two years away, and here at least the hindsight of a Kracauer seems for once justified.

The rather troubled atmosphere of close friendships between young adolescents, whose senses have still to come to rest on an object different from their own sex, is evoked throughout.

As in a military review, the young ladies are presented to a Royal Highness, an important person with an enormous hat and monstrous indifference. The satire comes across without exaggeration.

In the same way this film by a woman never exaggerates the tragic mode. A girl is expelled and her schoolfriends break bounds to try to see her again. The sequence in the immense forbidden staircase, with the constant shouts of 'Manuela! Manuela!' getting more and more anguished, is almost as effective as the staircase scene in *M* with the mother's frantic cries of 'Elsie! Elsie!'

With this work the pre-war German sound film reached its highest level. Leontine Sagan, a stage-actress, directed the dialogue admirably. She brings out the unselfconscious naïvety of the boarders' confidences whispered across the dormitory, and the flush of love trembling in the cracked voice of the adolescent – Hertha Thiele – in a counterpoint with the contralto of Dorothea Wieck. In *Anna und Elisabeth* (1933) Franck Wysbar made his own attempt at capturing the emotive quality found in this film; though he chose the same actresses, 'fluent speakers of the language of the heart' as Paul Gilson so rightly says, he did not succeed.

A few gay scenes in *Mädchen in Uniform* attest to the freshness which speech can bring to the image. The liveliness of the dialogue in Lamprecht's version of *Emil und die Detektive* (1931) likewise underlines this story of the fantastic chase of an adult thief by a band of boys.

### The Ufa style

The coming of sound unleashed, alas, a torrent of operettas (for example the extremely heavy *Drei von der Tankstelle* of 1930) and the even graver disaster of *Musikerfilme*, films on the love life of famous composers with broken hearts, and lashings of Lieder. *White Horse*

*Inn*, the operetta lavishly staged by Erik Charell, had captured the enthusiasm of the Berlin crowds. When Charell came to film *Der Kongress Tanzt* (1931) he did so with the same panoply of lush settings and costumes, and the images of his film influenced all the subsequent productions.

Yet *Der Kongress Tanzt* must not bear all the blame. German film-makers had exploited the chiaroscuro for so long that the commercial film was bound to take it over eventually and, of course, debase it. This danger was already imminent in the silent era – *Die Wunderbare Lüge der Nina Petrowna* (1929) and *Ungarische Rhapsodie* (1928), both by Hanns Schwarz, are striking examples – but it got rapidly worse in the days of the talkie. The Tobis company rushed into the mass production of daydreams and Ufa, beating its big drums at a time when the independent producers were still frightened of the expense involved in the talkie, matched sentimentality to melodrama: for instance, *Melodie des*

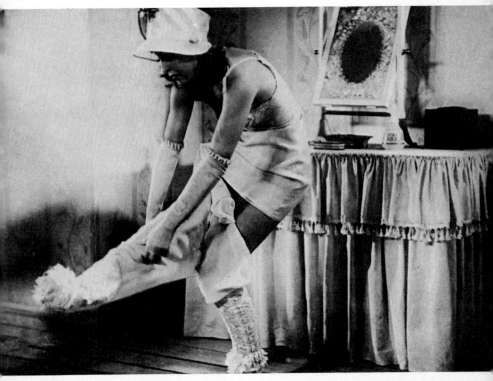

The Ufa style: *Der Kongress Tanzt*

The 'social décoratif': *Die Weber* and *So Ist das Leben*

*Herzens* (1929), in which, moreover, the usual chiaroscuro is watered down into a flat grisaille. This fault had already marred Hans Kyser's *Luther* (1927) and was to mar, still later, Ucicky's *Das Mädchen Johanna* (1935).

The mawkish perfection of the 'Ufa style' which cameramen of quality were obliged to adopt left its mark above all on the pseudo-historical film. It introduces a false note into all the costume film productions made during the Third Reich, from *Jud Süss* (1940) and *Rembrandt* (1942) to Pabst's *Paracelsus* (1943) and Riefenstahl's *Tiefland* (1944). Despite a few nuances due to the Agfacolor process, the Ufa style is unchanged in *Die Abenteuer des Baron Münchhausen* (1943) and is still there to mar Pabst's post-Nazi film *Prozess*, made in Austria in 1948.

For let there be no mistake: the antisemitic tendencies in Veit Harlan's *Jud Süss* have no more to do with this film's purely cinematic quality than philosemitism in any other, whether it be the English film *Jew Süss*, *Prozess*, or *Ehe im Schatten* (1947). We must try – though it is difficult – to consider the films made during the Third Reich altogether objectively, from the sole viewpoint of quality and style.

Apart from over-glossy images, we meet with the same faults in *Jud Süss* and another film by Harlan, *Der Grosse König* (1942), as in many pre-Nazi historical films. Their creators plumped either for the vast stylized fresco or for the sentimental 'little history' attested by the titles: *Napoleon und die Kleine Wäscherin* (*Napoleon and the Little Washergirl*), or *Napoleons Töchter* (*Napoleon's Daughter*). Karl Grune's *Waterloo* (1928) itself wavers between this anecdotal genre and the rip-roaring epic. Lupu Pick's *Napoleon auf Sankt Helena* (1929) and the numerous films about Frederick II, whether by Czerèpy, Froelich, Boese, or Lamprecht, though the last-named was sincere, all fail to avoid waxwork stiffness.

In his first speeches, made in 1933–34, Goebbels declared that the German film had the mission of conquering the world as the vanguard of the Nazi troops. He asked the studios to produce films with precise tendencies, 'mit scharfen völkischen Konturen', with sharp racial contours, portraying men and society 'as they are in reality'.

'Kraft durch Freude' (Strength through Joy) slammed the gates of dream and fantasy, and Nazi ideology was not of a nature to create an authentic reality capable of compensating for their loss.

Like the costume film, the social film was fond of composing fine images and, even before the advent of the Third Reich, was no more successful than the costume film in ridding itself of the sentimentality which had already sugared *Sylvester*. It is not possible to make films in studio slums for so long without something rubbing off when you leave them to go and film in the streets.

The studio-made *Joyless Street* was the ready-made prototype for the 'social décoratif' and all the 'Kaschemmen' (underworld films) and 'Sittenfilme' (moralizing sex films) made later. The exploitation of the picturesqueness of poverty – a typically German approach to the theme – marred all the so-called social films and even others more sincere than Zelnik's *Die Weber*. The films standing at the crossroads between the fantastic and the real, such as *M*, were always to have an intensity and power which films such as Piel Jutzi's *Mutter Krausens Fahrt ins Glück* (1929), made in the Berlin streets, or Leo Mittler's *Jenseits der Strasse* (1929), shot on the Hamburg docks, vainly tried to equal.

Piel Jutzi's film is an example of the influence wielded on all the social films of this period by *Berlin, die Symphonie der Grossstadt*, not because of the inordinate use of the Berlin Luna Park and Freibad Wannsee or the asphalt workers (whom Piel Jutzi in his turn hired for *Mutter Krausens* as Joe May had done for *Asphalt*), but because all these films display the same concern for documentary detail: the camera scrutinizes the life of humble people and shoots the trivial incidents of the street from life. *Mutter Krausens* also reveals the basic flaw in all these films which try their hand at imitating *Berlin*: the documentary passages are mixed with melodrama, when their quality is often such that these traces of the *Sittenfilm* are all the more unpleasant.

The actors are the first to suffer from this mixing of genres. Baranovskaya's acting is greatly superior under Pudovkin's direction in *Mother* than in *So Ist das Leben* (1929), a film made in Prague by Junghans. And in the

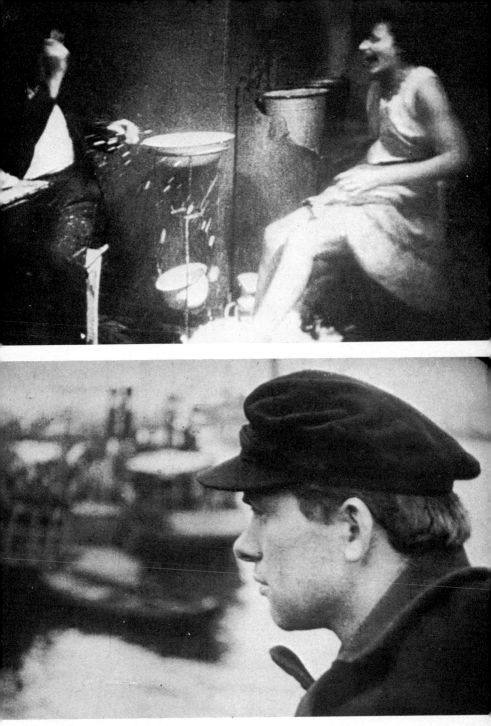

*Mutter Krausens Fahrt ins Glück; Jenseits der Strasse*

*So Ist das Leben; Berlin-Alexanderplatz*

Soviet film, despair is evident in a room's casual desolate emptiness; whereas in Junghans's film all the objects and situations have a function, corresponding to a predetermined framework. Such is life? Not quite, surely!

Lamprecht made several films in which he portrayed the misery of the Berlin slums. Though more convincing than Rossellini's *Germania, Anno Zero*, whose author appeared as ignorant of the German mentality as he is of the language, Lamprecht's post-Nazi film *Irgendwo in Berlin* (1946) does convey the eternal inconclusive hesitation between realism and sentimentality.

As a result, the cinema of the Nazi era, which portrays men and societies 'as they are in reality' is not vastly different from its predecessors; with regard to style, for example, *Hitlerjunge Quex* (1938) is not a great way away from its political opposite *Berlin-Alexanderplatz* (1931). Up to our own day the German social film, whatever its political colour, has never attained the

*Menschen am Sonntag:* the incidents of everyday life

*Menschen am Sonntag*

humanity of such films as *The Childhood of Maxim Gorky*, or *Bicycle Thieves*. And even the simplicity of Robert Siodmak's *Menschen am Sonntag* (1928) in which Schüfftan's skill with bold shooting-angles gives relief to the incidents of everyday life, or even *Kuhle Wampe* (1932), an extremely honest film made by the Bulgarian-born Slatan Dudow in collaboration with Brecht, in which the miserable existence of the unemployed is portrayed with documentary restraint enhanced by the rhythm of the montage and the violence of the music, cannot equal some of the Russian or Italian neo-realist films.

Nevertheless the precision of the reporting makes the opening sequence in *Kuhle Wampe* unforgettable. Men on bicycles chasing after work in a headlong race, dominated by Hanns Eisler's sublimely impetuous music, burst on to the screen in a paroxysmal fortissimo of sound and image. The pleasant comedy of the workman's betrothal-feast, which follows, jars in comparison, as

334

*Triumph of the Will:* 'use of close-up to confer gigantic proportions on the meanest of objects'

does the sports meeting, which unwittingly anticipates the Nazi parades. There remains a piece of pure Brecht – incomprehensible for a non-German audience, unfortunately – in the dialogue scene in a suburban train compartment: the trenchantly dialectic interlude of 'the coffee they're burning in Brazil'.

## Leni Riefenstahl

Leni Riefenstahl's *Triumph des Willens* (*Triumph of the Will*), made in 1935, an idealized documentary glorifying a Nazi rally at Nuremberg, is laden with elements from the old German school. In order to understand this type of propaganda film better, we have to try to ignore the nightmarish impression caused by certain passages, especially the one in which Hitler in person dedicates the new flags. The film leaves one finally with an impression of insanity, and can be seen as a case study.

As for the film's artistic conception, it unites all the

335

*Olympiade*

distinctive elements of German film-making; in her
*Olympiade* (1938), another idealized documentary, this
time celebrating the Berlin Olympic Games, Leni
Riefenstahl lingers at length over night views of torch-
light slashing the darkness and flags becoming transparent next to the flames – a high point of chiaroscuro.
In sunlight she seeks to catch figures against the light,
the shadows cast by a marching column, or men en-
veloped in the halo of phosphorescence that we have
already noted, and we perceive Hitler standing in his
car with a kind of nimbus round his head. The crowds
jostle around their Führer and raise their arms in a
studied parallelism similar to the compositions of the
classical German cinema. A sea of flags and poles undulates
like a field of ripe corn; the human body becomes
an ornament, and the columns filmed from above,
like the warriors in *Siegfried*, are suddenly transformed
into a blurred, hazy vision like the acrobat's view of the
crowd in *Variety*.

336

Another well-worn technique found here is the frequent use of the close-up to confer gigantic proportions on the meanest of objects; the policeman's hands linking against their cartridge belts take on the appearance of some giant-stopping palisade. Here man becomes statue. (Kracauer points out the resemblance of the horn-blowers with those who stand out 'architecturally' from the background in the *Nibelungen*.) The faces in close-up seem like granite, with their vast strongly-modelled surfaces and inhumanly sculptural chins. They evince the same impression of emptiness and boredom as the colossal hulking statues erected by Arnold Brecker, the Third Reich's most conspicuous sculptor. Since the ultimate aim of German *Kultur* is, in the words of Langbehn, the so-called 'Rembrandtdeutsche', to 'monu-mentalisieren', ponderous pomposity is inevitable and official art will always commission it in mistake for the heroic.

If in *Olympiade* the close-ups are less shocking, the reason is that the cult of the hero is not out of place in a film devoted to the athletic prowess of harmonious bodies. The credit for certain admirable shots in this film should perhaps go to the great talent of the camera-man, Hans Ertl, rather than to the eye of Leni Riefenstahl. It is he who captures the dynamism of a stance and the passion infusing the athletic exploit: a figure, filmed from a low angle, waits for the word 'go', then an action shot of the jump spreads in a victorious diagonal across the entire screen. All these oblique masses destroy the syntax of the cinema's two dimensions, they burst from within the framework of the flat image. Occasionally, one of these bronzed champions produces the effect of Murnau's grandiose celebration of the body in *Tabu*. But, alas, we are sometimes closer by far to the techniques underlying *Wege zu Kraft und Schönheit* (*Ways to Strength and Beauty*, 1925), in which Ufa propounded the clichés of the eugenics posters.

## The post-Nazi era

What remains of the wish to represent reality, as Dudow, Piel Jutzi and Junghans attempted to do before the Nazi era?

*Der Verlorene*

We know that Slatan Dudow made an implacable film, *Stärker als die Nacht*, denouncing the ravages of Nazism in a working-class milieu. This film goes much further than Staudte's anodyne *Die Mörder Sind unter Uns* (*The Murderers are among Us*).

One wonders why Wolfgang Staudte (who in *Rotation* had shown us, without ambiguity, and better than Stemmle in the over-complacent *Berliner Ballade*, the average German caught up in Nazism) and Helmut Käutner, the author of *In Jenen Tagen*, nowadays make nothing but fundamentally mediocre films. Why do films such as *Schwarzer Kies* (1961) or *Die Rote* (1962) – both by Käutner – testify to such an afflicting decline in the German cinema?

Are we to put it down to the behaviour of the all-important distributors, who by advancing money as 'angels' control the film from the first take of the very first scene? Or to the general public's tendency to prefer the mediocre and to denigrate any artistic ambitions in advance? Fritz Lang himself suffered from the prevailing atmosphere when he returned to film in Germany, despite the pains he took (as always) over the filming of his 'Indian' films and *Die Tausend Augen des Dr Mabuse*. It is not surprising that he abandoned the idea of filming in Germany *Und Morgen Mord*, which could well have been a second *M*.

In spite of some superficial attempts to do so, it is not possible to link to the German great period such films as Käutner's *Der Apfel Ist Ab*, with its pseudo-Expressionistic settings, Stemmle's *Berliner Ballade*, which marks a return to the chiaroscuro and the old schizoid evasion theme, or the version of *Wozzeck* by Klaren, the scenarist of many commercial films, who attempted an over-picturesque stylization of Büchner's violent drama. Compromises ruined this attempt at a renewal of Expressionism.

Unfortunately the Germans did not grasp the scope of one of their films whose quality recalls that of the best films from the period 1930–32. *Der Verlorene* (1951), by Peter Lorre, who was a remarkable actor in *M*, bears no trace of the numerous recent attempts to turn the clock back to pre-Nazi days. Though he owes certain debts to *M* – the obsession with murder and the tragically tense atmosphere recall Lang's old film – Lorre gives evidence of very personal inspiration. He has matured, his physique has improved with his art, he knows how to avoid false pathos and overemphasis, and how to give full weight to silences.

The scenario owes much to his subtlety: this film's suggestive power is the fruit of devices which always have their origin in the situation. We have to read between the lines. The Nazi rout felt to be imminent everywhere from 1943 onwards is made vividly present by a few tiny incidents and a few phrases slipped in here and there. To portray the reign of the Third Reich, many lesser directors deem it necessary to present a profusion of resistance fighters, people declaiming 'Heil Hitler', and torture scenes. Here there is nothing of the kind: the Nazi who plays an important part throughout the film is completely defined by his manner, his laugh, and his language, and only once do we see him in the extreme situation of the killer. And that's all.

Nor is there any need to resort to the ruins of Hamburg to get a picturesque setting: on the one occasion that the camera comes to rest on a house in ruins, the shot is necessary and totally integrated into the action.

This approach, and this tact, a quality which had been absent from German films for twenty years, are found constantly in the dialogue, the acting, and even the elocution. There is not a single slip, a single forced contrast, or a single false value. The editing also testifies to these rediscovered qualities: the flashbacks to 1943 are fitted into the action with perfect logic and great restraint.

Misunderstood and disillusioned, Peter Lorre went to the United States, where the roles he had to play were rarely suited to his talent. Frustration hounded him to an early death, and in him, and in Fritz Lang, who has given up hope of filming again in Germany, the German cinema lost for some years all its hopes of renewal.

Like the young French directors, the young film-makers of the Oberhausen Festival have tried to do away with the 'cinéma de papa'. A certain revival is apparent in the short film. But, as always in Germany, everybody wears himself out in demonstrations, conferences, and grandiloquent protestations, without ever getting round to actually doing something. Can we hope that, as has already happened in England, a new generation of talented directors will affirm itself through the short film?

Today the question seems settled, curiously enough owing to influences coming from France. The 1966 production of *Der Junge Törless* was made by Volker Schlöndorff, who lived in France for seven decisive years and was Louis Malle's assistant. His drama of the sexual miseries of puberty, and the latent sadism which seems to impregnate the youth of every country, is full of atmosphere and – despite its violent subject – remarkable sensibility. In hindsight this Austrian novel by Robert Musil, written in 1906, has become, in its cinematic transposition, a sombre prelude to Nazism; Schlöndorff attains this association of ideas with restraint – and is, of course, attacked for it by the neo-Nazis.

As for the rest, there are two films by Alexander Kluge, *Abschied von Gestern* (*Yesterday Girl*, 1966), in

340

which certain données of the best of Godard's films seem visible, and *Die Artisten in der Zirkuskuppel: Ratlos* (*The Artistes at the Top of the Big Top: Disorientated*, 1968). And there is a remarkable first feature by Werner Herzog, *Lebenszeichen* (*Signs of Life*, 1968), deriving indirectly from a story by Achim von Arnim.

All we can do is to hope that these films of quality spell a new departure for the German cinema.

*Die Dreigroschenoper*

# Appendix: the Dreigroschenoper Lawsuit

Brecht was profoundly shocked by Pabst's transposition, which he saw as an intolerable adulteration of the ideological and stylistic content of his play.

After many preliminary negotiations, Brecht, Leo Lania and Pabst tried to work together. If I remember rightly, they travelled down to a place in the South of France where Brecht often went, Le Lavandou. Soon disputes broke out between these very disparate personalities, and Brecht, after seeing his different proposals all refuted, departed, leaving Lania to safeguard his intentions. Lania relates in an interview published in *Cinémages* that after the first twenty-four hours any possibility of collaboration became illusory and Brecht 'just stepped out of the picture', and this corresponds more or less with my own recollection. Yet the film's still photographer, Hans Casparius, recently assured me that after this dispute Brecht still came along to the studios for the first few days' shooting, in the course of which the text was modified and even improvised. Sometimes recollections get mixed up; Pabst's film-editor, Jean Oser, in another *Cinémages* interview, confusing Weill's suit with Brecht's, states that the latter won his.

For in the autumn of 1930, Brecht and Weill, through the intermediary of their four lawyers, had lodged a common action against the production company, Nero Films. At the first hearing the common suit was split into separate actions at the judge's request. Brecht pleaded that the film was being shot from a scenario with which he had not been able to acquaint himself, despite an accessory clause granting him plenary power over the drafting of the script. Such an arbitrary procedure made it impossible to safeguard either the tenor or the style of the original.

Weill seconded the plea: his music had been transformed and an attempt had even been made to tack on passages not by him. In addition it had become apparent that his songs would not be inserted in the same places as in the play. This being so, both authors asked for the filming to cease entirely, preferring to give back the sums of money they had already received in order to recover their copyright.*

At the time, certain shots were being filmed, I remember, in the Efa studio, quite near the Kurfürstendamm. But as the crowd scenes required a lot of room, Pabst had begun filming – still before the end of the lawsuit – just outside Berlin, at Staaken, where the old Zeppelin Hall had been transformed into a studio some years earlier.

The lawsuit opened in the Copyright Court of one of the Berlin courthouses, a dismal building, on Friday 17 October 1930. It continued on Monday 20 October. All Berlin high society had tried to attend and the Court had to move into a larger courthouse for plenary hearings. So as to give the Berliners the chance of appreciating the play afresh, the Schiff-bauerdamm Theater had immediately envisaged taking the *Dreigroschenoper* back into its repertory as early as November. On this first Sunday, the Court went to the theatre for a performance organized specially for the needs of the lawsuit.

On the Monday, the discussions were particularly vehement. On several occasions the presiding judge had to call for silence among the rival parties, the public, and even the press, threatening to clear the court. Journalists from all over the country tirelessly took notes.

The ambience was curiously incongruous: besides the big businessmen of the cinema there was, as at theatre premières, the inevitable gathering of society women. Brecht's friends and his Nazi enemies were all present in force, though the latter did not quite know which leg to stand on; while detesting Brecht, the friends of Arnolt Bronnen† could not entirely support a producer who was both Jewish and American.

The literary élite of the day sided with Brecht, realizing that the outcome of the suit would establish a precedent affecting all German authors.

Counsel for the opposing party tried to turn the tables on Brecht by alleging that he himself had always challenged other authors' copyright and in particular had appropriated, for the songs in the *Dreigroschenoper*, whole lines from the verse translation of Villon's ballades by K. L. Ammer.‡

Brecht scornfully proved that Ammer had been in agreement and that he, Brecht, had even written a preface for a new edition of Ammer's poems. In the present instance, he declared, he was in no way defending his copyright, his literary property, but – and this is very significant as to Brecht's attitude

* The rights in *Die Dreigroschenoper* were sold for DM 40,000. Nero Films having obtained the cooperation of Tobis and Warner Bros, the film was budgeted at the then enormous sum of DM 800,000.

† Arnolt Bronnen, whose play *Vatermord* was first performed in 1922, at the same time as Brecht's first plays, was unjustifiably considered a serious rival to Brecht. Bronnen belonged to the Nazi Party from its inception.

‡ One day Brecht asked me to lend him a German translation of Villon's poems by Ammer. He kept this copy for a very long time and when, after some years, he gave it back to me, I found its margins crammed with notes and snatches of poems. Moreover he points out in his notes to *Die Dreigroschenoper* that his songs contain a few lines of Villon's ballads. As for Stendhal, all was grist to Brecht's mill. 'Copying', he was to write after the war in his *Theaterarbeit*, 'is an art which the master must dominate. He must handle it skilfully, for the sole reason that otherwise he could produce nothing worth copying in its turn'.

towards his audiences – *the property of the spectator*, who had the right to demand that a work be transmitted intact and according to the author's intentions. At another juncture he asked whether the cinematographic industry could arrogate, once and for all, the right to adulterate a work of literature.

In 1930, 'there still were judges in Berlin', and the presiding judge seemed to be of good faith. But what could a bureaucratic judge understand of the social implications of Bert Brecht's violent tragi-comedy?

Counsel for the producer Nebenzahl angered Brecht with insinuations and, after briskly riposting without being called upon to speak, Brecht swept out of the courthouse leaving his lawyers to carry on with the proceedings.*

On 4 November, Brecht's plea was rejected on the grounds that he had not fulfilled the requirements of his contract, considering that he had broken off all discussion during the work in common and voluntarily ended his collaboration in the script. As for his objection that the style of his play had been betrayed, it was treated as purely ideological and without bearing on the contract. Weill, always more pliable and rather inclined to make a few concessions, had more luck: having continued working until Nero Films themselves had dismissed him at the same time as Brecht, he won his case.

We were all very sad for Brecht, who was ordered to pay the costs of his suit. However, with his way of facing squarely up to everything, he shrugged and went back hard at work on his transposition of Gorky's *Mother*, realizing that all those who valued independence of mind did not have much longer to stay in Germany.

(Adapted from my article published in *Europe*, January/February, 1957.)

* 'A film scenario can't be treated as if it were a kettle of herrings', exclaimed Brecht's counsel. His client, who had never concealed the fact of using lines of Villon from Ammer's translation, had only used, in all, 40 lines from a work containing 500.

# Principal Works Mentioned in the Text

BALÁZS, BÉLA: *Der Sichtbare Mensch: Eine Film-Dramaturgie.* Deutsch-Osterreichischer Verlag, Vienna and Leipzig, 1924.

BARRY, IRIS: *Program Notes.* Museum of Modern Art Film Library, New York. (For Pabst and *The Love of Jeanne Ney*, see Series III, program 3.)

BENN, GOTTFRIED: *Kunst und Macht.* Deutsche Verlags-Anstalt, Stuttgart and Berlin, 1934.

CARRICK, EDWARD: *Designing for Films.* Studio Publications, London and New York, 1949.

EDSCHMID, KASIMIR: *Über den Expressionismus in der Literatur und die neue Dichtung* (Tribüne der Kunst und Zeit no. 1). Erich Reiss Verlag, Berlin, 1919.

EINSTEIN, CARL: *Bebuquin oder die Dilettanten des Wunders.* Verlag der Wochenschrift Die Aktion, Berlin, 1912.

EISNER, LOTTE: 'Sur le procès de l'*Opéra de Quat' Sous.*' Europe, Paris, Jan./Feb. 1957.

FECHTER, PAUL: *Der Expressionismus.* Piper Verlag, Munich, 1919.

FLEISCHMANN, BENNO: *Max Reinhardt.* Paul Neff Verlag, Vienna, 1948.

FREUND, KARL: Interviewed by Oswell Blakeston. *Close Up*, Territet, Switzerland, 1929.

IHERING, HERBERT: *Aktuelle Dramaturgie.* Verlag Die Schmiede, Berlin, 1924.

IHERING, HERBERT: *Kampf ums Theater.* Sybillen Verlag, Dresden, 1922.

JEAN-PAUL (pseud. of Johann Paul Friedrich Richter): *Quintus Fixlein* (1797) and *Titan* (1800–03).

KAPLAN, LEO: *Das Problem der Magie und der Psychoanalyse.* Heidelberg, 1927.

KLEE, WOLFHART GOTTHOLD: *Die charakteristischen Motive der expressionistischen Erzählungslitteratur.* Lichtwitz, Berlin, 1934.

KRACAUER, SIEGFRIED: *From Caligari to Hitler: a psychological history of the German film.* Princeton University Press, 1947.

KUBIN, ALFRED: *Die Andere Seite.* Originally published 1909; reissued 1962 by Deutscher Taschenbuch Verlag, Munich.

KURTZ, RUDOLF: *Expressionismus und Film.* Lichtbildbühne, Berlin, 1926.

LANG, FRITZ: 'Happily Ever After.' *Penguin Film Review*, 5. Penguin Books, London and New York, 1948.

LANGBEHN, JULIUS: *Rembrandt als Erzieher.* Hirschfeld, Leipzig, 1890 (and numerous subsequent editions).

LAURET, RENÉ: *Le Théâtre allemand d'aujourd'hui.* Gallimard, Paris, 1933.

LENI, PAUL: (Article in) *Der Kinematograph*, 911, Berlin, 1924.

MARZYNSKI, GEORGE: *Die Methode des Expressionismus.* Verlag von Klinkhardt & Diermann, Leipzig, 1920.

MAYER, CARL: *A Tribute to Carl Mayer, 1894–1944.* Memorial Programme, Scala Theatre, London, 1947.
Contents: (1) A note on the German cinema 1919–26; (2) 'Carl Mayer's debut' by Erich Pommer; (3) 'Carl Mayer, an Appreciation' by Paul Rotha; (4) 'The Impact of Caligari' by Ivor Montagu; (5) 'A Film Artist' by Karl Freund; (6) and (7) tributes by Anthony Asquith and Gabriel Pascal; (8) a list of films, with brief credits, on which Mayer worked.

MAYER, CARL: *Sylvester: Ein Lichtspiel* (scenario). With preface by Lupu Pick, Potsdam, 1924.

MESSELL, RUDOLPH: *This Film Business.* Ernest Benn, London, 1928.

MÖLLER, KAI (ed.): *Paul Wegener.* Rowohlt Verlag, Hamburg, 1954.

MOULLET, LUC: *Fritz Lang.* 'Cinéma d'aujourd'hui.' Editions Seghers, Paris, 1963.

PABST, G. W.: Interviewed on Realism by Jean Desternes. *Revue du cinéma,* 18, Paris, 1948.

PABST, G. W.: Articles by K. MacPherson and Bryher, including some interview material. *Close Up,* Territet, Switzerland, December 1927.

PABST, G. W.: 'Servitude et grandeur d'Hollywood.' *Le Rôle intellectuel du cinéma.* Institut international de co-opération intellectuel, Société des Nations, Cahier 3. Paris, 1937.

ROTHA, PAUL: *The Film Till Now.* Jonathan Cape, London, 1930. Revised with the help of Richard Griffith, and reissued, Vision Press, London, 1949; subsequently by Spring Books, Feltham.

SAGAN, LEONTINE: (Article in) *Cinema Quarterly,* Vol. 1, No. 4, Edinburgh, Summer, 1933.

SÖRGEL, ALBERT: *Dichtung und Dichter: Neue Folge: Im Banne des Expressionismus.* Voigtlander Verlag, Leipzig, 1925.

SPENGLER, OSWALD: *Der Untergang des Abendlandes,* two vols. Vienna and Leipzig, 1918–23. Eng. translation, *The Decline of the West,* two vols. Allen and Unwin, London, 1926–29; one-volume edition, 1934.

STORM, THEODOR: *Zur Chronik von Grieshuus,* 1884. Eng. translation, *A Chapter in the History of Grieshus,* 1908.

VISCHER, FRIEDRICH THEODOR: *Auch Einer.* Stuttgart and Leipzig, 1884.

WALDEN, HERWATH: *Die neue Malerei.* Berlin, 1919.

WERFEL, FRANZ: *Spiegelmensch.* Munich, 1920.

WORRINGER, WILHELM ROBERT: *Abstraktion und Einfühlung.* Doctorate thesis, 1907: published in Munich, 1921; Eng. translation by Michael Bullock, *Abstraction and Empathy,* Routledge and Kegan Paul, London 1953.

# Selective Filmography, 1913–33

This is an alphabetical listing of the principal films mentioned in the text made during the years 1913–33, the main period of the German Expressionist cinema.

Wherever possible the following information is given. 1: German title, usually followed by the English-language title by which the film is best known or, alternatively, a free, usable translation of the German title into English. 2: the name of the production company and the year(s) of production. 3: the name of the director (*Dir*). 4: the name of the scenarist, sometimes with additional information about the literary source (*Scr*). 5: the name of the artistic designer (*Ad*) and occasionally the name of the costume designer (*Cost*). 6: the name of the cameraman (*Ph*). 7: the name of the musical composer or arranger (*Mus*). 8: the names – these lists vary in comprehensiveness – of the actors (*Cast*).

Various published sources have been consulted, in particular: the two volumes so far compiled on the silent period (covering the years 1923–31) by Gerhard Lamprecht for the Deutsche Kinemathek; the *Deutscher Spielfilm Almanach, 1929–1950*, published by Filmblätter Verlag, Berlin, in 1950; the listings originally published in the last French edition of the present work, compiled with the help of Rolf Burgmer and Werner Zurbuch; the filmographies in *Fritz Lang in America* by Peter Bogdanovich (Movie Paperbacks, Studio Vista, London, 1967) and *The Lubitsch Touch* by Herman G. Weinberg (E. P. Dutton & Co. Inc., New York, 1968); the magazine *Cahiers du Cinéma* for Pabst, Lubitsch, and Lang; and Mme Eisner's *F. W. Murnau* (Le Terrain Vague, Paris, 1964). The Publishers also wish to acknowledge the help afforded them by the Librarian and staff of the British Film Institute Library in granting them access to unpublished or otherwise recondite reference material.

## Abwege (Crisis)
Erda-Film, 1928
*Dir*: G. W. Pabst
*Scr*: Adolf Lantz, Ladislaus Vayda, from a treatment by Franz Schulz
*Ad*: Hans Sohnle, Otto Erdmann
*Ph*: Theodor Sparkuhl
*Cast*: Brigitte Helm, Gustav Diessl, Jack Trevor, Hertha von Walther, Fritz Odemar, Nico Turoff, Ilse Bachmann, Richard Sora, Peter Leschka, Irm Cherry, Irma Green, Immy Lygett, Tita Christensen, Andreas von Horn

## Abschied (Adieu)
Universum-Film, 1930
*Dir*: Robert Siodmak
*Scr*: Emmerich Pressburger, Irma von Cube
*Ad*: Robert Herlth
*Ph*: Eugen Schüfftan
*Mus*: Erwin Bootz
*Cast*: Brigitte Horney, Aribert Mog, Emilia Unda, Konstantin Mic, Frank Günther, Edmée Symon, Gisela Draeger, Erwin Bootz, Martha Ziegler, Wladimir Sokoloff

## Alraune (Mandrake)
Ama-Film, 1928
*Dir*: Henrik Galeen
*Scr*: Henrik Galeen, from a novel by Hanns Heinz Ewers
*Ad*: Walter Reimann, Max Heilbronner
*Ph*: Franz Planer
*Cast*: Brigitte Helm, Paul Wegener, Ivan Petrovich, Mia Pankan, Georg John, Valeska Gest, Wolfgang Zilzer, Louis Ralph, Hans Trautner, John Loder, Heinrich Schroth, Alexander Sascha

## Alraune (Mandrake)
Ufa, 1930
*Dir*: Richard Oswald
*Scr*: Charlie Roellinghoff, R. Weisbach, based on Hanns Heinz Ewers
*Ad*: Otto Erdmann, Hans Sohnle
*Ph*: Günther Krampf
*Mus*: Bronislaw Kaper
*Cast*: Brigitte Helm, Albert Bassermann, Agnes Straub, Harald Paulsen, Liselot Schaatz, Bernhard Geotzke, E. A. Licho, Iwan Kowal-Samborski, Käthe Haack, Paul Westermeier, Henry Bender, Martin Kosleck

## Das Alte Gesetz (The ancient law)
Comedia-Film, 1923
*Dir*: E. A. Dupont
*Scr*: Paul Reno
*Ad*: Alfred Junge, Curt Kahle
*Cost*: Ali Hubert
*Ph*: Theodor Sparkuhl
*Cast*: Henny Porten, Alice Hechy, Ruth Weyher, Margarete Schlegel, Grete Berger, Olga Limburg, Ernst Deutsch, Werner Krauss, Jacob Tiedtke, Avram Morewsky, Robert Garrison, Robert Scholz, Albert Krafft-Lortzing, Dominik Löscher, Dr Albert Manning, Fritz Richard

## Anna Boleyn
Union Film-Ufa, 1920
*Dir*: Ernst Lubitsch
*Scr*: Hans Kräly, Fred Orbing
*Ad*: Kurt Richter
*Cost*: Ali Hubert
*Ph*: Theodor Sparkuhl
*Cast*: Henny Porten, Emil Jannings, Aud Egede-Nissen, Paul Hartmann, Ludwig Hartan, Ferdinand von Alten, Hedwig Pauli, Paul Biensfeldt, Wilhelm Diegelmann, Friedrich Kühne, Maria Reisenhöfer

## Anna und Elisabeth
Kollektiv-Film/Terra-Film, 1933
*Dir*: Frank Wysbar
*Scr*: Frank Wysbar
*Ad*: Fritz Maurischat
*Ph*: Franz Weihmayr
*Mus*: Paul Dessau
*Cast*: Dorothea Wieck, Hertha Thiele, Mathias Wieman, Maria Wanck, Carl Balhaus, Willi Kaiser-Heyl, Roma Bahn, Dorothea Thiess, Carl Werg, Karl Platen, Robert Eckert, Margarete Kestra, Dora Thalmer, Sybill Smolowa

## Ariane
Nero-Film, 1931
*Dir*: Paul Czinner
*Scr*: Paul Czinner, Carl Mayer from a novel by Claude Avet
*Ad*: Erich Zander
*Ph*: Adolf Schlasy
*Mus*: Richard Strauss
*Cast*: Elisabeth Bergner, Rudolf Forster, Annemarie Steinsieck, Hertha Guthmar, Theodor Loos, Alfred Gerasch, Nikolas Wassilieff

## Asphalt
Joe May-Film/Ufa, 1928/29
*Dir*: Joe May
*Scr*: Fred Majo, Rolf E. Vanloo, from a film-story by Rolf E. Vanloo
*Ad*: Erich Kettelhut
*Ph*: Günther Rittau
*Cast*: Betty Amann, Gustav Fröhlich,

Albert Steinrück, Else Heller, Hans Adalbert Schlettow, Hans Albers, Arthur Duarte, Paul Hörbiger, Trude Lieske, Karl Platen, Rosa Valetti, Hermann Vallentin, Kurt Vespermann

**Atlantik**
Deutsch-englische Gemeinschafts- produk tion/British International Pictures, 1929
*Dir:* E. A. Dupont
*Scr:* E. A. Dupont from *Der Berg*, a play by Ernest Raymond
*Ad:* Alfred Junge
*Ph:* Charles Rosher
*Mus:* John Reynders
*Cast:* Fritz Kortner, Elsa Wagner, Heinrich Schroth, Julia Serda, Elfriede Borodin, Lucie Mannheim, Franz Lederer, Willi Forst, Hermann Vallentin, Theodor Loos, Georg John, Philipp Manning, Georg August Koch, Syd Crosley

**Backstairs** see **Hintertreppe**

**Berlin-Alexanderplatz**
Allianz-Tonfilm, 1931
*Dir:* Piel Jutzi
*Scr:* Alfred Döblin, Hans Wilhelm, Karl Heinz Martin, from Döblin's novel *Alexanderplatz*
*Ad:* J. von Borsody
*Ph:* Nikolaus Farkas, Erich Giese
*Mus:* Allan Gray, Artur Guttmann
*Cast:* Heinrich George, Maria Bard, Margarete Schlegel, Bernhard Minetti, Gerhard Bienert, Albert Florath, Paul Westermeier, Oskar Höcker, Hans Deppe, Käthe Haack, Julius Falkenstein, Jakob Tiedtke, Siegfried Berisch, Arthur Mainzer, Karl Stepanek, Ernst Behmer, Paul Rehkopf, Anna Müller-Lincke, Hermann Krehan, Heinrich Schroth, Heinrich Gretler, Willi Schur, Walter Werner, Karl Harbacher, Franz Weber

**Berlin, die Symphonie der Grossstadt (Berlin, symphony of a great city)**
Deutsche-Verenis-Film, 1927
*Dir:* Walther Ruttmann
*Scr:* Walther Ruttmann, Karl Freund, from an idea by Carl Mayer
*Ad:* Erich Kellelhut
*Ph:* Reimar Kuntze, Robert Baberske, Lászlo Schäffer

**Der Blaue Engel (The blue angel)**
Ufa, 1930
*Dir:* Josef von Sternberg
*Scr:* Robert Liebmann, from Heinrich Mann's novel *Professor Unrat*
*Ad:* Otto Hunte, Emil Hasler
*Ph:* Günther Rittau, Hans Schneeberger
*Mus:* Friedrich Holländer
*Cast:* Emil Jannings, Marlene Dietrich, Kurt Gerron, Rosa Valetti, Hans Albers, Reinhold Bernt, Eduard von Winterstein, Hans Roth, Rolf Müller, Roland Varno, Carl Balhaus, Robert Klein-Lörk, Karl Huszar-Puffy, Wilhelm Diegelmann, Gerhard Bienert, Ilse Fürstenberg

**Das Blaue Licht (The blue light)**
Leni Riefenstahl/Sokal Film, 1932
*Dir:* Leni Riefenstahl
*Scr:* Béla Balázs, from an idea by Leni Riefenstahl
*Ad:* Leopold Blonder
*Ph:* Hans Schneeberger
*Mus:* Giuseppe Becce
*Cast:* Leni Riefenstahl, Mathias Wieman, Beni Führer, Max Holzboer, Franz Maldacca, Martha Mair

**Der Brennende Acker (The burning earth)**
Goron-Deulig Exklusiv Film, 1922
*Dir:* F. W. Murnau
*Scr:* Willy Haas, Arthur Rosen, Thea von Harbou
*Ad:* Rochus Gliese
*Ph:* Karl Freund, Fritz Arno Wagner
*Cast:* Werner Krauss, Eugen Klöpfer, Vladimir Gaidarow, Eduard von Winterstein, Stella Arbenina, Lya de Putti, Greta Dierks, Emilie Unda, Alfred Abel, Olga Engl, Elsa Wagner, Unda Faliansky, Eugen Rex, Leonhard Haskel, Gustav Botz, Adolf Klein, Albert Patry

**Die Büchse der Pandora (Pandora's box)**
Nero Film, 1928
*Dir:* G. W. Pabst
*Scr:* Ladislaus Vayda, from two plays by Frank Wedekind, *Erdgeist* and *Büchse der Pandora*
*Ad:* Andrei Andreiev, Gottlieb Hesch
*Ph:* Günther Krampf
*Cast:* Louise Brooks, Fritz Kortner, Daisy d'Ora, Franz Lederer, Gustav Diessl, Siegfried Arno, Alice Roberts, Carl Groetz, Krafft-Raschig, Michael von Newlinski

**Die Buddenbrooks**
Dea Film, 1923
*Dir:* Gerhard Lamprecht
*Scr:* Alfred Fekete, L. Heilborn-Körbitz, Gerhard Lamprecht, from Thomas Mann's novel
*Ad:* Otto Moldenhauer
*Cast:* Peter Esser, Mady Christians, Alfred Abel, Hildegard Imhof, Mathilde Sussin, Franz Egenieff, Rudolf del Zopp, Auguste Prasch-Grevenberg, Ralph Arthur Roberts, Charlotte Böcklin, Karl Platen, Kurt Vespermann, Elsa Wagner, Rudolf Lettinger, Emil Heyse, Friedrich Taeger, Philipp Manning, Hermann Vallentin, Robert Leffler

**The Cabinet of Dr Caligari**
see **Das Kabinett des Dr Caligari**

**Carlos und Elisabeth**
Richard Oswald-Film, 1924
*Dir:* Richard Oswald
*Scr:* Richard Oswald
*Ad:* O. F. Werndorff
*Ph:* Karl Hasselmann, Karl Puth, Karl Vass, Theodor Sparkuhl

*Cast:* Conrad Veidt, Eugen Klöpfer, Aud Egede-Nissen, Wilhelm Dieterle, Adolf Klein, Martin Herzberg, Robert Taube, Friedrich Kühne, Dagny Servaes, Rudolf Biebrach

**Congress Dances**
see **Der Kongress tanzt**

**Die Chronik von Grieshuus (The chronicle of Grieshus)**
Ufa, 1925
*Dir:* Arthur von Gerlach
*Scr:* Thea von Harbou, from the story by Theodor Storm
*Ad:* Robert Herlth, Walter Röhrig
*Ph:* Fritz Arno Wagner, Carl Drews, Erich Nitzschmann
*Cast:* Arthur Kraussneck, Lil Dagover, Paul Hartmann, Rudolf Rittner, Gertrud Welcker, Rudolf Forster, Gertrud Arnold, Hans Peter Peterhans, Christian Bummerstedt, Ernst Gronau, Josef Peterhans, Hermann Leftler

**Danton**
1921
*Dir:* Dimitri Buchowetzki
*Ad:* Hans Dreier
*Ph:* Arpad Viragh
*Cast:* Emil Jannings, Werner Krauss, Hilde Wörner, Eduard Winter, Maly Delschaft, Eduard von Winterstein

**Destiny** see **Der Müde Tod**

**Diary of a lost girl**
see **Tagebuch einer Verlorenen**

**Dirnentragödie (Tragedy of a street)**
Pantomim-Film, 1927
*Dir:* Bruno Rahn
*Scr:* Ruth Goetz, Leo Heller, from a play by Wilhelm Braun
*Ad:* Carl L. Kirmse
*Ph:* Guido Seeber
*Cast:* Asta Nielsen, Oskar Homolka, Hilde Jennings, Werner Pittschau, Hedwig Pauly-Winterstein

**Dr Mabuse der Spieler (Dr Mabuse the gambler)**
Ullstein-UCO Films/Ufa, 1922
*Dir:* Fritz Lang
*Scr:* Fritz Lang, Thea von Harbou, from a novel by Norbert Jacques
*Ad:* Otto Hunte, Stahl-Urach
*Ph:* Carl Hoffmann
*Cast:* Rudolf Klein-Rogge, Paul Richter, Alfred Abel, Bernhard Goetzke, Schlettow, Georg John, Aud Egede-Nissen, Gertrude Welcker, Lil Dagover, Forster Larrinaga, Paul Richter, Hans Adalbert von Schlettow, Grete Berger, Julius Falkenstein, Lydia Potechnia, Anita Berber, Paul Biensfeldt, Karl Platen, Karl Huszar, Edgar Pauly, Julius Hermann

349

**Die Dreigroschenoper (The threepenny opera)**
Warner Bros/Tobis/Nero-Film, 1931
*Dir:* G. W. Pabst
*Scr:* Leo Lania, Béla Balázs, Ladislaus Vayda, after the play by Bertolt Brecht inspired by John Gay's *The Beggars' Opera*
*Ad:* Andrei Andreiev
*Ph:* Fritz Arno Wagner
*Mus:* Kurt Weill
*Cast:* Rudolf Forster, Carola Neher, Reinhold Schünzel, Fritz Rasp, Valeska Gert, Lotte Lenya, Hermann Thimig, Ernst Busch, Wladimir Sokoloff, Paul Kemp, Gustav Püttjer, Oskar Höcker, Krafft-Raschig, Herbert Grünbaum
(*Die Dreigroschenoper* was made simultaneously in German and French versions. For the French version Solange Bussi, André Mauprey and Ninon Steinhoff worked on the scenario, and the cast was changed.)

**Emil und die Detektive (Emil and the detectives)**
Ufa, 1931
*Dir:* Gerhard Lamprecht
*Scr:* Billy Wilder, from the novel by Erich Kästner
*Ad:* W. Schlichting
*Ph:* Werner Brandes
*Mus:* Allan Gray
*Cast:* Fritz Rasp, Käthe Haack, Rolf Wenkhaus, Rudolf Bilbrach, Olga Engl, Martin Baumann, Gerhard Dammann, Rudolf Lettinger, Margarete Sachse, G. H. Schnell, and children

**Erdgeist (Earth spirit)**
Leopold Jessner-Film, 1923
*Dir:* Leopold Jessner
*Scr:* Carl Mayer
*Cast:* Asta Nielsen, Rudolf Forster, Albert Bassermann, Carl Ebert, Alexander Granach, Gustav Rickelt, Julius Falkenstein, Heinrich George, Erwin Biswanger

**Faust**
Ufa, 1926
*Dir:* F. W. Murnau
*Scr:* Hans Kyser, from Goethe
*Ad:* Robert Herlth, Walter Röhrig
*Ph:* Carl Hoffmann
*Cast:* Gösta Ekman, Camilla Horn, Emil Jannings, Frieda Richard, Wilhelm Dieterle, Yvette Guilbert, Hanna Ralph, Werner Fütterer, Eric Barclay, Hans Rameau, Hertha von Walther, Emmy Wyda

**Die Frau im Mond (Woman on the moon)**
Fritz Lang Film/Ufa, 1929
*Dir:* Fritz Lang
*Scr:* Thea von Harbou
*Ad:* Otto Hunte, Emil Hasler, Karl Völlbrecht
*Ph:* Curt Courant, Otto Kanturek, Konstantin Tschetwerikoff, Oskar Fischinger

*Cast:* Gerda Maurus, Willy Fritsch, Klaus Pohl, Gustav von Wangenheim, Gustl Stark-Gstettenbauer, Fritz Rasp, Tilla Durieux, Hermann Vallentin, Max Zilzer, Mahmud Terja Bey, Borwin Walth, Margarethe Kupfer, Max Maximilian, Alexa von Porembsky, Gerhard Dammann, Heinrich Gotho, Karl Platen, Alfred Loretto, Edgar Pauly, Julius E. Herrmann

**Die freudlose Gasse (The joyless street)**
Sofar-Film-Produktion, 1925
*Dir:* G. W. Pabst
*Scr:* Willy Haas, from a novel by Hugo Bettauer
*Ad:* Hans Sohnle, Otto Erdman
*Ph:* Guido Seeber, Curt Oertel, Robert Lach
*Cast:* Asta Nielsen, Greta Garbo, Werner Krauss, Einar Hanson, Karl Etlinger, Ilka Grüning, Jaro Fürth, Gräfin Agnes Esterhazy, Alexander Murski, Henry Stuart, Robert Garrison, Gregori Chmara, Hertha von Walther, Max Kohlhase, Sylvia Torf, Valeska Gert, Tamara, Kl. Loni Nest, Mario Cusmich, Gräfin Tolstoi, Frau Markstein, Otto Reinwald, Raskatoff, Krafft-Raschig

**Geheimnisse einer Seele (Secrets of a soul)**
Neumann-Film-Produktion, 1926
*Dir:* G. W. Pabst
*Scr:* Colin Ross, Hans Neumann
*Ad:* Ernö Metzner
*Ph:* Guido Seeber, Curt Oertel, Robert Lach
*Cast:* Werner Krauss, Ruth Weyher, Ilka Grüning, Jack Trevor, Pawel Pawlow, Hertha von Walther, Renata Brausewetter

**Genuine**
Cecla-Bioscop, 1920
*Dir:* Robert Wiene
*Scr:* Carl Mayer
*Ad:* César Klein
*Ph:* Willy Hameister
*Cast:* Fern Andra, Harald Paulsen, Ernst Gronau, John Gottoht, Hans Heinz von Twardowski

**Der Golem (The golem)**
Bioscop, 1914
*Dir:* Paul Wegener, Henrik Galeen
*Ad:* Robert A. Dietrich, Rochus Gliese
*Ph:* Guido Seeber
*Cast:* Paul Wegener, Lyda Salmonova, Henrik Galeen, Carl Ebert

**Der Golem: Wie er in die Welt kam (The golem: how he came into the world)**
Ufa, 1920
*Dir:* Paul Wegener, Carl Boese
*Scr:* Paul Wegener, Henrik Galeen
*Ad:* Hans Poelzig
*Cost:* Rochus Gliese
*Ph:* Karl Freund
*Cast:* Paul Wegener, Albert Steinrück,

Ernst Deutsch, Lyda Salmonova, Lothar Müthel, Otto Gebühr, Grete Schröder, Hans Sturm, Max Kronert, Dora Paetzold

**The Hands of Orlac**
see **Orlacs Hände**

**Das Haus ohne Tür (The house without a door)**
1914
*Dir:* Stellan Rye
*Ph:* Guido Seeber
*Cast:* Theodor Loos

**Heimkehr (Homecoming)**
Joe May-Film/Ufa, 1928
*Dir:* Joe May
*Scr:* Fred Majo, Dr Fritz Wendhausen, from a story by Leonhard Frank
*Ad:* Julius von Borsody, Arthur Schwarz
*Ph:* Günther Rittau
*Cast:* Lars Hanson, Dita Parlo, Gustav Fröhlich, Theodor Loos, Philipp Manning

**Die Herrin von Atlantis (Mistress of Atlantis)**
Nero-Film, 1932
*Dir:* G. W. Pabst
*Scr:* Ladislaus Vayda, Hermann Oberländer from Pierre Benoit's novel *Atlantide*
*Ph:* Eugen Schüfftan, Ernst Koerner
*Mus:* Wolfgang Zeller
*Cast:* Brigitte Helm, Gustav Diessl, Tela Tschai, Heinz Klingenberg, Wladimir Sokoloff, Mathias Wieman, Georges Toureil, Florelle

**Hintertreppe (Backstairs)**
1921
*Dir:* Leopold Jessner, assisted by Paul Leni
*Scr:* Carl Mayer
*Ad:* Paul Leni
*Ph:* Karl Hasselmann, Willy Hameister
*Cast:* Fritz Kortner, Henny Porten, Wilhelm Dieterle

**Homunculus**
Bioscop, 1916. A six-part serial
*Dir:* Otto Rippert
*Scr:* Otto Rippert, Robert Neuss
*Ph:* Carl Hoffmann
*Cast:* Olaf Fønss, Frederich Kuhn, Theodor Loos, Mechtild Their, Maria Carmi, Gustav Kühne, Aud Egede-Nissen

**Hungarian rhapsody**
see **Ungarische Rhapsodie**

**Das Indische Grabmal (The Indian tomb)**
Joe May Company-Efa, 1921; originally in two parts
*Dir:* Joe May
*Scr:* Fritz Lang, Thea von Harbou, from Thea von Harbou's novel
*Ad:* Martin Jacoby-Boy, Otto Hunte
*Cast:* Lya de Putti, Olaf Fønss, Conrad Veidt, Erna Morena, Mia May, Bernhard Goetzke, Paul Richter

**I.N.R.I.**
Neumann-Produktion, 1923
*Dir:* Robert Wiene
*Scr:* Robert Wiene
*Ad:* Ernö Metzner
*Ph:* Axel Graatkjär, Reimar Kuntze,
  Ludwig Lippert
*Cast:* Gregori Chmara, Henny Porten,
Asta Nielsen, Werner Krauss, Theodor
Becker, Emanuel Reicher, Robert Taube,
Bruno Ziener, Hans Heinrich von
Twardowski, Emil Lind, Max Kronert,
H. Magnus, Walter Neumann, Guido
Herzfeld, Wilhelm Nagel, Les Reuss,
Eduard Kandl, Walter Werner, Alexander
Granach, Paul Graetz, Mathilde Sussin,
Maria Kryschanowskaja, Erwin Kalser,
Elsa Wagner, Erich Walter, Ernst
Dernburg, Gustav Oberg, Jaro Fürth,
Pawel Pawlow, Rose Veldtkirch

**Jenseits der Strasse** ( US title:
**Harbour drift)**
Prometheus Film, 1929
*Dir:* Leo Mittler
*Scr:* Jan Fethke, Willy Döll
*Ad:* Robert Scharfenberg, Karl Haacker
*Ph:* Friedel Behn-Grund
*Cast:* Lissi Arna, Paul Rehkopf, Fritz
Genschow, Siegfried Arno, Friedrich
Gnass, Margarete Kupfer

**The joyless street**
see **Die freudlose Gasse**

**Das Kabinett des Dr Caligari**
**(The Cabinet of Dr Caligari)**
Decla-Bioscop, 1919
*Dir:* Robert Wiene
*Scr:* Carl Mayer, Hans Janowitz
*Ad:* Hermann Warm, Walter Reimann,
  Walter Röhrig
*Ph:* Willy Hameister
*Cast:* Werner Krauss, Conrad Veidt,
Friedrich Feher, Lil Dagover, Hans Heinz
von Twardowski, Rudolf Klein-Rogge,
Rudolf Lettinger

**Kameradschaft (Comradeship)**
Nero-Film, 1931
*Dir:* G. W. Pabst
*Scr:* Ladislaus Vayda, Karl Otten, Peter
  Martin Lampel
*Ad:* Ernö Metzner, Karl Vollbrecht
*Ph:* Fritz Arno Wagner, Robert Baberske
*Cast:* Alexander Granach, Fritz Kampers,
Ernst Busch, Elisabeth Wendt, Gustav
Püttjer, Oskar Höcker, Daniel Mendaille,
Georges Charlia, Andrée Ducret, Alex
Bernard, Pierre Louis, Heléna Manson
(*Kameradschaft* was made simultaneously
in German and French versions. For the
French version the cast was altered.)

**Der Kongress tanzt (Congress**
**dances)**
Ufa, 1931
*Dir:* Erich Charell
*Scr:* Norbert Falk, Robert Liebmann
*Ad:* Ernst Stern

*Ph:* Karl Hoffmann
*Mus:* Werner R. Heymann
*Cast:* Lilian Harvey, Willy Fritsch, Otto
Walburg, Conrad Veidt, Carl Heinz
Schroth, Lil Dagover, Alfred Abel,
Eugen Rex, Alfred Gerasch, Adele
Sandrock, Margarete Kupfer, Julius
Falkenstein, Max Gülstorff, Paul Hörbiger,
Trude Brionne, Franz Nicklisch, Hermann
Blass, Sergius Sax

**Kriemhild's Rache**
see **Die Nibelungen**

**Kuhle Wampe (**US title:
**Whither Germany?)**
Prometheus/Praesens, 1932
*Dir:* Slatan Dudow
*Scr:* Bertolt Brecht, Ernst Ottwald
*Ad:* Robert Scharffenberg, Karl Haaker
*Ph:* Günther Krampf
*Mus:* Hanns Eisler, Josef Schmid
*Cast:* Hertha Thiele, Ernst Busch, Martha
Wolter, Adolf Fischer, Lili Schönborn,
Max Sablotzki, Alfred Schaefer, Gerhard
Bienert, Martha Burchardi, Carl Heinz
Charell, Karl Dahmen, Fritz Erpenbeck,
Josef Hanoszek, Richard Pilgert, Hugo
Werner-Kahle, Hermann Krehan, Paul
Kretzburg, Anna Müller-Lincke, Rudolf
Pehls, Erich Peters, Olly Rummel, Willi
Schur, Martha Seemann, Hans Stern,
Karl Wagner

**Der Letzte Mann (**lit. **The last**
**man,** usually known as **The**
**last laugh)**
Ufa, 1924
*Dir:* F. W. Murnau
*Scr:* Carl Mayer
*Ad:* Robert Herlth, Walter Röhrig
*Ph:* Karl Freund (assistant: Robert
  Baberske)
*Cast:* Emil Jannings, Hermann Vallentin,
Maly Delschaft, Emilie Kurz, Georg John,
Max Hiller, Hans Unterkircher, Olaf
Storm, Erich Schönfelder, Neumann-
Schüler, Emmy Wyda

**Die Liebe der Jeanne Ney (The**
**Love of Jeanne Ney)**
Ufa, 1927
*Dir:* G. W. Pabst
*Scr:* Ilya Ehrenburg, Ladislaus Vayda,
  from the novel by Ehrenburg
*Ad:* Otto Hunte
*Ph:* Fritz Arno Wagner, Walter Robert
  Lach
*Cast:* Edith Jehanne, Brigitte Helm,
Hertha von Walther, Uno Henning,
Fritz Rasp, Adolf Edgar Licho, Eugen
Jensen, Hans Jaray, Wladimir Sokoloff,
Siegfried Arno, Jack Trevor, Mammey
Terja-Basa, Josefine Dora

**Lukrezia Borgia**
1922
*Dir:* Richard Oswald
*Ad:* Robert Neppach
*Ph:* Karl Freund

*Cast:* Liane Haid, Conrad Veidt, Albert
Bassermann, Heinrich George, Lothar
Müthel, Paul Wegener, Wilhelm Dieterle

**M**
Nero-Film, 1931
*Dir:* Fritz Lang
*Scr:* Thea von Harbou
*Ad:* Otto Hasler
*Ph:* Fritz Arno Wagner
*Cast:* Peter Lorre, Ellen Widman, Inge
Landgut, Gustaf Gründgens, Friedrich
Gnass, Fritz Odemar, Paul Kemp, Theo
Lingen, Ernst Stahl-Nachbaur, Franz
Stein, Otto Wernicke, Theodor Loos,
Georg John, Rudolf Blümner, Karl Platen,
Gerhard Bienert, Rosa Valetti, Hertha
von Walther, Carl Balhaus, Josef Dahmen,
Else Ehser, J. A. Eckhoff, Karl Elzer, Ilse
Fürstenberg, Heinrich Gotho, Günther
Hadank, Albert Hörmann, Albert
Karchow, Werner Kepich, Rose
Lichtenstein, Lotte Löbinger, Sigurd
Lohde, Paul Mederow, Margarete Melzer,
Trude Moos, Hadrian M. Netto, Maya
Norden, Edgar Pauly, Klaus Pohl, Franz
Poland, Paul Rehkopf, Hans Ritter,
Leonard Steckel, Wolf Trutz, Borwin
Walth, Bruno Ziener

**Madame Dubarry**
Union Film-Ufa, 1919
*Dir:* Ernst Lubitsch
*Scr:* Hans Kraly, Fred Orbing
*Ad:* Karl Machus, Kurt Richter
*Cost:* Walter Reimann
*Ph:* Theodor Sparkuhl
*Cast:* Pola Negri, Emil Jannings, Eduard
von Winterstein, Reinhold Schünzel,
Harry Liedtke, Karl Platen, Elsa Berna,
Frederich Immler

**Mädchen in Uniform (Girls in**
**uniform)**
Deutsche Film, 1931
*Dir:* Leontine Sagan, under the
  supervision of Carl Froelich
*Scr:* Christa Winslow, F. D. Andam
*Ad:* Fritz Maurischat
*Ph:* Reimar Kuntze, Franz Weihmayr
*Mus:* Hansom Milde-Meissner
*Cast:* Dorothea Wieck, Hertha Thiele,
Ellen Schwanneke, Emilie Unda, Hedwig
Schlichter, Gertrud de Lalsky, Marte Hein,
Lene Berdolt, Lisi Scheerbach, Margory
Bodker, Erika Mann, Else Ehser, Ilse
Winter, Charlotte Witthauer, Erika-
Margot Biebrach, Margarete Reschke,
Annemarie von Rochhausen, Ilse Vigdor,
Barbara Pirk, Dora Thalmer

**Der Mann, der den Mord**
**beging (The man who murdered)**
Terra-Film, 1931
*Dir:* Kurt Bernhardt
*Scr:* Heinz Goldberg, Hermann
  Kosterlitz, Harry Kahn
*Ad:* Hermann Warm, Heinrich Richter
*Ph:* Curt Courant
*Mus:* Hans J. Salter

*Cast:* Conrad Veidt, Trude von Molo, Heinrich George, Friedl Haerlin, Frida Richard, Friedrich Kayssler, Gregori Chmara, Erich Ponto, Hans Joachim Moebis, Yvette Rodin

## Manon Lescaut
Ufa, 1925/26
*Dir:* Arthur Robison
*Scr:* Arthur Robison, after the novel by the Abbé Prevost
*Ad:* Paul Leni
*Ph:* Theodor Sparkuhl
*Cast:* Lya de Putti, Wladimir Gaidarow, Eduard Rothauser, Fritz Greiner, Hubert von Meyerinck, Frieda Richard, Emilie Jurz, Lydia Potechina, Theodor Loos, Siegfried Arno, Trude Hesterberg, Marlene Dietrich, Olga Engl, Karl Harbacher

## Die Melodie der Welt (World melody)
Tonbild Syndikat, 1929
*Dir:* Walter Ruttmann
*Scr:* Walter Ruttmann
*Ph:* Reimar Kuntze, Wilhelm Lehne, Rudolph Rathmann, Paul Holzki
*Mus:* Wolfgang Zeller

## Menschen am Sonntag (People on Sunday)
Filmstudio 1929, 1929
*Dir:* Robert Siodmak, Edgar Ulmer
*Scr:* Billy Wilder, from an idea by Kurt Siodmak
*Ph:* Eugen Schüfftan
*Cast:* Brigitte Borchert, Christl Ehlers, Annie Schreyer, Wolfgang von Waltershausen, Erwin Splettsösser

## Metropolis
Ufa, 1926
*Dir:* Fritz Lang
*Scr:* Thea von Harbou, Fritz Lang
*Ad:* Otto Hunte, Erich Kellethut, Karl Vollbrecht
*Cost:* Anne Willkomm (sculpture, Walter Schulze-Mittendorf)
*Ph:* Karl Freund, Günther Rittau (special effects, Eugen Schüfftan)
*Cast:* Brigitte Helm, Alfred Abel, Gustav Fröhlich, Rudolf Klein-Rogge, Fritz Rasp, Theodor Loos, Erwin Biswanger, Heinrich George, Olaf Storm, Hanns Leo Reich, Heinrich Gotho, Margarete Lanner, Max Dietze, Georg John, Walter Kuhle, Arthur Reinhard, Erwin Vater, Grete Berger, Olly Böheim, Ellen Frey, Lisa Gray, Rose Liechtenstein, Helene Weigel, Beatrice Garga, Anny Hintze, Helen von Münchsfen, Hilde Woitscheff, Fritz Alberti

## Monna Vanna
1922
*Dir:* Richard Eichberg
*Ad:* Kurt Richter
*Ph:* Werner Geofred Lemki, Max Lutze
*Cast:* Lee Parry, Paul Wegener, Albert Steinrück, Lyda Salmonova

## Der Müde Tod (lit. The weary death, usually known as Destiny, sometimes as The three lights or Between worlds)
Decla-Bioscop, 1921
*Dir:* Fritz Lang
*Scr:* Fritz Lang, Thea von Harbou
*Ad:* Robert Herlth, Walter Röhrig, Hermann Warm
*Ph:* Fritz Arno Wagner, Erich Neitzschmann, Hermann Salfrank
*Cast:* Bernhard Goetzke, Lil Dagover, Walter Janssen, Rudolf Klein-Rogge, Georg John, Eduard von Winterstein, Max Adalbert, Paul Biensfeldt, Karl Huszar, Hermann Valentin, Erika Unruh, Wilhelm Diegelmann, Lothar Müthel, Hermann Picha, Hans Sternberg

## Mutter Krausens Fahrt ins Glück (Mother Krausen's journey to happiness)
Prometheus Film, 1929
*Dir:* Piel Jutzi
*Scr:* Dr Döll, Jan Fethke
*Ad:* Robert Scharfenberg, Karl Haacker
*Ph:* Piel Jutzi
*Cast:* Alexandra Schmitt, Holmer Zimmermann, Ilse Trantschoed, Gerhard Bienert, Vera Sacharowa, Friedrich Gnass

## Mutter und Kind (Mother and child)
Froelich-Film, 1924
*Dir:* Carl Froelich
*Scr:* Robert Liebmann, Walter Supper, from Friedrich Hebbel
*Ad:* Hans Sohnle, Otto Erdmann
*Ph:* Gustave Preiss, Willy Gaebel
*Cast:* Henny Porten, Friedrich Kayssler, Erna Morena, Willy Fritsch, Wilhelm Diegelmann, Arnold Risck, Hanne Brinkmann-Schünzel, Wilhelm Dieterle, Hans Land, Loni Nest

## Narkose (Narcosis)
G.P. Films, 1929
*Dir:* Alfred Abel
*Scr:* Béla Balázs, from a story by Stefan Zweig
*Ad:* Julius von Borsody, Willy Brummer
*Ph:* Günther Krampf
*Cast:* Renée Héribel, Alfred Abel, Jack Trevor, Fritz Alberti, Gustav Rickelt, Karl Platen

## Die Nibelungen
*Part I,* Siegfried
1922–24;
*Part II,* Kriemhilds Rache (The vengeance of Kriemhild)
1923–24
Decla-Bioscop
*Dir:* Fritz Lang
*Scr:* Thea von Harbou
*Ad:* Otto Hunte, Karl Vollbrecht, Erich Kettelhut
*Cost:* Paul Gerd Gudesian, Anne Willkomm
*Ph:* Carl Hoffmann, Günther Rittau
*Cast:* Paul Richter, Margarete Schön,

Hanna Ralph, Gertrud Arnold, Theodor Loos, Hans Carl Müller, Erwin Biswanger, Bernhard Goetzke, Hans Adalbert Schlettow, Hardy von François, Georg John, Frieda Richard, Georg Jurowski, Iris Roberts, Rudolf Klein-Rogge, Hubert Heinrich, Rudolf Rittner, Fritz Alberti, Georg August Koch, Grete Berger, Ernst Legal, Rose Liechtenstein

## Nju
Rimax-Film, 1924
*Dir:* Paul Czinner
*Scr:* Paul Czinner, from a play by Ossip Dymow
*Ad:* Paul Rieth, Gottlieb Hesch
*Ph:* Axel Graatkjär, Reimar Kuntze
*Cast:* Elisabeth Bergner, Emil Jannings, Conrad Veidt, Migo Bard, Nile Edwall, Anne Röttgen, Margarete Kupfer, Karl Platen, Max Kronert, Walter Werner, Grete Lund, Maria Foreseu, Fritz Ley

## Nosferatu, eine Symphonie des Grauens (Nosferatu, a symphony of horror)
Prana, 1922
*Dir:* F. W. Murnau
*Scr:* Henrik Galeen, from Bram Stoker's novel *Dracula*
*Ad:* Albin Grau
*Ph:* Fritz Arno Wagner
*Cast:* Max Schreck, Gustav von Wangenheim, Alexander Granach, Grete Schröder, Ruth Landschoff, G. H. Schnell, John Gottowt, Gustav Botz, Max Nemetz, Wolfgang Heinz, Albert Venohr, Herzfeld, Hardy von François, Heinrich Witte

## Orlacs Hände (The hands of Orlac)
Pan-Film (Austria), 1924
*Dir:* Robert Wiene
*Scr:* Ludwig Nerz, from the novel by Maurice Renard
*Ad:* Stefan Wessely
*Ph:* Günther Krampf, Hans Andreschin
*Cast:* Conrad Veidt, Alexandra Sorina, Carmen Cartelleri, Fritz Kortner

## Othello
1922
*Dir:* Dimitri Buchowetzki
*Ad:* Karl Machus
*Ph:* Karl Hasselmann
*Cast:* Emil Jannings, Werner Krauss, J. von Lenkeffy, Lya de Putti

## Pandora's Box
see Die Büchse der Pandora

## People on Sunday
see Menschen am Sonntag

## Peter der Grosse (Peter the Great)
1923
*Dir:* Dimitri Buchowerzki
*Ad:* Hans Dreier
*Ph:* Curt Courant
*Cast:* Emil Jannings

352

**Phantom**
Uco-Becla Bioscop, 1922
*Dir:* F. W. Murnau
*Scr:* Thea von Harbou, Hans Heinrich
  von Twardowski, from a novel by
  Gerhart Hauptmann
*Ad:* Hermann Warm, Erich Czerwonski
*Ph:* Axel Graatkjär, Theophan Ouchakoff
*Cost:* Vally Reinecke
*Cast:* Alfred Abel, Frieda Richard, Aud
Egede-Nissen, Hans Heinrich von
Twardowski, Karl Ettlinger, Lil Dagover,
Grete Berger, Anton Edthofer, Ilka
Grüning, Lya de Putti, Adolf Klein, Olga
Engl, Heinrich Witte

**Raskolnikow**
Lionardi-Film der Neumann Produktion,
1923
*Dir:* Robert Wiene
*Scr:* Robert Wiene, from Dostoevsky's
  *Crime and Punishment*
*Ad:* Andrei Andreiev
*Ph:* Willy Goldberger
*Cast:* Gregori Chmara, Maria
Krishanovskaja, Pawel Pawloff, Michael
Tarschanow, Maria Germanowa,
Elisaweta Skulskaja

**Der Rattenfänger von Hameln
(The pied piper of Hamelin)**
1918(?)
*Dir:* Paul Wegener
*Ad:* Rochus Gliese
*Ph:* Guido Seeber(?)
*Cast:* Paul Wegener, Lyda Salmonova,
Wilhelm Diegelmann, Jakob Tiedtke

**Revolt of the fishermen**
see **Vostaniye rybakov**

**Rosenmontag (Rose Monday,**
i.e. the Monday before Lent**)**
Ufa, 1930
*Dir:* Hans Steinhoff
*Scr:* Ludwig A. Wohl, Philipp Lothar
  Mayring
*Ph:* Werner Brandes
*Mus:* Willy Schmidt-Gentner
*Cast:* Lien Deyers, Mathias Wieman,
Eduard von Winterstein, Karl Ludwig
Diehl, Peter Voss, Harry Halm, Lutz
Altschul, Hubert von Meyerinck, Fritz
Alberti, Hanna Waag, Gertrud Arnold,
Lucie Enler, Lotte Spira, Heinz John,
Paul Heidemann, Erich Kestin, Karl
Platen, Alexander Sascha

**Schatten (Warning shadows)**
Pan-Film der Dafu-Film-Verleih, 1923
*Dir:* Arthur Robison
*Scr:* Rudolf Schneider, Arthur Robison
*Ad:* Albin Grau
*Ph:* Fritz Arno Wagner
*Cast:* Fritz Kortner, Ruth Weyher,
Gustav von Wangeheim, Alexander
Granach, Eugen Rex, Max Gülstorff,
Ferdinand von Alten, Fritz Rasp, Karl
Platen, Lilli Herder

**Der Schatz (The treasure)**
Froelich-Film, 1923
*Dir:* G. W. Pabst
*Scr:* Willy Hennings, G. W. Pabst, after
  a story by Rudolf Häns Bartsch
*Ad:* Robert Herlth, Walter Röhrig
*Ph:* Otto Tober
*Cast:* Albert Steinrück, Ilka Grüning,
Lucie Mannheim, Werner Krauss, Hans
Brausewetter

**Scherben (Shattered fragments)**
1921
*Dir:* Lupu Pick
*Scr:* Carl Mayer
*Ph:* Friedrich Weimann
*Cast:* Werner Krauss, Edith Posca, Paul
Otto

**Secrets of a Soul**
see **Geheimnisse einer Seele**

**Siegfried** see **Die Nibelungen**

**So Ist das Leben (Such is life)**
1929; made in Prague
*Dir:* Carl Junghans
*Ad:* Ernst Meiwers
*Ph:* Laszlo Schäffer
*Cast:* Vera Baranovskaya, Valeska Gert

**Die Spinnen (The spiders)**
*In two parts:* (1) **Der Goldene See
(The Golden lake),**
  (2) **Das Brillantenschiff (The
diamond ship)**
Decla-Bioscop, 1919
*Dir:* Fritz Lang
*Scr:* Fritz Lang
*Ad:* Otto Hunte, Carl Hirmse, Hermann
  Warm, Heinrich Umlauff
*Ph:* (1) Emil Schünemann, (2) Karl Freund
*Cast:* Carl de Vogt, Ressel Orla, Lil
Dagover, Georg John, Paul Morgan,
Bruno Lettinger, Edgar Pauly, Paul
Biensfeldt, Friedrich Kühne, Meinhardt
Maur, Gilda Langer

**Spione (Spies)**
Fritz Lang-Film/Ufa, 1928
*Dir:* Fritz Lang
*Scr:* Thea von Harbou
*Ad:* Otto Hunte, Karl Vollbrecht
*Ph:* Fritz Arno Wagner
*Cast:* Lien Deyers, Lupu Pick, Hertha
von Walther, Gerda Maurus, Rudolf
Klein-Rogge, Julius Falkenstein, Willy
Fritsch, Paul Hörbiger, Georg John,
Louis Ralph, Fritz Rasp, Paul Rehkopf,
Craighall Sherry, Hermann Vallentin

**Die Strasse (The street)**
Stern Film, 1923
*Dir:* Karl Grune
*Scr:* Karl Grune, Julius Urgiss, from a
  treatment by Carl Mayer
*Ad:* Karl Görge, Ludwig Meidner
*Ph:* Karl Hasselmann
*Cast:* Eugen Klöpfer, Lucie Höflich, Aud
Egede-Nissen, Leonhard Haskel, Anton
Edthofer, Hans Trautner, Max Schreck

**Der Student von Prag (The
student of Prague)**
Bioscop, 1913
*Dir:* Stellan Rye
*Scr:* Hanns Heinz Ewers
*Ad:* Robert A. Dietrich, Kurt Richter
*Ph:* Guido Seeber
*Cast:* Paul Wegener, John Cottowt, Grete
Berger, Lyda Salmonova, Lothar Körner

**Der Student von Prag (The
student of Prague)**
H. R. Sokal-Film, 1926
*Dir:* Henrik Galeen
*Scr:* Henrik Galeen, Hanns Heinz Ewers
*Ad:* Hermann Warm
*Ph:* Günther Krampf, Erich Nitzschmann
*Cast:* Conrad Veidt, Werner Krauss,
Agnes Esterhazy, Elizza La Porta,
Ferdinand von Alten, Fritz Alberti,
Sylvia Torf, Erich Kober, Max
Maximilian, Marian Alma

**Sumurun**
Union Film-Ufa, 1920
*Dir:* Ernst Lubitsch
*Scr:* Hans Kraly, after the Max
  Reinhardt pantomime by
  Friedrich Freksa and Viktor
  Hollander
*Ad:* Kurt Richter, Ernö Metzner
*Cost:* Ali Hubert
*Ph:* Theodor Sparkuhl
*Cast:* Ernst Lubitsch, Pola Negri, Paul
Wegener, Aud Egede-Nissen, Jenny
Hasselquist, Carl Clewing, Harry Liedtke,
Jakob Tiedtke, Paul Biensfeldt, Margarete
Kupfer

**Sylvester**
Rex-Film, 1923
*Dir:* Lupu Pick
*Scr:* Carl Mayer
*Ad:* Robert A. Dietrich, from an outline
  by Klaus Richter
*Ph:* Karl Hasselmann (interiors), Guido
  Seeber (street-scenes)
*Cast:* Edith Posca, Eugen Klöpfer, Frieda
Richard, Karl Harbacher, Julius E.
Herrmann, Rudolf Blümner

**Tagebuch einer Verlorenen
(Diary of a lost girl)**
G. W. Pabst Film, 1929
*Dir:* G. W. Pabst
*Scr:* Rudolf Leonhardt, from a novel by
  Margarete Böhme
*Ad:* Ernö Metzer, Emil Hasler
*Ph:* Sepp Allgeier
*Cast:* Louise Brooks, Fritz Rasp, Josef
Rovensky, Sybille Schmitz, Franziska
Kinz, André Roanne, Vera Pawlowa,
Arnold Korff, Andrews Engelmann,
Valeska Gert, Edith Meinhard, Siegfried
Arno, Kurt Gerron, Jaro Fürth, Sylvia
Torf, M. Kassaskaja, Speedy Schlichter,
Emmy Wyda, Hans Casparius, Michael
von Newlinski

353

**Tartüff (Tartuffe)**
Ufa, 1925
Dir: F. W. Murnau
Scr: Carl Mayer, after Molière
Ad: Robert Herlth, Walter Röhrig
Ph: Karl Freund
Cast: Emil Jannings, Lil Dagover,
Werner Krauss, Lucie Höflich, André
Mattoni, Rosa Valetti, Hermann Picha

**Das Testament des Dr Mabuse
(The testament of Dr Mabuse)**
Nero-Film, 1933
Dir: Fritz Lang
Scr: Thea von Harbou
Ad: Emil Hasler, Karl Vollbrecht
Ph: Fritz Arno Wagner
Mus: Hans Erdmann
Cast: Rudolf Klein-Rogge, Gustav Diessl,
Rudolf Schündler, Oskar Hökker, Theo
Lingen, Camilla Spira, Paul Henckels,
Otto Wernikke, Theodor Loos, Hadrian
M. Netto, Paul Bernd, Henry Pless,
A. E. Licho, Oskar Beregi, Wera Liessem,
Karl Meixner, Klaus Pohl, Gerhard
Bienert, Josef Dahmen, Georg John, Karl
Platen, Paul Rehkopf, Franz Stein,
Ludwig Stoessel, Eduard Wesener, Bruno
Ziener, Heinrich Gotho, Michael von
Newlinski, Anna Goltz, Heinrich Gretler

**The Threepenny Opera**
see **Die Dreigroschenoper**

**Torgus**
1920
Dir: Hans Kobe
Cast: Eugen Klöpfer, Herta Russ-
Schillinger, Herta Arnold

**Der träumende Mund (The
dreaming mouth; Mélo)**
Pathe/Matador, 1932
Dir: Paul Czinner
Scr: Paul Czinner, Carl Mayer from
Henri Bernstein's play Mélo
Ad: Robert Scharffenberg, Karl Haaker
Ph: Jules Krueger
Cast: Elisabeth Bergner, Rudolf Forster,
Anton Edthofer, Margarete Hruby, Jaro
Furth, Peter Kröger, Karl Hannemann,
Ernst Stahl-Nachbaur, Werner Pledath,
Gustav Püttjer, Willi Schur
(Der träumende Mund was made
simultaneously in German and French
versions.)

**Überfall (Accident)**
1928
Dir: Ernö Metzner
Ph: Ernö Metzner
Cast: Kurt Gerron, Hans Casparius

**Ungarische Rhapsodie
(Hungarian rhapsody)**
Ufa, 1928
Dir: Hanns Schwarz
Scr: Fred Majo, Hans Skekely
Ad: Erich Kettelhut
Ph: Carl Hoffmann

Cast: Willy Fritsch, Dita Parlo, Lil
Dagover, Fritz Greiner, Gisela Bathory,
Erich Kaiser-Titz, Leopold Kramer,
Andor Heltai, Harry Hardt, Oswaldo
Valenti

**Vanina**
1922
Dir: Arthur von Gerlach
Scr: Carl Mayer
Ad: Walter Reimann
Ph: F. Fuglsang
Cast: Asta Nielsen, Paul Wegener, Paul
Hartmann

**Varieté (Variety)**
Ufa, 1925
Dir: E. A. Dupont
Scr: E. A. Dupont, based on a novel by
Friedrich Hollaender
Ad: O. F. Werndorff
Ph: Karl Freund
Cast: Emil Jannings, Maly Delschaft,
Lya de Putti, Warwick Ward, Alice
Hechy, Georg John, Kurt Gerron, Paul
Rehkopf, Charles Lincoln

**Der Verlorene Schuh
(Cinderella)**
Decla-Bioscop, 1923
Dir: Ludwig Berger
Scr: Ludwig Berger
Ad: Rudolf Bamberger
Ph: Günther Krampf
Cast: Helga Thomas, Paul Hartmann,
Mady Christians, Lucie Höflich, Olga
Tschechowa, Frieda Richard, Hermann
Thimig, Leonhard Haskel, Max Gülstorff,
Paula Conrad-Schlenther, Emilie Kurz,
Werner Hollmann, Gertrud Eysoldt,
Georg John, Karl Eichholz, Edyth Edwards

**Von Morgens bis Mitternachts
(From morn to midnight)**
1920
Dir: Karl Heinz Martin
Scr: Karl Hainz Martin, Herbert Juttke,
from a play by Georg Kaiser
Ad: Robert Neppach
Ph: Carl Hoffmann
Cast: Ernst Deutsch, Roma Bahn, Erna
Morena, Elsa Wagner, Frieda Richard,
Hugo Döblin

**Vostaniye rybakov (Revolt of
the fishermen)**
Mezhrabpomfilm, 1934
Dir: Erwin Piscator
Scr: Georgy Grebner, from a novel by
Anna Seghers
Ad: Vladimir Kaplunovsky
Ph: Pyotr Yermolov, M. Kirillov
Mus: F. Sabo, V. Ferre, N. Chemberzhi
Cast: Alexei Diky, Emma Tsesarskaya,
Vera Yanukova

**Das Wachsfigurenkabinett
(Waxworks)**
Neptun-Film, 1924
Dir: Paul Leni

Scr: Henrik Galeen
Ad: Paul Leni, Ernst Stern
Ph: Helmar Lerski
Cast: Emil Jannings, Conrad Veidt,
Werner Krauss, Wilhelm Dieterle, Olga
Belajeff, John Gottowt, Ernst Legal,
Georg John

**Warning shadows** see **Schatten**

**Die Weber (The Weavers)**
Friedrich Zelnik Film, 1927
Dir: Friedrich Zelnik
Scr: Fanny Carlsen, Willy Haas
Ad: Andrei Andreiv
Ph: Frederik Fuglsang, Friedrich
Weinmann
Cast: Paul Wegener Dagny Servaes,
Wilhelm Dieterle, Theodor Loos,
Valeska Stock, Hermann Picha, Hertha
von Walther, Camilla von Hollay,
Arthur Kraussneck, Hans Heinrich von
Twardowski, Georg John, Georg
Burghardt, Hanne Brinkmann, Julius
Brandt, Emil Lind, Hans Sternberg,
Emil Birron, Willy Kruszinski, Georg Gartz

**Das Weib des Pharao (Pharaoh's
wife)**
Efa-Ufa/Ernst Lubitsch Film, 1921
Dir: Ernst Lubitsch
Scr: Norbert Falk, Hans Kräly
Ad: Ernst Stern, Ernö Metzner, Kurt
Richter
Cost: Abi Hubert
Ph: Theodor Sparkuhl, Alfred Hansen
Cast: Paul Wegener, Dagny Servaes,
Albert Bassermann, Harry Liedtke, Emil
Jannings, Lyda Salmonova, Paul
Biensfeldt, Friedrich Kühne, Mady
Christians, Tina Dietrich

**Die Weisse Hölle von Piz Palü
(The white hell of Piz Palu)**
H. R. Sokal-Film, 1929
Dir: Arnold Fanck, G. W. Pabst
Scr: Arnold Fanck, Ladislaus Vayda
Ad: Ernö Metzner
Ph: Sepp Allgeier, Richard Angst,
Hans Schneeberger
Cast: Leni Riefenstahl, Gustav Diessl,
Ernst Petersen, Ernst Udet, Mizzi Götzel,
Otto Spring

**Westfront 1918**
Nero Film, 1930
Dir: G. W. Pabst
Scr: Ladislaus Vayda, Peter Martin
Lampel, after a novel Vier von der
Infanterie by Ernst Johannsen
Ad: Ernö Metzner
Ph: Fritz Arno Wagner, Charles
Métain
Cast: Fritz Kampers, Gustav Diessl, Hans
Joachim Moebis, Claus Clausen, Gustav
Püttjer, Jackie Monnier, Hanna Hoessrich,
Else Heller, Carl Balhaus, Aribert Mog,
André Saint-Germain

**Woman on the Moon** see **Die
Frau im Mond**

# Index

Page numbers in *italic* refer to the illustrations and those in **bold** type to the Filmography.

357

## Sources of Illustrations

The Author and Publishers are grateful to the following organizations and individuals for the use of illustrations which appear in this book: Aguettand; Atlas Film; J.-G. Auriol; Bruckmann; Chmara-Volmane; the Cinémathèque Française, including the Casparius, Grune, Lang, Poelzig and Skladanovsky collections; Jean Delmas; the Deutsche Kinemathek, Berlin; the Deutsches Filmarchiv, Wiesbaden; the Staatliches Filmarchiv der D.D.R.; Hopkins-Stern; Standish D. Lawder; Lo Duca; Jean Mitry; the National Film Archive, London; the Nederlands Filmmuseum; the Bildarchiv of the Oesterreichische Nationalbibliothek; Poulaille.

2266 013

The Golden Age of German cinema began at the end of the
First World War and ended shortly after the coming of
sound. From *The Cabinet of Dr Caligari* onwards the
principal films of this period were characterized by two
influences: literary Expressionism, and the innovations of
the theatre directors of the period, in particular
Max Reinhardt. This book demonstrates the connection
between German Romanticism and the cinema through
Expressionist writings. It discusses the influence of the
theatre: the handling of crowds; the use of different levels,
and of selective lighting on a predominantly dark stage; the
reliance on formalized gesture; the innovation of the intimate
theatre. Against this background the principal films of the
period are examined in detail. The author explains the key
critical concepts of the time, and surveys not only the work of
the great directors, such as Fritz Lang and F. W. Murnau,
but also the contribution of their writers, cameramen and
designers. As *The Times Literary Supplement* wrote, 'Mme
Eisner is first and foremost a film critic, and one of the best
in the world. She has all the necessary gifts.' And it
described the original French edition of this book as 'one of
the very few classics of writing on the film and arguably the
best book on the cinema yet written'.

$5.45

UNIVERSITY OF CALIFORNIA PRESS

Berkeley 94720